A Theory of Secession

The Case for Political Self-Determination

A Theory of Secession: The Case for Political Self-Determination offers an unapologetic defense of the right to secede. Christopher Heath Wellman argues that any group has a moral right to secede as long as its political divorce will leave it and the remainder state in a position to perform the requisite political functions. He explains that there is nothing contradictory about valuing legitimate states while permitting their division. Once political states are recognized as valuable because of the functions that they are uniquely suited to perform, it becomes apparent that the territorial boundaries of existing states might permissibly be redrawn as long as neither the process nor the result of this reconfiguration interrupts the production of the crucial political benefits. Thus, if one values self-determination, then one has good reason to conclude that people have a right to determine their political boundaries.

Christopher Heath Wellman teaches in the Department of Philosophy at Washington University in St. Louis. He works in ethics, specializing in political and legal philosophy, and is coauthor, with A. John Simmons, of *Is There a Duty to Obey the Law?* (2005).

A Theory of Secession

The Case for Political Self-Determination

CHRISTOPHER HEATH WELLMAN
Washington University in St. Louis

CAMBRIDGE UNIVERSITY PRESS
Cambridge, New York, Melbourne, Madrid, Cape Town,
Singapore, São Paulo, Delhi, Mexico City

Cambridge University Press
The Edinburgh Building, Cambridge CB2 8RU, UK

Published in the United States of America by
Cambridge University Press, New York

www.cambridge.org
Information on this title: www.cambridge.org/9781107407237

First published 2005
First paperback edition 2012

A catalogue record for this publication is available from the British Library

Library of Congress Cataloguing in Publication data
Wellman, Christopher Heath.
A theory of secession: the case for political self-determination/
Christopher Heath Wellman.
p.   cm.
Includes bibliographical references and index.
ISBN 0-521-84915-2 (hardback)
I. Secession.   2. Self-determination, National.   3. Sovereignty.   I. Title.
JC327.W46   2005
320.1′ 5–dc22   2004030403

ISBN 978-0-521-84915-9 Hardback
ISBN 978-1-107-40723-7 Paperback

For Tim

Contents

Acknowledgments

I began thinking about secession in graduate school, so my debts date back to my time at the University of Arizona. I was a terribly raw and uncensored student, and I shudder to think how things might have turned out had I not studied alongside such supportive classmates and under the direction of such an attentive and nurturing faculty. I am fond of many places, but Tucson is my movable feast.

Portions of this book draw upon essays that have already appeared in print, and I would like to thank the following journals and presses for allowing me to incorporate parts of my previously published work into this project. "A Defense of Secession and Political Self-Determination" and "Liberalism, Political Legitimacy, and Samaritanism" were both published in *Philosophy and Public Affairs*; "Lincoln on Secession" first appeared in *Social Theory and Practice* (this article was coauthored with Peter Lindsay, so I am especially grateful to Peter for allowing me to draw upon our jointly authored work here); "Nationalism and Secession" was written for Blackwell's *A Companion to Applied Ethics*; "The Paradox of Group Autonomy" was published in *Social Philosophy and Policy*; and "The Truth in the Nationalist Principle" first appeared in the *American Philosophical Quarterly*.

Many friends and colleagues have generously commented on my work over the years, and I would like to reiterate my thanks to the following people for helping me with either the articles just listed or portions of earlier drafts of this book: Patrick Boleyn-Fitzgerald, Bernard Boxill, Jan Boxill, Allen Buchanan, Thomas Christiano, David Copp, Nancy Daukas, Joel Feinberg, Ray Frey, Will Kymlicka, Jonathan Malino, Larry May, David Miller, Ron Milo, Christopher Morris, Wayne Norman, Alan Patten, Ellen

Frankel Paul, Geoff Sayre-McCord, David Schmidtz, and James Stacey Taylor. Andy Altman, Russ Shafer-Landau, John Simmons, and Carl Wellman deserve special credit (and sympathy) for reading numerous unpublished papers. In addition, I have been very lucky to have worked under three ideal department chairs: Jonathan Malino, Robert Arrington, and George Rainbolt.

It has been a pleasure to work with everyone at Cambridge University Press. I am particularly indebted to the two anonymous reviewers for their detailed feedback and for being so flexible about my reluctance to change aspects of the manuscript. Beatrice Rehl and Eric Schwartz made the production process easier than I could have asked for, and the late Terry Moore exhibited the patience of Job during the years it took me to revise the bloody thing. Above all, I would like to thank Russell Hahn for his extraordinary care, skill, and imagination in editing the manuscript.

Among the many people who have helped me with this project, Allen Buchanan stands out. Everyone who works on secession profits from his peerless work, but none owes him as much as I. Over the last fifteen years, he has been an inspiring professor, a generous mentor, and a cherished friend. Allen is rightly prized for his rigorous argumentation and crystal clear writing, but I have always been most struck by his enthusiasm for philosophy and his (not unrelated) passionate concern with issues that impact people's lives. He and I do not agree on all points, but I suspect that the important ways in which Allen and his work continue to be models for me will be readily apparent to many who read this book.

Naturally, my greatest debts are also the most personal. I am ever thankful that someone as lovely as Donna continues to put up with the likes of me; I rely more than I care to admit on her boundless love, patience, and support. Finally, my deepest and least calculable debts are to my parents, who sacrificed mightily to ensure that my life would be easier than theirs. Those who know Carl professionally will recognize his influence on every page that follows, and those who know me best understand that I could not advance the theses I do unless I were quintessentially my mother's son.

February 2005

A Theory of Secession
The Case for Political Self-Determination

1

Introduction

This book aims to supply a thorough and unapologetic defense of the right to secede. In particular, it argues that any group has a moral right to secede as long as its political divorce will leave it and the remainder state in a position to perform the requisite political functions.

To call this thesis a minority position is an understatement. Though the twin doctrines of state sovereignty and territorial integrity are currently undergoing a dramatic reassessment, and though most theorists now acknowledge that a group may have a remedial right to secede when it has suffered severe and long-standing injustices at the hands of its state, it remains highly controversial to suggest that a group might have a right to separate even when its state has in no way treated it unjustly. Moreover, the majority of those who champion a primary right to secede presume that such political self-determination must come under a nationalist banner. Thus, my view is doubly controversial: Not only does it allow for the unilateral division of perfectly legitimate states, it does not mandate that the separatists be a culturally distinct minority group.

It would not be surprising for an anarchist to be so open to state breaking, but I defend secessionist rights despite being a statist. As I shall argue, there is nothing contradictory or otherwise problematic about valuing legitimate states, on the one hand, and permitting their division on the other. Once one recognizes that political states are valuable because of the functions (e.g., securing a just peace) that they are uniquely suited to perform, it becomes apparent that the territorial boundaries of existing states might permissibly be redrawn as long as neither the process nor the result of this reconfiguration interrupts the production of the crucial political benefits. In short, there is nothing about insisting upon the importance of states that requires us to preserve existing states in their present forms. And, once one concedes that states might permissibly be reconfigured, this raises the question of why the territorial boundaries of current states may not be redrawn in accordance with the wishes of their inhabitants. Admittedly, there is no chance that we can redo political boundaries in a way that pleases everyone, but this in no way implies that we must refrain from making changes that leave a greater percentage of people happy. The bottom line is that, if one values self-determination, then one has good reasons to conclude that people have a right to determine their political boundaries. These reasons are subject to being outweighed, of course, but I will argue that they are typically not outweighed whenever political boundaries can be redrawn without jeopardizing the requisite political functions.

Before summarizing the chapters to follow, let me explicitly acknowledge two features of my position. First, my argument is conditional: I suggest that *if* self-determination is valuable, then there is a primary right to secede from legitimate states. Those who come to this book skeptical of the importance of self-determination will not find a full defense of it here. Rather, I assume without argument that, other things being equal, people should be left free to be the authors of their own lives. The purpose of this book is to argue from this modest assumption to some striking conclusions regarding the morality of state breaking. Thus, my argument will admittedly have no purchase with those who do not share my view that this initial assumption is both modest and plausible.

Second, let me emphasize that I here defend the *right to secede* rather than *secession* itself. I stress this distinction because I am emphatically *not* a fan of secession. Although there are clearly some cases in which many lives could be dramatically improved by the division of existing states, I do not yearn for a world populated by countless tiny, more homogenous political units. On the contrary, I suspect that lives would more likely be improved if states continued to form more extensive international unions (if not outright mergers) that minimize the significance of political borders for the purposes of travel, trade, immigration, economic redistribution, and even culture. Still, just as one might defend the right to no-fault divorce for married couples even though one believes adamantly that people too often wrongly choose to separate, I defend the right to secede despite being no fan of state breaking. Put simply, whether it is wise for one to do X and whether one has a moral right to do X are separate issues. We are often morally entitled to act in ways that are not in our best interests, and here I defend the right to secede without offering any assurances that separatist parties would exercise this right only in cases of which I (and others) would approve.

In Chapter 2, "The Case for Statism," I show that one cannot merely appeal to freedom of association to ground secessionist rights. There are good reasons to allow people to choose their associates, but an unqualified defense of freedom of association is a recipe for anarchism. Statism is inconsistent with unrestricted freedom of association because states must be territorially contiguous in order to perform their crucial functions, and this contiguity would not be possible if states coerced only those subjects who freely consented. In the end, then, we must choose between viable political states and unqualified freedom of association. Anarcho-libertarians suggest that this choice shows why all existing states are illegitimate, but I argue that the converse is true. I propose that the legitimacy of territorially defined states implies that freedom of association must be qualified in the political context and that, as a consequence, it is implausible to posit unlimited rights to secede based upon an absolute right to freedom of association.

Chapter 3, "Valuing Self-Determination," is the pivotal chapter of the book. Here I argue that a commitment to statism does not force us to turn our backs on the importance of self-determination. It is true that one cannot consistently affirm political states and endorse unlimited secessionist rights, but this does not imply that there can be no primary rights to secede. Drawing upon the account of political legitimacy advanced in chapter 2, I suggest that we must allow those secessions that would not interfere with the production of essential political benefits. Thus, I propose that all separatist groups that can adequately perform the requisite political functions (and would leave their remainder states politically viable) have a primary right to secede. The central point is that, even if the benefits of political stability are important enough to outweigh conflicting claims to freedom of association, self-determination remains valuable and should be accommodated in those cases in which doing so does not conflict with the procurement of those political benefits. In short, our choices are not limited to either enduring anarchic chaos or retaining our existing states in their present form; statists who value self-determination can and should point toward a third option: reconfiguring the territorial boundaries of existing states according to the preferences of constituents whenever this reordering will not interrupt the benefits of political stability.

In Chapter 4, "Lincoln on Secession," I examine my permissive stance on unilateral state breaking in light of Abraham Lincoln's objections to the Confederacy's bid to secede. Discussing this case is instructive not only because it illustrates how my theory of secession would address an actual secessionist conflict, but also because it forces me to counter Lincoln's objections to state breaking, some of which remain popular today. After explaining the ten objections Lincoln raised against the South's separatist movement, I argue that none of them is cogent. I ultimately conclude that, though Lincoln's arguments did not themselves suffice, my account points the way toward an alternative argument that better explains why the Union was justified in resisting the political divorce.

In Chapter 5, "The Truth in Nationalism," I argue that a group need not be a cultural nation in order to qualify for the right to secede. Traditionally, the most vociferous advocates of political self-determination have been nationalists who propose that every nation has a right to form its own state. I acknowledge that national groups typically have the greatest interest in political self-determination, but I argue that cultural features are not central to secessionist conflicts. In my view, political abilities are paramount, and a group's status as a nation can at most play a secondary role in qualifying it for the right to secede, chiefly in cases where the group's cultural capital buttresses its capacity to perform the requisite political functions.

In Chapter 6, "Political Coercion and Exploitation," I address the worry that institutionally recognizing the right to secede will corrupt democratic decision making by allowing minority groups to hold their compatriots hostage. The basic worry here is that, by threatening to secede unless their demands are met, groups will be able to coerce and/or exploit their fellow citizens out of more than their fair share of the benefits of political cooperation. In response, I acknowledge that the dynamics of political decision making might well change, and that groups may occasionally capitalize on their ability to exit, but (after offering an analysis of the morality of coercion and exploitation) I suggest that my theory of secession does not permit a group to *impermissibly* exploit or coerce its compatriots. Moreover, I regard these changes largely as providing reasons *in favor* of constitutionally recognizing the right to secede. In my view, democracies are currently corrupt and stand to be improved by extending groups the political leverage that would likely accompany an effective right to exit.

In Chapter 7, "Secession and International Law," I explore whether the best international legal system would institutionally recognize and enforce the moral right to secede. I argue both that the moral rights to secede place the argumentative burden of proof on those who would deny political self-determination and that there are reasons to doubt that the skeptics can defeat this presumption in favor of political liberty. In the end, I concede that this is not a question best answered solely by moral philosophers; international lawyers, sociologists, and theorists of international relations are among those better equipped to answer some of the empirical questions that must be asked en route to settling this matter. However, even if it turns out that it would be imprudent or even irresponsible to institutionalize the right to secede in the international law at this juncture, this implies neither that the moral right does not currently exist nor that we should not work to reform the immoral international actors who currently make it inadvisable to institutionalize the ideal of political self-determination.

Finally, in Chapter 8, "The Velvet Transformation," I offer an optimistic prediction: We are not far from the day when political theorists and international actors respect the importance of political self-determination, and when that day arrives, groups will not vote in favor of secession. My hope and expectation is that as the continued emergence of international cooperation, international law, democracy, human rights, group rights, and self-determination gradually transforms the international landscape, we will witness corresponding decreases in injustice, group grievances, separatist passion, and, most significantly, the importance of state sovereignty. If so, there is every reason to expect that the charged tension of secessionist conflicts will ease as states offer less resistance to separatist movements and the motivations to achieve independent statehood correspondingly diminish.

2

The Case for Statism

At first blush, it would not seem terribly difficult to construct a compelling argument in defense of unlimited, unilateral rights to secede: One need only appeal to the right to freedom of association. Think, for instance, of how we regard marital and religious self-determination. Freedom of association is paramount in marital relations; we insist that a marriage should take place only between consenting partners. I may not be forced against my will to marry anyone, and I likewise have no right to force an unwilling partner to marry me. Not only do we have the right to determine whom we would like to marry, each of us has the discretion to decide whether or not to marry at all, and those of us who are married have the right to unilateral divorce. In short, any law requiring us to marry by a certain age, specifying whom we may or may not marry, or prohibiting divorce would impermissibly restrict our freedom of association.

Freedom of religion is in many ways more complicated, but most of us feel similarly about religious affiliation: Whether, how, and with whom I attend to my humanity is up to me as an individual. If I elect to explore my religious nature in community with others, I have no duty to do so with anyone in particular and no right to demand that others allow me to join them in worship. This freedom of association explains why it would be objectionable for my parents or my country to force me, as an adult, to attend my family church or the official church of the state.

Against this backdrop, it is easy to see what is potentially worrisome about a political state requiring its citizens to remain in the union. If I have the right to choose my marital and religious partners, why may I not also choose my political partners? As David Gauthier explains: "Just as secession may be compared to divorce, so political association may be compared to marriage. I may have the right to marry the woman of my choice who also chooses me, but not the woman of my choice who rejects me."[1] Moreover, invoking the analogies of marriage and religious self-determination highlights how dissatisfying it would be to allege that political self-determination allows one merely to secede from a country that treats one unjustly. Certainly, groups victimized by their states have a right to secede, but it is wrong to think that this remedial claim exhausts our rights to political self-determination. Imagine, for instance, if we required children to marry spouses chosen by their parents. Would we claim that these children had freedom of association if they were allowed to divorce only when their spouses mistreated them? Presumably not. Similarly, no one would label it religious self-determination if one were allowed to leave the church into which one was born just in case that church treated one unjustly. On the contrary, we recognize that freedom of association gives one much more than a right to leave an abusive arranged marriage, and that religious self-determination gives one greater discretion than merely to break from a church that mistreats one. As Margaret Moore emphasizes, freedom of association includes freedom of dissociation: "Freedom of association involves the ability to associate with other freely consenting individuals, and to dissociate from some others. If dissociation is implicit in a freedom of association principle, freedom of association cannot imply a right to associate with others against their will."[2] Given this, it is clear that an account of political self-determination inspired by freedom of association would give citizens much more than simply a right to secede from a country that treated them unjustly. Rather, each citizen would have the unilateral right to secede at any point in order either to form a new political alliance with others or even to withdraw and live in a state of nature, without any political association at all.

It does not take long to recognize that respecting freedom of association in the political context would be a recipe for anarchy. Just as freedom of association in personal relationships has led to a dramatic increase in the number of divorces and religious self-determination has weakened many organized religions, respecting unfettered political self-determination would be disastrous for existing states. If everyone were given the opportunity freely to withdraw from their countries,

[1] David Gauthier, "Breaking Up: An Essay on Secession," pp. 360–361.
[2] Margaret Moore, *The Ethics of Nationalism*, p. 170.

the institutions that remained would be so diminished in population and fragmented in territory that they would no longer merit the title of states. Most importantly, these territorially porous, voluntary associations would not be able satisfactorily to perform the functions of a modern state. If existing states were forced to draw upon only those who freely remained, the peace and security present in modern liberal democracies would be a thing of the past. Put bluntly, the price of unqualified freedom of association would be anarchy.

Of course, while some of those who champion the importance of freedom of association do not flinch at its anarchical implications, most deny that it has such radical consequences.[3] In particular, it has been common to suggest either (1) that we have all freely consented to our states or (2) that if given the opportunity, the vast majority would do so. Either option would allow advocates of freedom of association to avoid anarchism, because (1) explains how, despite our initial freedom, we are not currently at liberty to secede from our existing states, and (2) suggests that allowing unlimited secession would not in fact greatly diminish existing states, let alone result in anarchy. Upon closer examination, however, neither option satisfactorily reconciles unbridled freedom of association with statism.

The obvious problem with positing consent is that it seems baldly historically inaccurate. Other than naturalized citizens, very few of us have even been asked for, let alone given, our consent to be governed. In response to this difficulty, many have followed Locke in suggesting that citizens have *tacitly* consented to their state's imposition. This is not the place to address each of the various accounts on offer, but let me briefly explain why I think that even the most promising attempt to show the citizens' consent fails. In particular, consider why even those who vote for the winning side in a democratic election are not morally bound as if they had consented.[4]

The problem with this approach is that voting on political options in existing democracies is significantly disanalogous to (morally valid) acts of tacit consent in other arenas because the voter is never given the most important option of whether or not there will be a government. Instead, she is given only a (typically negligible) voice in what particular

---

3 For instance, Harry Beran and David Gauthier are two prominent advocates of secession grounded in consent/freedom of association, and neither advocates anarchy.

4 Carole Pateman, in *The Problem of Political Obligation*, and Peter Singer, in *Democracy and Disobedience*, are among those who explore the connection between voting and political obligation.

form the government will take. Therefore, even if a citizen *could singularly control* the results of a given election, she would not be morally bound by its outcome because she never consented to the restricted options of the election. Unless a voter is given the option of being exempt from the political imposition (i.e., allowed to secede), she cannot be morally bound by the outcome of an election in which she voted.[5] Indeed, to say that citizens are bound to those laws for which they vote (given the practice of current democracies) is morally tantamount to saying that an abductee has consented to being shot if she has expressed a preference that her abductor shoot rather than stab her. One might object that the analogy between having a vote and being abducted is inapt, since one can opt not to vote but cannot choose not to be killed, but this objection misses the point of the comparison. The two positions are importantly analogous, because neither the citizen nor the abductee can choose whether or not she will be coerced. Just as the abductee will be killed no matter how she responds (and even if she does not answer the abductor's question), the citizen will be subjected to coercive laws no matter how she votes (and even if she does not vote).

I believe that other explanations of tacit consent suffer from the same problem as the voting account. If so, most citizens have neither explicitly nor tacitly consented to their state's imposition.[6] As a consequence, a defender of unqualified freedom of association appears committed to insisting that everyone who has not given her morally binding consent (i.e., virtually all of us) must be given the option to secede unilaterally from her existing state. Even so, such a theorist might deny that this implication is a recipe for anarchism on the grounds that few would actually choose to secede. The basic idea here is that because virtually everyone would recognize the benefits of political cooperation, very few would opt out, and there would therefore be no appreciable diminution in existing states' capacities to perform their functions.

---

[5] It is important to appreciate that it is not enough that citizens be allowed to emigrate; they must be allowed to secede. The state would be entitled to force one to "love it or leave it" only if it had somehow already achieved a position of moral sovereignty over its territory before it had gained the consent of its constituents. Thus consent theorists of this stripe face a dilemma: If (1) the state has no claim to its territory prior to the consent of its citizens, then it has no right to demand that citizens either play by the state's rule or leave, but if (2) the state does have a claim to its territory before it has garnered the consent of its citizens, then it is no longer true that each citizen enjoys a position of privileged dominion over her own affairs until she voluntarily relinquishes it.

[6] The best critique of tacit consent remains John Simmons's treatment of the subject in *Moral Principles and Political Obligations*.

The view that very few would elect to secede from our existing states is inspired by an appreciation of the profound benefits of political order. Because virtually all of us recognize that life in the absence of political stability would be hazardous, each of us would voluntarily pay our political dues in order to avoid the insecurity of an apolitical environment. Thus, even if we insist that existing states are morally required to give those citizens who have not consented the option to secede (as a consistent advocate of freedom of association must), a proponent of this response would predict that only the most irrational or politically ignorant among us would choose to withdraw. And because it is unduly pessimistic to think that more than a handful of us are that spectacularly irrational or ignorant, we need not worry about the wholesale defections it would take to threaten the functional efficacy of existing states.

This response is inadequate, however, because it is not clear that it would necessarily be irrational to secede. I do not doubt that the benefits of political order are extraordinary, but the irrationality of secession would follow from this only if political withdrawal would cause the feared political instability, and it is implausible to think that an individual's defection would have this effect. The relevant point here is a well-worn one in political theory: Even if a state's capacity to perform its functions depends upon a general level of cooperation, a single individual's participation typically has no discernible effect. As a consequence, it would not be irrational to secede, regardless of what one expected the bulk of others to do. If one expects that most others will not secede, then it might be rational to secede, because one could stop making political sacrifices without worrying about the perils of anarchy. If we expect that most people will secede, on the other hand, it clearly becomes rational to secede oneself rather than sacrifice and still enjoy no benefits of political stability.

In light of this reasoning, one should conclude that, even if we would all be markedly better off if no one seceded, the dominant strategy would be for each individual to secede. Moreover, each of us should presume that others will reason similarly, and thus it seems more accurate to suppose that most of us would (quite reasonably) secede with an expectation that others will do so as well. Of course, this mass defection might build gradually rather than occur all at once, but as the secessions increasingly cause a diminution in the benefits of political cooperation (which in turn inspires further defections, and so on), we should expect the vast majority of citizens to eventually opt out of political states if given the choice.

Thus, it appears neither that most citizens have consented nor that the great majority would do so if given the chance to opt out. If this is the case, then we face a watershed choice between either leaving enough normative room for the legitimacy of political states or insisting upon unbridled freedom of association in the political realm. In the remainder of this chapter, I explain why we should embrace statism and eschew freedom of association and the case for virtually unlimited secessionist rights it entails.

Samaritanism and Political Legitimacy

Consider the plight of Antonio and Bathsheba. Imagine that Antonio is driving along a highway when he stops to pick up a hitchhiker, Bathsheba. Bathsheba asks for a ride to Pleasantville, a town about twenty miles ahead. Antonio's route will take him through Pleasantville, so he agrees to take her. But Antonio is *very explicit* that he prefers driving alone; he is taking her only as a favor (suppose that he picks her up only because a storm is on the horizon), and under no condition would he be willing to take her any further. Bathsheba nods in understanding and thanks him profusely for the favor. After a twenty-mile drive during which no words are uttered, they arrive only to find that Pleasantville is anything but pleasant. In fact, it is a lawless town, a contemporary Hobbesian state of nature. The only people visible are the roving gangs of thugs responsible for the burning buildings, broken glass, and other signs of chaos that litter the scene. Antonio looks around in horror as Bathsheba begs him to escort her safely out of Pleasantville.

Is Antonio at liberty to leave Bathsheba in Pleasantville (where the car has already attracted the gangs' attention), or does Antonio have a moral duty to transport her far enough away that she will no longer be in jeopardy? I assume that Antonio has a duty to deliver Bathsheba to safety. But notice: Antonio's duty cannot be attributed to his consent, nor to a special relationship to Bathsheba, nor to the harm-to-others principle.[7] The obligation cannot be grounded in consent, because Antonio explicitly refused to take her any further than Pleasantville. There is no

---

[7] The "harm-to-others" principle to which I refer is the liberty-limiting principle (often called the "liberty principle" or simply the "harm principle") that J. S. Mill advocated in *On Liberty*. Joel Feinberg has offered the most sophisticated analysis of this principle in his book *Harm to Others*. Feinberg suggests that the harm principle forbids an agent to wrongly cause a second party to be worse off than she would be otherwise.

special moral relationship between Antonio and Bathsheba, since the two have just met and exchanged only a few words.[8] And, as I will argue, the duty cannot fall under the harm principle because any harm done to Bathsheba would subsequently come at the hands of a gang member rather than Antonio. Most importantly, Antonio has not *wrongfully* harmed Bathsheba (as is necessary to violate the harm principle) by taking her to Pleasantville, because she requested to be taken there, and *Volenti non fit injuria.*[9]

Antionio's duty can be explained only in terms of samaritanism. Bathsheba has a right to assistance from Antonio, and he has a correlative duty to her. Antonio's samaritan duty results from the combination of (1) Bathsheba's extreme peril and (2) Antonio's ability to assist her at no unreasonable cost to himself.[10] Both conditions are necessary for a samaritan duty to obtain, so that if the scenario were altered on either count, no duty would exist. If Bathsheba were not imperiled in Pleasantville (suppose, for instance, that she was anxious to leave only because Pleasantville reminded her of troubled times she had spent there in the past), then Antonio would have no duty to escort her out of town. Alternatively, even if Bathsheba were in dire need of help, Antonio would be at liberty to refuse if assisting would be unreasonably costly (if, for example, Antonio's car had such poor acceleration or so little gas that Bathsheba's additional weight would jeopardize his own escape from Pleasantville). Because Bathsheba's life is at stake and Antonio need sacrifice only his

---

[8] One might object that sharing this brief ride is enough somehow either to signal Antonio's consent or to create a special bond between the "carmates." This strikes me as far-fetched, but those persuaded by this objection can simply alter the scenario, so that Bathsheba first appears as a hitchhiker in Pleasantville. I did not change my story in this way because it would require me to add a number of cumbersome conditions about Antonio's knowing that Bathsheba would not harm him or otherwise jeopardize his safety.

[9] In *Harm to Others*, pp. 105–125, Feinberg explains why the harm principle prohibits one only from *wrongfully* setting back another's interests. This is important to this case because one's consent to be placed in a particular situation or to undergo certain risks or treatment vitiates any wrongdoing on the part of another who does what has been consented to.

[10] My requirement that Antonio's assistance not be "unreasonably" costly is deliberately vague. Some would insist that all but the most minimal costs would be unreasonable (and perhaps that Bathsheba should compensate Antonio for whatever costs he incurs), while others believe that much more robust costs would qualify as samaritan. I am not sure how this disagreement could be conclusively settled; for now, I seek merely to make the general point that Bathsheba's peril would not bind Antonio if he could not have saved her without unreasonable cost to himself.

preference for driving in solitude in order to save her, however, he has a duty to assist Bathsheba.

Because consent, special relations, and the harm principle have all been ruled out, this samaritan duty must fall under a "benefit-to-others principle."[11] It constitutes a duty to benefit because it is a duty to make Bathsheba *better off* (outside of Pleasantville) than she would be otherwise (left in Pleasantville). It is tempting to subsume a duty to prevent harm under the harm principle, but this temptation should not be indulged. The mere fact that harm may occur does not show that everyone's action is forbidden/required by the harm principle. When B is on the verge of harming C, A may have a duty to shield C from harm. B's action may be prohibited by the harm principle, but A's assistance cannot be required without a benefit principle, because A's action makes C better off (shielded) than she would be otherwise (unshielded). One might object that benefit-to-others principles implausibly require one ceaselessly to assist others, but a principle that requires some benefits need not require all benefits. As the samaritan account advocated here confirms, there is nothing implausible about a *limited* benefit-to-others principle according to which one is required to assist others only when they are in dire need and one can help them at no unreasonable cost to oneself. In endorsing samaritanism as I do, I am merely confirming John Stuart Mill's judgment that "[t]o make anyone answerable for doing evil to others is the rule; to make him answerable for not preventing evil is, comparatively speaking, the exception. Yet there are many cases clear enough and grave enough to justify that exception."[12]

This much is neither novel nor controversial. What is striking, however, is that the moral relations of political legitimacy are echoic of those between Antonio and Bathsheba.[13] Just as Antonio has no liberty-right to drive off in solitude and leave Bathsheba vulnerable in Pleasantville, citizens have no claim-right to be free from political coercion when this will leave others in a condition of political instability. Just as Antonio's

---

[11] The "benefit-to-others principle" (or simply the "benefit principle") is analogous to the harm principle mentioned in note 7. A benefit-to-others principle forbids wrongly failing to make a second party better off than she would be otherwise. As I will explain, one's failure to benefit another is wrong when the other is in peril and one can rescue her at no unreasonable cost to oneself.

[12] John Stuart Mill, *On Liberty*, p. 11.

[13] As Bernard Boxill has pointed out to me, there is one point of disanalogy in that, unlike one's compatriots, Bathsheba clearly consents to be taken from Pleasantville. This consent does not disrupt the analogy, however, because the comparison is between a citizen and Antonio, and neither of them has given his morally valid consent.

car is the only vehicle in which Bathsheba can flee Pleasantville, political society is the only vehicle with which people can escape the perils of the state of nature. Just as Antonio's samaritan duty to Bathsheba is not grounded in consent, special relations, or the harm-to-others principle, a state's justification for limiting the liberty of its citizens does not stem from consent, special relations, or the harm principle. In the end, the only plausible justification for a state's coercion must spring from the same samaritan source as Antonio's duty to benefit Bathsheba. The state's right to coerce its citizens correlates to the latter's lack of rights to be free from political coercion, an absence that exists only because of the way in which samaritanism can limit our normal sphere of moral dominion. In short, my account of political legitimacy capitalizes upon the intuitive appeal of samaritanism and uses it to connect a state's benefits to its justification.

To appreciate fully this analogy between a citizen and Antonio, we must understand why political states offer the only hope of escaping the state of nature. A stateless environment would be an insecure place in which peace would be unavailable and moral rights would be disrespected because, among other things, there will always be people unwilling to honor the moral rights of others if violating them has no legal repercussions. Moral rights will be respected and peace will be ensured only if police effectively protect individuals and recognized judges impartially adjudicate conflicts according to established rules.[14]

But even if one acknowledges the value of peace and security, one might deny the necessity of territorially defined states. If the primary function of a political state is to protect rights and secure peace, then why could these same benefits not be supplied by private protection agencies or via some other arrangement? Why not sort people into protective agencies according to religion, eye color, preference for a particular set of rules, or by consent? Most importantly, how can we justify coercing people into territorially defined political units when the benefits of these states might be achieved through less coercive or even consensual means? The proper response is that political coercion is permissible because (and only when) no other arrangement is feasible. It is no mere historical accident that states are territorially defined; they are territorial because this is the only way for them to perform their functions.[15] Peace would be

---

[14] As authors such as Joseph Raz, in "On the Authority and Interpretation of Constitutions," and Thomas Christiano, in "The Authority of Democracy," point out, states are also needed to establish – not just to enforce – justice.

[15] Insofar as the requisite political functions involve securing peace and protecting moral rights, the more precise list of these functions will depend upon which moral rights states

unavailable in the absence of a decisive and accepted method of enforcing common rules and adjudicating conflicts. Because conflicts typically occur between parties in spatial proximity (since conflicts require interactions, and we most often interact with those nearby), and because a judge can peacefully and decisively settle conflicts only if she has authority over both parties, a judge must have power over all those who share spatial proximity.[16] Thus, since conflicts will proliferate and escalate if those around us follow different rules and appeal to competing authorities, we cannot politically sort ourselves according to religious affiliation, sexual preference, or eye color as long as we live among people of varying religions, sexual preferences, and eye colors. I will return to the necessity of political society later, but hopefully this quick sketch explains why states must be territorially defined.[17]

Given that states must be territorial, it is easy to see why the consent of their constituents is a luxury they can ill afford. The benefits of political society accrue only if all those in close proximity are similarly bound, so a state must insist that residents either play by the promulgated rules or

are specifically charged to protect. On this question there will inevitably be controversy, both because theorists disagree about the extent of our samaritan responsibilities to one another, and because it is unclear what political functions might be justified on nonsamaritan grounds (once a samaritan state is justified, for instance, considerations of political equality, fairness, or democratic governance might explain why all citizens have additional rights). Because discussing these issues would take us too far afield (and because we need not settle these matters in order to develop a general theory of secession), I will not try to settle them definitively here. For now, let me merely specify that the requisite political functions involve *at least* securing peace and protecting the most minimal moral rights to live free from peril.

[16] We increasingly interact (and come into potential conflict) with others to whom we are spatially disparate. In international business, for instance, conflicts frequently arise between parties who are thousands of miles apart. Unless special arrangements are made, these conflicts are typically adjudicated by the local authorities having jurisdiction over the territory where the product is sold. Increasingly, however, international organizations are being designed to establish and enforce a uniform set of rules. This arrangement confirms that interacting/conflicting parties must appeal to the same authority and submit to the same power.

[17] One might object that the territoriality issue is a red herring because private schemes can and often do supply lifesaving (or otherwise very important) benefits to those they serve. I agree that private agencies provide important benefits, and I admit that private agencies should be preferred when they can adequately replace coercive ones. The fact that private agencies currently provide many essential services is not necessarily a good objection, however, because it is doubtful that they could do so in a state of nature. Even if voluntary businesses could provide these benefits in the state of nature, however, I believe that they could not eliminate the perils of a state of nature. I develop and defend this empirical claim (which is admittedly necessary for my account of political legitimacy) later in this chapter when I consider the anarchist's rejoinder to the samaritan account.

leave. If each citizen were at liberty to secede (as opposed to emigrate) and citizenship were established consensually, the numerically diminished and spatially disparate remaining people could not perform the functions of securing peace and protecting rights.[18] Indeed, the fact that emigration does not threaten a state's capacity to secure peace and protect rights confirms that states must be territorial. Whereas unlimited secession precludes a country from uniformly coercing all those in spatial proximity, emigration does not lead to conflicts between parties who play by different rules and appeal to different authorities. Thus, the fact that emigration is not as disruptive as secession is further evidence for the link between states being territorial and their being capable of performing their political functions.[19]

In short, freedom of political association is incompatible with political stability, and samaritanism is an ineliminable ingredient of political legitimacy, because people cannot enjoy the benefits of political stability without uniformly restricting the political liberty of those around them. To emphasize: The reason that *I* have no moral right to be free from political coercion (i.e., to secede) is that, even if *I* would rather forego

[18] There are a number of ways in which a citizen can "opt out," so it is important to reiterate that an absence of political legitimacy leaves normative room for unlimited secession. Here the distinction between political legitimacy and political obligation is paramount: An absence of political obligation does not entail a corresponding lack of political legitimacy, and the former has much less striking implications. If there is no political obligation, citizens are morally free to break the law and to emigrate if they so choose. If there is no political legitimacy, on the other hand, then the state's presence is impermissible and it has no right to force those within its jurisdiction to "play by the rules or leave." In the absence of political legitimacy, citizens have a moral claim to stay put and to be free from any legal interference; in other words, they may secede.

[19] John Simmons has cautioned me against alleging that it is inconceivable that samaritanism would prohibit emigration as well as secession. Because my account of political legitimacy draws upon the moral force of samaritanism, I must admit that emigration may permissibly be limited where such limitation is compatible with samaritanism. This may seem an awkward implication, but I suspect this is only because the circumstances would have to be radically counterfactual for this to be so. In particular, the chances are slim that all three of the following conditions would be met: (1) A society's population is so diminished that it could not perform its political functions if more citizens left; (2) those citizens who would voluntarily remain cannot find political stability elsewhere, i.e., they cannot also emigrate; and (3) for those who would prefer to leave, the burden of staying is not unreasonable. In the end, limiting emigration is normally impermissible because it is typically either unnecessary or too costly to those denied emigration, but limiting secession is more often permissible because it is more likely to be both necessary and not unreasonably costly to those who would prefer to secede. If circumstances were different and all three of the above conditions obtained, however, then samaritanism could be invoked to limit emigration.

the benefits of political society, my state may permissibly coerce me in order to secure political stability for *my fellow citizens*. To return to the analogy, the justification for my state's coercive presence stems from the same samaritan source as Antonio's duty to Bathsheba. The only normative difference between Antonio and me is a Hohfeldian one: Samaritanism gives Antonio a duty (correlative to Bathsheba's claim-right) where ordinarily he would have a liberty-right, and it leaves me with no moral claim (correlative to the state's liberty-right) where ordinarily I would have a claim-right.[20] In less Hohfeldian terms, this difference is merely that samaritanism requires Antonio to do something (escort Bathsheba safely from Pleasantville) that he would not ordinarily have to do, and it leaves me morally liable to an imposition (the state's coercion) that I would ordinarily not be required to endure. Once one recognizes the two facts (1) that a political state is necessary to avoid the hazards of the state of nature and (2) that a government can successfully eliminate these dangers only if it is territorially defined, one appreciates why political legitimacy has the same grounds as Antonio's samaritan duty to Bathsheba.

At this point, some are likely to complain that a citizen's moral relationship to her compatriots is disanalogous to Antonio's relationship to Bathsheba. A critic might contend that the two are importantly different because (1) citizens have consented to the imposition of their states, (2) there are morally significant allegiances among compatriots, or (3) the limitation of political liberty is covered by the harm principle.

As I explained earlier, the consent theory of political legitimacy is doubly flawed, because (1) citizens almost never consent to their governments and (2) any act even resembling that which implies consent (such as voting) is a moral nullity because it is performed under coercion (the voter in a political election will be – and has been – subject to the state's laws no matter how, or if, she votes). The notion that special, associative duties obtain among fellow citizens has been riding a recent wave of popularity, but it is no more plausible than consent theory.[21] As I argue elsewhere, compatriots do not have associative responsibilities

---

[20] In his *Fundamental Legal Conceptions*, Wesley Hohfeld carefully distinguishes among the various distinct relations to which the general term "right" refers. In light of Hohfeld's analysis, I deliberately invoke the moral force of "samaritanism," rather than merely "samaritan duties," to acknowledge that our responsibilities to strangers may arise in a variety of Hohfeldian forms.

[21] Ronald Dworkin, in *Law's Empire*, and Yael Tamir, in *Liberal Nationalism*, develop "associative" accounts of political obligation, for instance.

toward one another, and even if they did, these responsibilities could not solve the problem of political legitimacy.[22] The principal problem with this approach is that, while associative theorists are united in emphasizing the "Uncle" in "Uncle Sam," citizens are not connected to compatriots as they are to uncles (or contrapositively, no one would posit associative allegiances to uncles if they were as numerous and interpersonally distant as compatriots in a modern bureaucratic state). In response to this worry, authors like Ronald Dworkin and Yael Tamir suggest impersonal, nonintimate attachments that might ground associative allegiances in existing states. Each of these proposals ultimately proves unsuccessful for its inability to offer a realistic description of political identification while simultaneously explaining how this bond can generate associative responsibilities. As a matter of fact, the more realistic and clear the account of political connection provided, the more apparent the absence of associative obligations becomes.

Given the failure of both the consent and associative approaches, the most tempting way to distinguish between Antonio's duty to Bathsheba and the source of political legitimacy is to associate the latter with the harm principle. Since the state is justified in virtue of the harmful conditions it helps us to avoid, it seems natural to subsume political legitimacy under the harm principle. After all, limiting political liberty appears justified for the same reasons that the state may restrict other liberties, such as free speech. (Even if an individual has a right to express her beliefs, we may still permissibly prohibit her from screaming "Fire!" in a crowded movie theater, for instance.) The rationale for both restrictions is apparently that exercising one's liberty is harmful to others and, therefore, can permissibly be curtailed by the state. Contrary to initial appearances, however, there is an important point of disanalogy between restricting political liberty and standard appeals to the harm principle. Specifically, stabbing or shooting someone *causes* the victim to be worse off in a way that exercising political liberty would not. If one stabs someone, or even yells "Fire!" in a crowded movie theater, one is the *proximate cause* of another's harm. If everyone were to secede individually from the existing political unions, on the other hand, it would lead to a harmful state of affairs, but the political fragmentation would not itself be the proximate cause of the harm. The post-political environment is harmful because of its many attendant rights violations, but in each case it is the

[22] See my "Associative Allegiances and Political Obligations" and John Simmons's article "Associative Political Obligations."

particular rights violation, rather than the antecedent secession, that is the proximate cause of the harm. To see this point more clearly, imagine a political state with only three citizens: A, B, and C. We might prohibit A from seceding, not because the secession itself would harm either B or C, but because B and C would be vulnerable to harm after A had seceded (perhaps because B would violate C's rights once A were no longer there to support C). In this case, B's action, rather than A's secession, is the proximate cause of C's wrongful harm. Thus, justifying political states for the harmful consequences they help us to avoid is not tantamount to limiting political liberty with the harm principle, because the mere exercise of political liberty does not *cause* harm in the manner required by the harm principle.[23] In short, if A's conduct does not cause B to be worse off than B would be otherwise, A's conduct does not harm B in the requisite sense, and, therefore, A's conduct cannot be forbidden by the harm principle.

A critic might object, however, that this case demonstrates merely that the harm principle must be expanded to include cases in which one's action leads to conditions where rights are violated. But this proposal is unacceptable for the inaccuracy with which it assigns responsibility for harm to an agent. To see this, consider a country that denied women's suffrage. Suppose that male supremacists respond to a growing women's movement by threatening to murder one hundred women if females are allowed to vote. This threat provides reasons to deny women the right to vote, but clearly it does not show the harm principle to be against women voting. Similarly, the fact that B will violate C's rights if A does not protect C does not mean that A's failure to protect C harms C; it is B who harms C, and expanding the harm principle to pin the harm on A only confuses the issue. (Of course, none of this shows that A cannot have a duty to protect C; it demonstrates only that such a duty would fall under a *benefit* rather than a *harm* principle.) Thus we must not abandon the harm principle's proximate cause requirement and, therefore, cannot restrict political liberty in the name of the harm principle.

At this point, a persistent critic might retort that exercising political liberty does harm others because it disrupts *existing* political stability. The idea here is that, since one's compatriots currently enjoy peace and security, the insecurity accompanying unlimited secession would leave

---

[23] For an explanation of the causal component of the harm principle, see Joel Feinberg, *Harm to Others*, pp. 165–171. Later I will critically assess Feinberg's stance on the causal efficiency of samaritan omissions.

them worse off and thereby harm them. The problem with this reply, however, is that the mere fact that one's compatriots currently enjoy a level of political security is insufficient to invoke the harm principle; it is essential that one's fellow citizens have a *valid claim* to this level of security. Unless one's compatriots have a *right* to the advantages of political stability, they are harmed but not wronged when they lose those benefits. And since the harm principle limits only conduct that *wrongfully* harms others, it would not restrict secession and its undeniable potential for harm. To see this, imagine that Jill daily extorts Jack's lunch money. Even if Jill became accustomed to her daily heist, she still would have no right to it. And, absent Jill's right to Jack's lunch money, Jack would not *wrongfully* harm Jill if he suddenly withheld his money. Or, in terms of slavery, a slave owner cannot appeal to the harm principle to justify retaining her slaves on the grounds that she currently enjoys a level of comfort possible only via slavery. Thus, *without a justification for the initial use of political coercion,* citizens cannot cite their current political benefits to invoke the harm principle any more than Jill can appeal to the harm principle to defend her continued robbery of Jack. In the end, we must conclude that the harm principle cannot cover political legitimacy.

Before I say more about the samaritanism invoked in my account, it is worth recapitulating my reasoning as plainly as possible. I believe that Antonio has a duty to escort Bathsheba away from the perils of Pleasantville, and I suggest that this duty is a samaritan chore required by a (duly limited) benefit-to-others principle. Similarly, I believe that the presumption in favor of each citizen's freedom of association is outweighed by the state's samaritan liberty to save others from the hazards of the state of nature. Because the only practical way to ensure peaceful interaction among people is to impose a common power over all those in spatial proximity, a territorially defined monopolistic authority is the only vehicle capable of rescuing us from the state of nature. In those cases in which a state can perform its political functions without requiring more of its citizens than is allowed by a duly limited benefit-to-others principle (i.e., when the state eliminates the perils of the state of nature without excessively curtailing the dominion of its constituents), the state permissibly limits the liberty of its citizens. In short, if citizens do not have unlimited rights to be free from political coercion, it is because samaritanism grounds the state's right to coerce those within its territory, and this liberty defeats the citizen's normal right to be free from political coercion.

If the foregoing analysis is on target, political legitimacy joins Antonio's duty to Bathsheba in being grounded in samaritanism. I have also alleged that samaritanism is best explained in terms of a benefit-to-others principle. This account is not without competition, however, so let me explain my dissatisfaction with the competing analyses of samaritanism.[24]

The Duty to Benefit Others

Because samaritanism is the key normative premise in my account of political legitimacy, it is important to say more about how I understand the peril of others to affect our moral relations. In particular, many have been reluctant to endorse samaritanism because it appears to be both (1) required by duty and (2) not covered by the harm principle. Although it has been common to deny either (1) or (2), I contend that it is better to include a "benefit-to-others" principle alongside the harm-to-others principle.

Jeffrie Murphy is among those who explicitly deny that there are samaritan rights and correlative duties. He writes:

> ...I can be morally lacking even in cases in which I violate no one's rights. For example: I am sitting in a lounge chair next to a swimming pool. A child (not mine) is drowning in the pool a few inches from where I am sitting. I notice him and realize that all I have to do to save him is put down my drink, reach down, grab him by the trunks, and pull him out (he is so light I could do it with one hand without even getting out of my seat). If I do not save him I violate no rights (strangers do not have a right to be saved by me) but would still reveal myself as a piece of moral slime properly to be shunned by all decent people.[25]

---

[24] Before considering objections to my view, let me quickly explain how and why my samaritan approach differs from the standard liberal account, which emphasizes that political order is a public good. Political theorists often stress the *nature* of the benefits of political stability – their joint consumption and nonexludability – to argue that fairness justifies political coercion. In short, we are justified in coercing all citizens in order to ensure that none free rides on the public good of political order. I eschew this approach, however, because of its paternalism: I think each of us has a right against having benefits coercively imposed on us without our consent. The samaritan approach avoids this paternalism insofar as it does not justify coercing me in terms of how *I* benefit; rather, it allows me to be coerced (whether I consent or not) only if this coercion is essential to rescuing *others* from the perils of the state of nature. In this regard, the samaritan approach is more reminiscent of Kant's account, which explains our requirement to avoid the state of nature as a duty of justice owed to the humanity in ourselves and others. (The samaritan account differs from Kant's, of course, not only because Kant did not label this responsibility a positive duty – nor would he likely characterize it as a samaritan duty – but also because I do not endorse his account of positive and negative freedom.)

[25] Jeffrie G. Murphy, "Blackmail: A Preliminary Inquiry," p. 168, n. 6.

Certainly Murphy is correct that there is more to morality than merely respecting rights, but one can agree with Murphy on this general point and still reject his analysis of the drowning child. I take issue with Murphy's description of the poolside encounter because I believe there are samaritan rights and correlative duties. One need posit only the existence of positive rights in order to allege that the lounger has a duty to save the drowning child. I shall return to positive rights in the next section when I consider the rigorous libertarian position, but for now let me make plain that I reject Murphy's analysis because I believe that, even if the lounger has no special relation to the child, this child has a positive right against the lounger.[26]

Joel Feinberg exemplifies another approach to samaritanism. He argues that the harm principle covers the drowning child's right to be saved and the lounger's correlative duty.[27] I grant that there are perfect duties to assist strangers, but I question Feinberg's claim that these duties stem from the harm principle. Expanding upon my earlier discussion, I will argue that Feinberg fails to reconcile samaritanism with the causal component of the harm principle.

As Feinberg acknowledges, conduct can be limited by the harm principle only if it *causes* harm.[28] If one fails to act, however, it is difficult to see how one's inaction can be a causal factor at all, let alone the proximate cause. In Antonio's case, it seems curious to allege that he is the proximate cause of Bathsheba's harm when Antonio takes no action to harm her. Feinberg concedes that most inactions cannot be causes but argues that some can. Consider, for instance, a causal explanation for Itchy's broken arm. Suppose Itchy broke her arm falling down a flight of stairs. Itchy's fall was her first after thousands of trips up and down these stairs, and she slipped on a patch of ice that had never collected there before. Assume further that ice had never formed on that stair because Itchy's landlord, Scratchy, had always put salt on the stairs before winter storms. If we discovered that Scratchy had not salted Itchy's stairs before this particular storm, we might cite Scratchy's omission as the cause of Itchy's broken arm.

---

[26] Patricia Smith has offered what is (to my knowledge) the most extensive and sophisticated analysis of samaritan responsibilities in her book *Liberalism and Affirmative Obligation*. See also her essay "Bad Samaritans, Acts, and Omissions." I am encouraged that she defends an account similar to the one I advocate here.

[27] Feinberg, *Harm to Others*, pp. 126–186.

[28] Feinberg provides a full account of why the harm principle prohibits only conduct that produces or causes harm in ibid., pp. 105–125.

Rather than allege that just any inaction could be causally cited, Feinberg specifies that *omissions* can cause. Thus, not everyone who failed to prevent another's harm could be causally responsible, only those who *omitted* to prevent the harm. According to Feinberg, a failure to act constitutes an omission only when the following criteria are met.

A omitted to do X when

1. A did not in fact do X.
2. A had a reasonable opportunity to do X.
3. A had the ability to do X.
4. A believed that there is at least a good chance that there is a person in peril and that he has sufficient ability and a reasonable opportunity to rescue that person.
5. It was in some way reasonable to expect A to do X in the circumstances, either because
   a. A or people in A's position ordinarily do X, or because
   b. A had a special duty to do X in virtue of his job, his socially assigned role, or his special relationship to B, or because
   c. A had a moral obligation to B to do X in virtue of a prior agreement between them, or a promissory commitment, or because
   d. For some other reason there is a moral requirement that people in the position A found himself in, do X.[29]

It is noteworthy, I think, that on Feinberg's list of circumstances in which it is reasonable to expect A to act (a–d of condition 5), the samaritan condition (d) is the only one in which no special moral or statistical relationship exists between A and B. (Indeed, the samaritan case is a shorthand label that specifically designates the absence of a special bond or relationship.) I highlight this because I believe that it is precisely these special relationships, rather than moral duties, that prompt our causal citations. To see this, imagine two possible scenarios involving samaritans. In the first, A encounters B, who requires assistance in manner Y. A has no duty to assist B in manner Y, but as a matter of fact, almost everyone in A's position does offer this assistance. In the second scenario, C encounters D, who requires assistance in manner X. C has a moral duty to assist D in manner X, but as a matter of fact, almost everyone in C's position withholds this aid. I suggest that we would causally cite A's inaction rather than C's, because we typically single out deviations from the

[29] Feinberg states and explains these conditions in ibid., pp. 159–163.

normal circumstances (including aberrant behavior) rather than moral relationships. As Feinberg acknowledges: "We ask what caused the surprising event and expect an explanation that will cite a factor normally present but absent this time, or normally absent but present this time, that made the difference. The occasion for explanation is a breach of routine; the explanatory judgment cites another deviation from routine to correlate with it."[30]

Given Feinberg's recognition that causal citations involve deviations from normality, it is curious that condition (d) (which refers to moral relations rather than statistical normality) is included. Perhaps the inclusion of conditions (b) and (c) (in which inactions qualify as omissions in virtue of the special obligations) led him to believe that mere duties make inactions omissions, but even in these cases I think it is more than the duty itself that prompts our causal citation. For instance, we speak of a lifeguard's failure to prevent a drowning as an omission, not simply because they have duties to do so but because it is their job to prevent drowning, and they *normally* do. What is more, morality might indirectly influence our causal citations, because if people are generally moved by their duties, we can reasonably expect one to do one's duty. But even in these cases, any failure to perform a duty invokes causal citations for its *abnormality*, not for its *immorality*.

In the end, though, I suspect Feinberg wants to suggest that samaritan inactions can be considered causes from a nonexplanatory standpoint. According to Feinberg, this nonexplanatory cause need not be an abnormal interference, because the causal citation is used not to explain how the harmful state of affairs occurred but to fix the blame upon a certain agent.[31] This notion of causation may be illuminating in some contexts, but it cannot be useful in samaritan cases for two reasons. First, this nonexplanatory cause seems incompatible with the causal component of the harm principle, which requires that the conduct *produce* the harmful state of affairs. Perhaps Feinberg could relax the causal requirement, but this procrustean move reconciles samaritanism with the harm principle only by distorting the latter's initial dimensions, not by showing that samaritan cases fit our previous concepts. Second and more importantly, we cannot use causal citations to fix the blame in samaritan cases because we must already know that the agent is blameworthy in order to know that her

---

[30] Ibid., p. 176.
[31] Feinberg discusses explanatory and nonexplanatory causal citations in ibid., pp. 176–177.

inaction constitutes a cause. This is because, of inactions, only omissions are causes. And since we know that a samaritan's inaction is an omission only when we posit that she has a duty to act, we must already know that she is blameworthy before we can make any causal claims, so the causal citation does no work in fixing the blame. (In other words, we need not reason that [1] duty implies omission, and [2] omission implies cause, and [3] cause implies harm, so that we can conclude that [4] harm implies blameworthiness, because we can infer the blameworthiness directly from the duty with which we began in [1].) Thus it appears that the appeal to nonexplanatory causation will not reconcile samaritan omissions with the harm principle.

Moreover, even if Feinberg could establish that samaritan inactions should be considered omissions (that is, even if he could explain why clause d should be included in condition 5), he would still need to show that *all* omissions could cause before he has proven that samaritan inactions can cause harm. Not only has he not done so, I have countered even a presumptive case for this conclusion. Furthermore, I have indicated why expanding the causal condition to include nonexplanatory causes is not helpful. We may safely conclude that Feinberg has not shown that duties to prevent harm derive from the harm principle. So, while authors like Murphy reject Feinberg's analysis because of skepticism about samaritan duties, I accept these duties but dispute that they are subsumed under the harm principle. If samaritan duties exist, they must stem from a benefit-to-others principle.

The Anarchist's Challenge

In the absence of consent, one cannot get political legitimacy for free. With this in mind, we must acknowledge that the samaritan justification for political coercion is not without its costs. In particular, it requires one to grant two premises: (1) that positive rights exist, and (2) that a political state is essential to secure peace and protect rights. In response to these twin premises, one might contest the samaritan approach on either normative or descriptive grounds. Questioning the normative assumption, anarchists might counter that, even if states are necessary to supply vital benefits, our inviolable moral rights make nonconsensual political coercion impermissible. And against the descriptive premise, one might contest whether states in fact supply benefits that could not be generated in the state of nature. Consider each of these potential objections in turn.

The most rigorous form of libertarianism denies positive rights and alleges that, even if there are vital functions that only a state can perform, the state may not permissibly limit the political liberty of its constituents without their consent. If I am right that samaritanism is required to justify the state, the question of political legitimacy forces us to make a watershed choice. On the one hand is the rigorous libertarian position that allows a person absolute and unlimited personal autonomy as long as her conduct does not harm others, and on the other is a characterization of agents as liable to having their moral dominion curtailed by the peril of others. I have no deductive proof for samaritanism, but I can offer a prima facie case for the benefit principle and then defend this stance against the arguments of the libertarians.

Combining the harm principle with a benefit principle accords better with our considered judgments than the libertarian alternative. I say this not only because it seems counterintuitive that every person in existing states has a right to secede, but also because there are countless other circumstances in which our considered moral judgments affirm our moral responsibility to help others. One's duty to rescue a drowning baby from a swimming pool when doing so requires only reaching down and grabbing the infant is just one example. We should abandon these moral convictions in favor of an uncompromising version of rights-libertarianism, then, only if we discover weighty arguments for this move.

Some theorists recommend revising our considered moral judgments in order to make them coherent. In particular, some libertarians assert that any theory that seeks to combine negative rights with the positive rights entailed by a benefit principle is conceptually incoherent. They argue that negative rights place individuals in positions of moral dominion that are inconsistent with positive rights. For instance, one's rights to life and liberty preclude one's incurring a duty without one's consent, and one's right to property implies that others can have no claim to what one owns. This argument constitutes more than a mere assertion that there are no positive rights; it is a deduction that they cannot exist given the presence of conflicting negative rights. This argument is still question-begging, though, because it assumes not only that these negative rights exist, but also that they must take a form that logically excludes positive rights. Strict libertarians understand the moral rights to life, liberty, and (often) property to be general and absolute positions of dominion that can never be transgressed without injustice. From this, some infer that the existence of a few negative rights would rule out positive rights.

While arguments supporting such a conception can be given, the balance of reasons clearly indicates that rights should not be understood as both absolute and general.

Because of the problem of rights conflicts, few contemporary rights theorists understand rights as both absolute and general. Virtually all who now work in this area are either specificationists or prima facie theorists. I advocate a version of the specificationist approach, but accepting the particular position I recommend is not essential to rejecting libertarianism, since both models deny the incompatibility of negative and positive rights.[32] The specificationist contends that negative rights do not rule out positive rights, since the two ultimately do not conflict, and the prima facie theorist maintains that they do conflict but that these clashes can be adjudicated in such a way that the supremacy of one does not preclude the existence of the other.

Specificationists insist that there are no actual conflicts between positive and negative rights, because once the two apparently conflicting rights are fully specified (or at least sufficiently specified for a particular conflict), there will be an exceptive clause in one of the rights that ensures that at most one of the parties occupies the relevant position of dominion. Consider, for example, a potential conflict between Chip's right to defend himself and Dale's right to life. If Chip's act of killing Dale is genuinely an instance of Chip defending himself, then Chip is justified in doing so and has no duty to the contrary. The specificationist asserts that since Chip has no duty not to kill Dale, Dale has no right to life against Chip in this case. According to the specificationist, then, Dale's right to life does not conflict with Chip's right to self-defense, because in this potential conflict there is an exceptive clause in Dale's right that gives him no advantage *in these particular circumstances.* So despite initial appearances, there is only one right and, consequently, no rights conflict. The prima facie theorist describes the relationship between Chip and Dale differently. She allows for rights conflict, but suggests that this conflict does not eliminate either right. The prima facie theorist alleges that Dale has a right to life that conflicts with Chip's right to defend himself, and that the former right persists despite being overridden by the latter. Regardless of which account is preferable, the important point for our purposes is that both models of rights can resolve apparent rights conflicts, and thus the mere fact that positive rights would initially seem

[32] I defend a specificationist theory of rights conflicts in my article "On Conflicts between Rights."

to come into conflict with negative rights is insufficient to show that the former cannot exist.

While this example shows that the specificationist and prima facie theorists can account for the logical possibility of positive rights, it is open to the libertarian to argue against these models of rights conflict. The libertarian might respond that, although the coexistence of negative and positive rights is not incoherent, there are good reasons to conceive of rights as general and absolute. Perhaps the greatest advantage of understanding rights in this way is that it brings clarity and simplicity to rights matters, thereby giving rights claims the greatest explanatory power. This libertarian model is more powerful because it allows reference to rights to determine the deontic status of actions without any further deliberation. In other words, according to this conception, if one has a right to life, liberty, or property, then we may safely infer that any action encroaching upon this right is impermissible. To see that this is not also true for the alternative models, notice how each would deal with Chip and Dale. For the specificationist, Dale's right to life does not establish the impermissibility of Chip's action, because additional scrutiny of the right's exceptive clauses is necessary before we could know whether Chip could permissibly kill Dale. Additional deliberation is also required on the prima facie model, because even after Dale's right to life is recognized it remains to be determined whether this right is overridden by more pressing moral concerns. If we conceive of rights as general and absolute, on the other hand, then Dale's right to life is sufficient to establish the impermissibility of Chip's conduct. If Dale's right is general, it holds against all others, including Chip; and if it is absolute, it trumps all competing moral concerns. Thus only a conception of rights as general and absolute is able fully to determine the deontic status of second-party actions with reference only to rights.

Ironically, while some may trumpet the virtues of clarity and simplicity, it is precisely those qualities that lead most theorists to reject a model of rights as general and absolute. The plain truth is that ethical issues do not always admit of simple solutions; quite the contrary, moral quandaries are often convoluted matters involving complex responses that cannot be deduced from simple rules or explained in terms of general and absolute rights. Above all, we should not accept counterintuitive substantive conclusions for the sake of preserving explanatory simplicity. There is no harm in striving for conceptual elegance, but this goal should not trump our moral phenomenology. The problem for strict rights-libertarianism, then, is that we should and do hold firm to our considered moral convictions even when we recognize that they conflict with the most simple model of rights. To see this, notice how our considered moral convictions have difficulty with a model of rights as general and absolute in a much-discussed example recounted by Joel Feinberg:

Suppose that you are on a backpacking trip in the high mountains when an unanticipated blizzard strikes the area with such ferocity that your life is imperiled. Fortunately, you stumble onto an unoccupied cabin, locked and boarded up for the winter, clearly somebody else's property. You smash in a window, enter, and huddle in a corner for three days until the storm abates. During this period you help yourself to your unknown benefactor's food supply and burn his wooden furniture in the fireplace to keep warm. Surely you are justified in doing all these things, and yet you have infringed the clear rights of another person.[33]

Feinberg is correct to judge that "[s]urely you are justified in doing all these things," and yet this conclusion is inconsistent with the model of rights as general and absolute. If the cabin owner's property right to the cabin is perfectly general, then it holds against everyone, including the hiker; if this same right is absolute, then it signals the presence of a decisive duty for all the second parties against whom it holds. Thus, the right's generality and absoluteness combine to entail the impermissibility of the hiker entering the cabin. But this is directly counter to our considered judgment that her entrance is permissible. In short, since we believe that the hiker is at liberty to enter the cabin, we conclude that the cabin owner's right cannot be both general and absolute. Either its generality is suspended so that it does not apply to the hiker, or its absoluteness is limited so that the hiker's peril overrides the property right. Thus we see that, while it would admittedly be nice if all rights questions could easily be answered by quick reference to simple rules regarding rights, such rules do not always generate answers that we can accept. It is perhaps lamentable that we must develop very elaborate models of rights in order to capture fully the dynamics of our moral relations, but the regret is not so great that we should amend our substantive conclusions in the interest of conceptual simplicity. In sum, the libertarian thinker cannot insist upon the impossibility of positive rights merely by appealing to what her traditional account of rights allows, because there are alternatives to this conception of rights. If the libertarian still wants to *argue*

---

[33] Feinberg, "Voluntary Euthanasia and the Inalienable Right to Life," p. 102.

for this traditional conception, she may do so, but the arguments seem not to be in her favor.[34]

To review: Libertarians begin with the appealing presumption in favor of individual liberty. Problems arise, however, when they proceed from this intuitively acceptable assumption to conclusions that are sharply at odds with commonsense morality. They move from an intuitively appealing departure point to these less tenable positions by making the unwarranted assumption that rights must be general and absolute. (One can value individual liberty without concluding that this liberty may never permissibly be limited.) Just as it is often impermissible to *harm* another, sometimes it can be equally impermissible to fail to benefit others. When one can prevent substantial harm to others at minimal cost to oneself, then one is not at liberty to do otherwise. The imperiled person has a right against you that limits your liberty. A duly qualified benefit-to-others principle makes it impermissible for Antonio to drive off and leave Bathsheba in Pleasantville, and this same principle limits one's claim to be free from political coercion when secession will leave others in a harmful state of affairs.

If the preceding is correct, rigorous libertarians are wrong to infer the absence of positive rights from the presence of negative rights. Statists should not be too quick to claim victory, however, because there is another way to attack the samaritan account of political legitimacy. A more popular (and promising) anarcho-libertarian approach is to assert that political coercion would be justified if it were necessary to secure vital benefits, but that states in fact perform no vital function that could not be provided by private enterprise in the state's absence.[35] As a consequence,

---

34 Someone sympathetic to rights-libertarianism might object that my discussion has included no specific libertarian's criticism of rights to assistance. This objection is totally reasonable; after all, it is a lot easier to defeat a view if you do not let anyone defend it! In response, let me say that I discuss the rigorous libertarian position in general terms because – unlike Feinberg's treatment of samaritan duties – there is no one libertarian whose treatment of this subject is widely regarded as definitive. (Robert Nozick is by far the most prominent rights-libertarian, but he is famously silent on the question of whether negative rights can be overridden.) Thus, if I focused on one or two particular accounts, I could be accused of neglecting others, and if I surveyed all the various accounts it would require much more space than addressing the issue in general terms. Thus, let me explicitly acknowledge that my discussion presumes that no one could conclusively argue against positive rights. If I am wrong, then my account of political legitimacy fails.

35 Authors like David Friedman, Bruce Benson, and Randy Barnett argue in this manner. To my knowledge, the most impressive attempts to show that the state cannot be justified

states that lack consent are not justified; and because existing states lack consent, all are illegitimate.

I argued earlier that unlimited political liberty precludes peace and security because the voluntarily remaining citizens would be unable to construct an effective legal regime. This counterfactual hypothesis relies on the assumption that, for a variety of interrelated reasons, many of us would not respect moral reasons without an effective legal system providing self-interested reasons for doing so. The recent looting in Iraq following the overthrow of Saddam Hussein's regime supports this view. As in other cases in which the political authorities have been disabled, masses of people took advantage of the inoperative legal system by selfishly violating the rights of others. Many ignored the moral rights of others simply because there were no longer sufficient self-interested reasons motivating them to respect those rights, but clearly this is just one element of a more complex story.[36]

An anarchist need not assert that everyone will respect moral reasons in the absence of self-interested motivation; she can make the more plausible claim that private companies can effectively protect moral rights. In my view, this is a very real possibility that has been given short shrift by traditional political theorists. Federal Express is an excellent example of a private company that provides a service that most of us assumed could be performed only by a (state's) monopoly. But, while I am impressed with Federal Express and am open to privatizing other services currently reserved for governments, I remain skeptical of trading our states for private protection agencies. The principal difficulty is that there is no reason to suppose that all people in a given territory would gravitate toward a single protective company, and stability would be threatened by clashes between competing enforcement agencies. More specifically, because private companies are concerned principally with profits, each would strive maximally to attract and retain clients. Since people would select agencies for self-interested reasons, they would select agencies offering the most enticing combination of low cost and secure protection. Problems would inevitably arise, then, since maximally protecting clients could lead companies to disrespect the moral rights of nonclients. Because the nonclients

---

in terms of the functions that cannot be performed in its absence are Benson's book *The Enterprise of Law,* Friedman's paper "Anarchy and Efficient Law," and Barnett's article "Restitution: A New Paradigm of Criminal Justice."

[36] I offer a more detailed explanation of why life in the absence of political order would necessarily be perilous in Chapter 1 of *Is There a Duty to Obey the Law?*

of one agency would likely be customers of another agency that similarly strove to protect its clients, however, there is apt to be constant strife and struggle between competing protective agencies that would threaten peace and leave individuals vulnerable.

I suspect that a system of private protection agencies would experience additional difficulties, but we need not catalogue these here.[37] For now, it is enough to note that the state appears to be the only effective vehicle to maintain peace and protect rights, because such peace and security requires a territorial monopoly of power that cannot be achieved if everyone's consent is required. No private agency would be selected by all, and competing agencies would clash in a manner that undermines peace. I must confess, though, that if someone could generate conclusive evidence that a just and secure peace could be established in the state of nature, I would embrace anarchism rather than statism. In the absence of such evidence, however, there is no reason to jettison the descriptive premise upon which the samaritan theory of political legitimacy relies.

Conclusion

If it were true either that we had consented to be governed or that very few of us would elect to secede if given the opportunity, then freedom of association would not be incompatible with statism. However, because it is historically inaccurate to posit widespread consent and unrealistically optimistic to predict that most of us would not secede if given the opportunity, we must choose between denying the legitimacy of existing states and qualifying freedom of association. The samaritan account of political legitimacy explains why states may permissibly coerce citizens without their consent and, in so doing, explains why we do not have a perfectly general and absolute right to freedom of association. Without denying the importance of being able to choose one's associates, we must acknowledge that this discretion may permissibly be restricted in the political context, because (unlike the case of choosing a marital partner or a religious community) its costs in the political arena are prohibitive. In the end, we are forced to choose between statism and unrestricted freedom

---

[37] For instance, problems would be created both by those who attempt to defend themselves rather than hire a protective agency and by those who cannot afford to hire a protective service (and there are likely to be many if there is no government to require welfare transfers).

of association, and the samaritan account makes plain why we must give up the latter and its permissive implications for secession. Thus we must confess that, while there may be unilateral rights to secede even from just states, these rights cannot be established merely by a straightforward appeal to the value of freedom of association.

3

Valuing Self-Determination

The samaritan theory of political legitimacy outlined in the preceding chapter illustrates that territorial states are necessary, but it is important to recognize that there is nothing about the necessity of political society that requires us to retain our current states in their existing configurations. There is no reason, for instance, why a statist cannot consistently recommend that territorial borders be redesigned so that states are made more stable, more efficient, more in keeping with historically legitimate claims to land, or perhaps more aligned with the ethno-cultural characteristics of their constituents. A theorist concerned with stability might suggest that states take whatever shape is least likely to change over time; someone interested in efficiency might reshape states so that they are best suited to perform their requisite functions; those concerned with historical claims to territory might seek to redraw political boundaries in an attempt to undo the history of unjust annexations, dubious treaties, and ethnic cleansing; and an advocate of nation-states could recommend tracing political borders along the lines of ethnic and cultural distinctions. While all four of these alternatives are consistent with statism, I advocate a fifth option that is more in line with that recommended by authors such as Harry Beran, David Copp, David Gauthier, and Daniel Philpott: Citizens ought to be allowed to redraw political boundaries in any way that is politically feasible.[1] In this chapter, I argue that anyone who properly

[1] See Harry Beran's essays "A Liberal Theory of Secession" and "A Democratic Theory of Political Self-Determination for a New World Order" and his book *The Consent Theory of Political Obligation,* David Copp's paper "Democracy and Communal Self-Determination," David Gauthier's article "Breaking Up: An Essay on Secession," and Daniel Philpott's

values self-determination should defend the right to secede whenever both the separatist group and the remainder state would be able and willing to perform the requisite political functions.

The Case for Secession Grounded in Self-Determination

A commitment to statism does not require us to deny the importance of political self-determination. The lesson from the last chapter is that one cannot consistently affirm the legitimacy of political states and endorse *unlimited* secessionist rights, but this does not imply that there can be *no* primary rights to secede. The crucial point is that, even if the benefits of political stability are important enough to outweigh conflicting claims to freedom of association, self-determination remains valuable and should be accommodated whenever it does not conflict with political order. Put simply, statists who value self-determination can give priority to the security of political states and yet still defend the right to reconfigure the territorial boundaries of existing states whenever this reordering will not interrupt the vital benefits of political society.

To appreciate the case for political self-determination, notice how we regard the state's interference with personal autonomy in other contexts. Consider, for instance, Locke's critique of Hobbes on this score. Hobbes was notoriously appreciative of the benefits of political security, and, in an effort maximally to secure those benefits, he recommended giving virtually unlimited power to the rulers. As a consequence, Hobbes suggested that the rulers should enjoy dominion over all aspects of their constituents' lives. Against this, Locke protested that there are many areas of our lives in which the government has no right to interfere. Locke appreciated Hobbes's point that political states are necessary to address some "inconveniences" that would inevitably remain in the state of nature, but he argued that this entitles the state to do only what is necessary to eliminate such inconveniences. Thus, while a government might permissibly impose various rules designed to prevent citizens from wrongly harming one another, it has no business interfering with its citizens' self-regarding behavior. Whereas the government may designate a side of the street on which all should drive, for instance, it has no right to tell its citizens what to believe, whether or how to worship, what sort

essays "In Defense of Self-Determination" and "Self-Determination in Practice." Although my views have been shaped by all of these authors, I do not know that any of them would agree with the specifics of the arguments I advance here.

of occupation to pursue, or how or with whom to pursue their erotic interests.

One might similarly disagree with Hobbes over who the rulers should be. Hobbes preferred monarchy over either aristocracy or democracy on the grounds that the former is apt to be the sturdiest form of government, and thus is least likely to dissolve into anarchic chaos. Virtually all contemporary theorists, on the other hand, prefer democracy. Thus, without denying that the necessity of political states entails that each person cannot enjoy unlimited dominion over her life, we might object to concluding from the fact that there are areas in which we cannot have *complete* say, that we therefore might as well have *no* say. On the contrary, many insist that each of us should have as much say as possible, and therefore that states must govern democratically.

These twin conclusions that (1) the authority of government is limited and that (2) democracy is required stem from the same root insight: The necessity of political states entails that individual dominion may permissibly be limited, but this in no way diminishes the importance of respecting self-determination. In other words, statists like Locke can insist that self-determination be given priority in all cases where a compelling justification could not be given for its restriction. In a nutshell, the aim of this chapter is to extend this stance regarding self-determination to state breaking. The bottom line is that we should insist upon the right to secede in all cases in which respecting this right would not be excessively harmful.

Given that states derive their legitimacy from the crucial functions they perform, it should come as no surprise that the cornerstone of a systematic theory of secession must be functional. In particular, I suggest that a group has a right to secede just in case it and its remainder state would be able and willing to perform the requisite political functions. If either the separatist group or the rump state would be unable or unwilling to protect its constituents' basic moral rights, then these harmful circumstances explain why the separatist group's political self-determination may permissibly be limited. If both the separatist group and the rump state are capable of maintaining a secure and just political environment, however, then the political divorce would not be excessively harmful, and there is no sufficiently compelling justification for denying political self-determination.

Against this, one might object that, while self-determination is important, its priority must be restricted to our self-regarding behavior. For instance, it would be ridiculous to claim that the importance of self-determination entitles one to rob others, because insofar as robbery wrongly harms those robbed, it is clearly not self-regarding behavior. Similarly, one might doubt the relevance of self-determination for unilateral rights to secede on the grounds that state breaking is obviously not self-regarding: Just as robbery harms those robbed, secession profoundly affects those left behind in the remainder state. To appreciate this, recall the difference between emigration and secession. When one emigrates, one does nothing to diminish one's former state's territory; when a group secedes, on the other hand, it takes a portion of the parent state's territory, thereby leaving those in the remainder state with jurisdiction over less territory. Accordingly, one might protest that, while self-determination is undoubtedly important, its importance cannot ground a unilateral right to secede.

To make this objection compelling, however, one cannot merely show that the citizens in the remainder state would be harmed by the loss of territory; one must establish that they would be *wrongly* harmed because they have a *valid claim* to all of the territory. Put another way, a secessionist conflict is fundamentally a territorial conflict between a separatist group, which cites its right to self-determination, and its state as a whole, which appeals to its political legitimacy. As we saw in the last chapter, a state's claim to jurisdiction over its territory stems from the necessity of the state's performing its political functions. Therefore, when a separatist group is politically viable, it is not true that the state as a whole is necessary to create a politically secure environment, and thus the state does not have a justification for denying the separatist group's political self-determination. Put plainly, while those in the remainder state will undeniably be *affected* by the loss of territory, they do not have a valid claim to preside over the contested territory and thus are not *wrongly harmed* by the political divorce. And because those left behind in the rump state are not wrongly harmed, their circumstances are not analogous to those of someone who is robbed. As a consequence, they cannot protest that the importance of the separatists' self-determination is irrelevant in this context.

In the end, then, I propose that a state should restrict political liberty in a manner analogous to the way it limits the liberty to drive a car. Because many people would be harmed if there were no legal restrictions on who could drive, states legitimately limit the right to drive based on age, health requirements, and demonstrated driving competence.[2] In

---

[2] As with the issuance of driver's licenses, I believe that a threshold concept is appropriate when adjudicating secessionist conflicts. This threshold may vary depending upon the historical and political context (it would clearly be wrong to hold a separatist group in

similar fashion, a state may initially restrict the right to secede to groups of a specific size, and then further require that interested parties demonstrate their ability and willingness to govern in a satisfactorily capable and just manner. This strikes me as a principled and systematic theory of secession that appropriately values self-determination without implausibly denying the crucial benefits of political stability. I shall explain this view in greater detail later, but first I should acknowledge that it requires a more substantial assumption than might at first be apparent.

The Assumption of Group Autonomy

The argument in this chapter is a conditional one: If you value self-determination, then you should endorse secessionist rights. My principal aim is not to defend this initial premise but to argue from it to some striking conclusions regarding state breaking. However, I should acknowledge that my premise is more ambitious and controversial than it might initially appear. In particular, my argument presupposes not just that we should value self-determination but that there are *deontological* reasons to respect *group* autonomy. This is potentially problematic, because even those who value self-determination might object on one of two fronts, alleging either that (1) there are only consequential reasons to respect self-determination or that (2) even if there are deontological reasons to respect an individual person's autonomy, there can be at most consequential reasons to respect a group's self-determination. Thus, before fleshing out my views on political self-determination, let me defend my understanding of group autonomy.

There is widespread agreement that individuals should be allowed to direct their own self-regarding affairs. There is some disagreement, however, about the proper justification for this position. Following John Stuart Mill, many emphasize that an appreciation of individual self-determination is conducive to the promotion of overall well-being.[3] This account rests upon the three plausible observations: Each person is likely to be the (1) most knowledgeable, (2) most interested, and (3) best positioned to promote her own welfare. In light of these three considerations, it seems reasonable to conclude that, in the absence of extenuating

---

1776 to a standard that would be appropriate today, or perhaps even to require that the Chechens be as just as the Scots in order to qualify for a right to secede), but the crucial point is that the preferences of the majority of the separatists should be decisive when the appropriate threshold of political competence has been satisfied.

[3] John Stuart Mill, *On Liberty*.

circumstances, each agent is likely to fare best when given authority over her self-regarding affairs. Thus, if we are concerned to promote overall or aggregate well-being, a sensible strategy would be to design the criminal law and other institutions so that each person is treated as sovereign over her own affairs. In short, considerations such as these explain why we should treat each person as enjoying what we might call a "right to autonomy."

Although I disagree with neither the premises nor the conclusion of this consequentialist defense of individual dominion, I do not think this approach provides the only, or even the primary, reasons to respect a person's autonomy. For two reasons, I ultimately favor a nonconsequentialist account of the value of autonomy. First, I am convinced that individuals retain their positions of dominion even when their decision making clearly does not maximize overall happiness. If we derive the value of autonomy exclusively from consequences, however, then it remains valuable only when and to the extent that it produces those consequences. Imagine, for instance, that if left to her own devices, Jezebel would quit her job and move to Santa Fe, where she would spend her time (and life savings) trying to pen the "Great American Novel." Suppose also that anyone who knows Jezebel (and her limited literary talents) even casually would recognize that such a move is a recipe for disaster. My view is that no one may rightfully interfere with Jezebel's plans even if it is abundantly clear that this interference would produce better consequences. That is to say, even if all the evidence suggests that Jezebel's move would be horribly detrimental to her well-being, she remains at liberty to make this move because it is *her life*. Of course, there is nothing wrong with trying to persuade Jezebel of the folly of such a move, but one may not forcibly interfere if one's best efforts fail to convince her.

The second reason I am dissatisfied with consequentialist explanations of the value of autonomy is that they do not adequately capture the sense in which our duties concerning autonomy are owed *to* the individual whose autonomy is in question. As Tom Beauchamp puts it, "To respect the autonomy of . . . self-determining agents is to recognize them as *entitled* to determine their own destiny."[4] According to the consequentialist, the reason that a government should not force me to practice a certain religion, for instance, is that a policy of religious coercion is unlikely to produce the best overall results. The real objection to such

---

[4] Tom L. Beauchamp and LeRoy Walters, *Contemporary Issues in Bioethics*, p. 23 (emphasis in original).

a policy, however, seems to me to be that this interference with my religious self-determination treats *me* wrongly. The chief problem with such intrusions into individual autonomy is not that they lead to a world containing less happiness; it is that my privileged position of moral dominion is violated. Thus, at the end of the day, I believe that no matter how the calculations come out, the balance of consequences is at best beside the most important moral point. If happiness might be maximized by disrespecting autonomy, then I would typically favor respecting autonomy to the detriment of overall well-being; and if happiness would be maximized by respecting autonomy, this strikes me as a lovely coincidence or perhaps even a buttressing consideration but not as the core argument in favor of respecting autonomy.

In fairness, I should acknowledge that consequentialists have designed sophisticated arguments to counter worries like the two I have just expressed. In particular, many emphasize that the best strategy for maximizing total welfare over the long haul would be to endorse a blanket prohibition against paternalistic meddling; others stress that a person's well-being is partly constituted by her autonomy or even that autonomy is among the intrinsic goods that must be considered when determining the right action. Although I think these attempts to better appreciate the value of autonomy are important improvements, I fear that no autonomy-related amendments within consequentialism will ultimately suffice because I remain convinced that agents are *entitled* to their self-determination, and *entitlement* is a fundamentally deontological notion that cannot be fully cashed out in consequentialist terms.[5] Thus, no matter how much one tinkers with either the action-guidance or the roster of intrinsic values of consequentialism, the latter will remain ill suited to capture an essential feature of autonomy. In other words, even if a consequentialist can explain why we ought not to interfere with Jezebel's self-regarding behavior (either because one should adopt a general rule against such interference or because autonomy is among the goods to be maximized), a consequentialist cannot adequately explain why we owe it *to* Jezebel not to interfere because she is *entitled* to live her own life.[6]

---

[5] I explain in greater detail these more sophisticated consequentialist approaches to autonomy and my dissatisfaction with them in my essay "The Paradox of Group Autonomy."

[6] To appreciate the essentially deontological nature of autonomy, consider the analogous case of promise keeping. Consequentialists can give very sophisticated explanations why we should keep our promises (they can even explain why we should keep our promises in cases where we could maximize well-being by breaking them), but consequentialists cannot fully capture the sense in which the promisor owes it *to* the promisee to keep

Although thoroughgoing consequentialists will no doubt bristle at this explanation of the deontological reasons to respect autonomy, I suspect that most will find it congenial. More work remains to be done in justifying my presumption of group autonomy, however, because one might concede all that I say regarding *personal* autonomy and still deny that we have deontological reasons to respect *group* self-determination. Before highlighting the problematic features of group autonomy, however, let me distinguish between two possible concepts of group dominion. To appreciate the difference between these two, first consider a country that prohibits women from voting in national elections or a municipality that forbids blacks from living on a certain side of the railroad tracks. I can understand why someone might say that such a country disrespects the group autonomy of women or that such a city disrespects the group autonomy of blacks; after all, the individuals are discriminated against on the basis of their membership in a given group, and it seems plausible to suggest that all members of the group suffer, even those women who do not care to vote and those blacks uninterested in living on the prohibited side of the tracks. However, without diminishing the importance of these types of discrimination, I want to stress that these cases do not constitute restrictions on group autonomy as I understand the term here.

I conceive group autonomy to be something that can be exercised by a collective *as a whole* rather than individually by persons in a group. Thus, on my understanding of group autonomy, examples might include the right of a corporation to choose its retirement policies, the right of a chess club to set its membership dues, the right of a condominium association to accept or reject the sale of a unit to a prospective buyer, the right of

---

the promise, because consequentialism can adequately explain neither why the promisor owes something *to* the promisee nor how the promisee would be *wronged* by the broken promise.

In insisting that the full story of autonomy cannot be told without invoking deontology, I mean to suggest neither that consequences are morally irrelevant nor that the deontological reasons we have to respect an agent's self-determination can never be outweighed by competing reasons generated by consequential considerations. Thus, by conceding that autonomy does not necessarily trump all appeals to consequences and yet maintaining that autonomy is a basic source of moral reasons, I regard myself as positing a pluralistic account reminiscent of the approach to ethics advanced by W. D. Ross (though I might not explain these moral reasons in terms of prima facie duties). That is, I conceive of autonomy as a basic moral value that provides others with deontological moral reasons not to interfere with one's self-regarding behavior irrespective of the expected consequences of such interference. Finally, I must confess that, like Ross, I have no fully codified algorithm specifying precisely when the moral reasons springing from autonomy prevail over competing reasons.

a Native American tribe to choose which language will be spoken in its schools, the right of a country to accept or reject an offer to merge with another country, and the right of a territorially concentrated group to secede from its host country. All of these examples are potential cases of group autonomy as I use the term here, insofar as they involve groups *qua groups* determining their own affairs. To reiterate: Group autonomy exists when the group as a whole rather than the individuals within the group stands in the privileged position of dominion over the affairs of the group.

Having specified what I mean by group autonomy, we can now apply the lesson of the preceding discussion to groups in particular. The fundamental point to this juncture has been that we have deontological moral reasons to respect an agent's autonomy. The moral duty we have not to interfere in Jezebel's affairs is a duty we owe *to Jezebel*, rather than some general, freestanding duty (owed to humanity? to no one? to the cosmos?) to maximize overall well-being. Extending this insight to groups, it seems as though any autonomy-based duties regarding collectives will be owed either to the group or perhaps to the members of the group. If we have a duty not to interfere with a chess club's plan to increase its membership dues, for instance, this duty is *owed to* the group. That is to say, the group's autonomy has a basic value, from which two things follow: (1) We might have a duty not to interfere with the group's self-determination even if interfering would maximize overall well-being, and (2) even if it turns out that not interfering would maximize aggregate welfare, the chief problem with interfering would be that it wrongs the group. These conclusions square with my pretheoretic intuitions (the principal reason that Iraq may not permissibly forcibly annex Kuwait, for instance, would seemingly have to be that it treats Kuwait and/or Kuwaitis wrongly), but, as I will now explain, it is surprisingly difficult to support these pretheoretic convictions.

To appreciate how difficult it is to explain the reasons for respecting group autonomy, notice that there are three salient accounts of collective self-determination, and none appears adequate. These three approaches feature (1) value-collectivism, (2) individual autonomy, and (3) individual well-being. Let us review each in turn.

First consider value-collectivism. The easiest and most seamless way to establish that group autonomy is perfectly analogous to individual autonomy is to suggest that groups are normatively analogous to individuals. That is, perhaps groups and individual persons enjoy the same positions of dominion over their own affairs simply because there is no morally relevant difference between the two. Although I am attracted to this position for the convenience with which it supplies the theoretical building blocks for a satisfying account of group autonomy, I must confess that I find it prima facie implausible. Michael Hartney captures the problem nicely when he suggests:

> ...people generally believe that communities are important because of their contribution to the well-being of individuals. Such a view is part of what might be called value-individualism: only the lives of individual human beings have ultimate value, and collective entities derive their value from their contribution to the lives of individual human beings. The opposite view we might call 'value collectivism': the view that a collective entity can have value independently of its contribution to the well-being of individual human beings. Such a position is counter-intuitive, and the burden of proof rests upon anyone who wishes to defend it.[7]

Thus, unless one can explain why groups, like individuals, have ultimate value, it is problematic to suggest that group autonomy is morally equivalent to individual autonomy. Of course, many theorists have argued on behalf of value-collectivism, but I know of none who has done so successfully. For instance, Michael McDonald defends the intrinsic value of groups on the ground that they possess all of the requisite properties. He writes: "Individuals are regarded as valuable because they are choosers and have interests. But so also do communities make choices and have values. Why not then treat communities as fundamental units of value as well?"[8]

To answer McDonald's question, my reservations about regarding groups as valuable in themselves stem from my interpretation of the sense in which groups can be said to have interests. I appreciate that groups can meaningfully be said to have interests insofar as groups can flourish or flounder depending upon the circumstances, and it makes sense to say that anything that contributes to the health of a group is in its interests. For example, it is perfectly intelligible to say that the emergence of the internet might prove detrimental to the interests of many community-based chess clubs, because the incentive to maintain membership in these clubs may diminish markedly with the newfound convenience of playing "virtual" chess with people all over the world. But, while there is nothing awkward about speaking of a chess club as having interests, it is important

---

[7] Michael Hartney, "Some Confusions Concerning Collective Rights," p. 297.

[8] Michael McDonald, "Should Communities Have Rights? Reflections on Liberal Individualism," p. 237.

to appreciate that these interests are not in and of themselves fundamentally morally significant in the way than an individual person's are. The key here is that a person has a vantage point from which she experiences the world, and thus her lived experience is better or worse depending upon the ways in which she flourishes or flounders. It is this experience that makes her interests fundamentally morally significant.

The problem with value-collectivism, then, is that while there is a sense in which groups might be said to have interests, groups themselves (that is, apart from the individuals who comprise them) have no vantage point from which they experience the realization or thwarting of their interests. Put another way, whereas people care desperately whether they flourish or flounder, it does not matter to a group itself whether or not its interests are promoted. Given this, we apparently must concede that group interests are not of fundamental moral value and, as a consequence, that there is in fact a morally important difference between groups and individual persons that explains why only the latter are of nonderivative moral value. And finally, the fact that groups are not valuable in themselves entails that group autonomy cannot be valuable in the same way as individual autonomy. As Charles Beitz puts it, given "that states, unlike persons, lack the unity of consciousness and the rational will that constitute the identity of persons. . . . [and are not] organic wholes with the unity and integrity that attaches to persons qua persons. . . . [i]t should come as no surprise that this lack of analogy leads to a lack of analogy on the matter of autonomy."[9] Thus, despite the difficulties it might pose for developing a satisfactory account of group autonomy, I must confess that I know of no adequate defense of value-collectivism. As a result, we should seek an account of group autonomy consistent with value-individualism.[10]

---

[9] Charles R. Beitz, *Political Theory and International Relations*, p. 81.

[10] One might object to my contention that an entity's interests are morally relevant only if these interests matter to the entity itself on the grounds that it unduly restricts the set of things that can have ultimate value. Among the unfashionable implications that follow from this stance, for instance, are the conclusions that ecosystems, great works of art, and various objects in nature can have no value apart from their contribution to the lives of sentient beings. Some will find this unpalatable insofar as it implies that there would be nothing wrong with burning the Mona Lisa, destroying the Great Barrier Reef, or chopping down all of the world's trees if one were the last sentient being alive. Although I too have reservations about these conclusions, I do not regard them as a reductio of my stance. Awkward or not, my considered conviction is that, although it is perfectly intelligible to say that various nonsentient things have interests, these interests are not morally significant in themselves.

Given the problems with value-collectivism, it seems natural to explore the possibility of deriving group autonomy from the individual autonomy of the members of the group. On this view, group autonomy creates duties that are owed to the members of the group. For instance, while the duty to allow the Augusta National Golf Club to choose its new members is not owed to the club itself, it may be owed to the club's members, which is to say that the members would be the ones wronged if someone unjustifiably interfered with the club's self-determination. Given my belief that, unlike groups themselves, the people who make up these groups are of ultimate moral importance, I find this way of understanding group autonomy very attractive. The question, however, is whether there is sufficient theoretical support for such a conception of group autonomy. In particular, what justifies the view that we owe it to individuals to respect the autonomy of the groups to which they belong?

The most salient answer to this last question, I think, is that respect for group autonomy is owed to the members of these groups because group autonomy is an extension of the autonomy of individuals. Another way of putting it is that group autonomy often matters morally because individual autonomy matters morally, and individuals sometimes exercise their autonomy in concert with others. Perhaps the best way to understand the view that a group's autonomy is an extension of the autonomy of its members is to think of the group as akin to a proxy for its constituents. Suppose, for instance, that I send my friend as a proxy to an important department meeting. If my colleagues refuse to count this proxy vote, they wrong *me*, not the person I have appointed as my proxy. I think that when our participation within a group enables a group to act on our behalf, this group can play a role analogous to an appointed proxy. And when some external party wrongly interferes with this group's activity, this interference wrongs the members of the group, those for whom the group is a proxy.

To see why this construal of group autonomy makes sense, consider again the golf club example. The position under consideration is that whatever autonomy-based moral reasons we have to refrain from forcing the Augusta National Golf Club either to accept or to reject certain new members exist in virtue of the value of the autonomy of the club's individual members. On this view, what is wrong with forcing Augusta to accept, say, Annika Sorenstam is neither that such forcible interference decreases overall well-being nor that it diminishes the welfare of any individuals who currently make up the club (it may do neither). The real problem is that it disrespects the autonomy of the club members.

Because this account depends upon the plausibility of regarding group autonomy as an extension of the autonomy of individuals, it is worth reflecting upon how groups like Augusta National are formed. Initially, a number of charter members get together to form a club. Often there are disagreements regarding what rules should govern the club, but no one has a gun held to her head, and most often people are able to work through these disagreements (though, occasionally, when the disagreements are significant enough, one or more of the potential members will abandon the project of forming the club). Once the club is created, new members may or may not be added. Any given new member may not be thrilled with every aspect of the existing arrangement, but again, no gun is held to her head, and those sufficiently concerned about the club's constitution are free not to join. Often, the rules or composition of a club will change over time (sometimes gradually, other times abruptly), and it is always possible that existing members will become so unhappy with these changes (or perhaps with the club's resistance to change) that they will want to leave. If so, they are free to exit. Finally, think about an individual member's control over adding new members. If these decisions are made collectively, then no one has complete control over this process. (Even if each member has veto power over new members, for instance, this gives each person only the power unilaterally to exclude others, not the ability to include them unilaterally. And, conversely, if anyone has the unilateral power to invite a certain number of new members, then the others have a correlative inability to exclude them.) Some might think that this last point undermines the understanding of group autonomy as an extension of individual autonomy insofar as individuals typically lack the requisite control over the group as a whole. In the imaginary case of Augusta and Annika Sorenstam, for instance, how can we conceive of interference with the group's decision as disrespecting the individual's autonomy when the individual did not have control over the process to begin with? Here I think the individual's history with the group is crucial. While it is true that any given member of Augusta may not have unilateral freedom to accept or reject Annika Sorenstam, each member was free not to join the club. And since each member freely joined the club with its rules about membership (as well as its secondary rules about how the primary rules regarding membership might be changed), it strikes me as plausible to regard the interference with the group's self-determination as an interference with each of the member's autonomy. Moreover, I think one's autonomy is infringed regardless of one's personal position on inviting Sorenstam to be a member. Thus, *even if*

I were among the outvoted minority who thought that Annika Sorenstam should have been invited to join, my autonomy would be violated by some party outside of the group forcing Augusta National to accept Sorenstam as a member. In short, each member of Augusta would equally have her autonomy disrespected by a third party's interference with the club's self-determination.

Understanding group self-determination as an extension of the autonomy of the individuals who comprise the group nicely captures ordinary moral thinking, but problems remain because this account does not appear broad enough. For example, legitimate political states are typically thought to be among the paradigm candidates for group autonomy, and yet it is not clear how they can be accommodated on this account. Imagine, for instance, that citizens in the United States become frustrated at being second-rate in hockey and seek to rectify their inferiority by uniting to form one country with Canada. It seems to me that Canada has the right to accept or reject this merger, and that if the United States forcibly annexed Canada after they rejected the offer, this annexation would be a violation of Canada's autonomy. Although this is more controversial, I also believe that those in Quebec might have the right to choose whether to remain in Canada or to secede and form their own country, and that Canada would be disrespecting Quebec's group autonomy if it forced them to remain in the union. The problem with explaining group autonomy as an extension of individual autonomy is that it appears unable to explain either of these cases.

The worry, of course, is that, unlike the Augusta National Golf Club, neither Canada nor Quebec owes its membership exclusively to the autonomous choices of its constituents. Crucial to regarding group autonomy as an extension of individual autonomy is that the group's actions derive at some basic level from the autonomous actions of the group's members. (This is why I emphasized that the members of Augusta freely chose to join the golf club and are equally free to withdraw if they become sufficiently dissatisfied with the rules, including those that govern the selection of new members.) Indeed, to see the importance of this condition, imagine that I believe myself to be a messianic figure whose calling is to start a religious community in Arizona. Because my repeated efforts to recruit a devoted flock garner no followers, I ultimately kidnap hundreds of people and transport them to Arizona, where I force them to set up a religious community. Under these circumstances, it strikes me as ludicrous to suggest that third parties have autonomy-based moral reasons to respect the group's self-determination. The key is that, because the individual members are not exercising their autonomy in concert with one another, it is unreasonable to construe the group's autonomy as an extension of the individual autonomy of the group's members. And if interfering with this group's self-determination is not tantamount to interfering with its members' autonomy, then it is hard to see how this interference wrongs anyone. As a result, there appear to be no autonomy-based moral reasons against interfering with such a group.

The problem for political states is that they are more like this imaginary religious community than the Augusta National Golf Club insofar as they are not comprised of constituents who have freely agreed to join them. In order to perform the functions that justify their existence, states are by necessity defined territorially, and thus voluntary compliance is a luxury they can ill afford to extend to those within their geographical boundaries. And, given that states nonconsensually coerce all those over whom they exercise sovereignty, it is not clear how we can, with intellectual integrity, regard their group autonomy as an extension of the individual autonomy of their citizens.

Of course, in pointing out that states are not constructed entirely from the autonomous choices of their constituents, I do not mean to suggest that they are therefore necessarily illegitimate. As I explained in the last chapter, nonconsensual political coercion can be justified by the vitally important benefits that could not be secured in its absence. And, given that states join consensual groups like Augusta in not impermissibly disrespecting the autonomy of their members, this suggests the possibility that a group's autonomy might be derived from the individual autonomy of its members just in case the group does not unjustly restrict the autonomy of its constituents.[11] I am attracted to this view for its ability to generate precisely the conclusions I favor (Augusta and just political states would be entitled to group autonomy, whereas our imaginary religious community and unjust states would not). I nonetheless reject this option because I do not see how a group's autonomy can be an extension of an individual's autonomy merely because the group has not impermissibly restricted that individual's self-determination.

The distinction between "extension of" and "permissible restriction of" autonomy can perhaps best be illustrated by returning to the analogy

---

[11] Beitz considers the view that all just states have a right to autonomy in *Political Theory and International Relations.* He does not necessarily endorse this view; his primary concern is to show that, even if it is true, it would not explain why we should not interfere with the self-determination of unjust states.

of a proxy. It seems plausible to understand group autonomy as an extension of an individual's autonomy if it is reasonable to regard the group's actions as a proxy for the individual, and a group acts as a proxy when an individual autonomously embraces that group as something of a proxy. When a group merely refrains from impermissibly infringing upon an individual's autonomy, however, this does not in itself make it a proxy for the individual, and thus there is not the same reason to regard the group's autonomy as an extension of the individual's. As a consequence, in the absence of an adequate story to bridge the gap between an "extension of" and "the permissible restriction of" autonomy, it strikes me as unwarranted to assert that a group's autonomy is derived from the individual autonomy of its members as long as the group does not unjustly restrict the autonomy of its constituents. As a result, while the more general approach of understanding group autonomy as derived from individual autonomy seems to work wonderfully for some types of groups, it cannot explain the importance of autonomy for all of the groups that we would like to include. Most notably, it does not explain the moral reasons we have to respect the self-determination of just states and suitably organized separatist groups.

Given the problems with conceiving of group autonomy as an extension of individual autonomy, it is worth considering a third potential account, which derives the value of group autonomy from the welfare of the members of the group in question. This approach is also value-individualist, and it promises to explain the value of autonomy for a broader set of groups, so it appears better able to accommodate our convictions regarding political states and separatist groups. Indeed, one of the chief lessons that contemporary liberals have learned from communitarians is the profound extent to which individual well-being depends crucially upon the health of the various noncontractual groups to which we belong. Thus, while social contract theorists have long emphasized the crucial benefits that political institutions supply by preventing the harmful chaos that would inevitably occur in their absence, only recently have writers begun to stress that healthy cultures are pivotal to the life prospects of their members.[12] Moreover, it seems only natural that groups like political states and cultural nations are more likely to flourish when they are left to direct their own affairs, free from the interference of others. Thus, perhaps the best way to account for the value of group autonomy is in

[12] For instance, see Will Kymlicka's landmark book, *Liberalism, Community and Culture*.

terms of its contribution to the well-being of the individuals within those groups.

Although this type of explanation appears capable of casting the net wide enough to include political states and many potential separatist units, I fear that it cannot generate a satisfying theory of group autonomy. In particular, because it ultimately derives the value of group autonomy from the promotion of welfare, it is vulnerable to the problems we discussed earlier in connection with Jezebel. To review, I offered the example of Jezebel to illustrate my dissatisfaction with explaining the value of (individual) autonomy in terms of its promotion of well-being. The problem with such an instrumental account is that it instructs one to respect autonomy only when and to the extent that doing so will maximize happiness. As I tried to show with Jezebel's ill-advised plan to move to Santa Fe, however, our convictions suggest that Jezebel retains her privileged position of dominion over her own affairs even when she is inclined to act in ways that are likely to cause her great unhappiness. Put plainly, we dismissed the consequentialist approach for its inability to capture our conviction that we may not permissibly interfere with Jezebel's move to New Mexico simply because it is Jezebel's life, and she is entitled to run the risk of ruining it if she wants.

The case of Jezebel is pertinent again here because analogous problems emerge if we conceive of group autonomy as valuable only to the extent that it promotes the well-being of the individuals within the group. To see this, let us return to the case of Canada's group autonomy, again assuming that the United States wants to merge with Canada in order to achieve world supremacy in hockey. The appeal of interpreting group autonomy's value as a function of individual happiness is that it allows us to explain Canada's group autonomy without importing the fiction of political consent. The problem, however, is that it leaves us with an anemic account of Canada's right to self-determination. To see this, imagine how the United States should act if Canada declined the invitation to merge. In particular, notice how this approach counsels the United States as to whether or not it may forcibly annex Canada. Because the value of Canada's group autonomy derives from its tendency to promote the welfare of Canadians, its autonomy is valuable only to the extent that it does so. Thus, just as we saw in the case of Jezebel, this approach does not require outsiders to respect Canada's group autonomy when Canada exercises its autonomy in a way that fails to maximize the welfare of its constituents. With this in mind, imagine that Canada rejects the U.S. merger offer because it recognizes that it can remain the preeminent hockey power all on its own. Suppose, though, that a strong case can be made that Canadians would, on balance, dramatically benefit from the merger; after all, uniting with the United States would instantly elevate Canada to world dominance in baseball, football, and basketball. Under these circumstances, it appears that the United States has no moral reason not to forcibly annex Canada. Given that Canada's group autonomy is valuable only to the extent that it serves to promote the welfare of Canadians, there appear to be no moral reasons to respect Canada's self-determination when Canada prefers to act in a way counter to that welfare. In short, this approach recommends that the United States may forcibly annex Canada whenever it reasonably expects this annexation to promote the well-being of Canadians.

Now, a sophisticated consequentialist might here invoke a long list of considerations as to why, in the real world, we could almost never reasonably expect that an annexation would produce the best results for those annexed. I am inclined to accept this stance, but – as in the case of Jezebel – these types of considerations strike me as being beside the most important moral point. No matter how seldom it would turn out to be the case that happiness would be maximized by disrespecting a country's wishes to remain independent, the consequentialist account of group autonomy seems to miss the mark. The real reason the United States may not permissibly forcibly annex Canada is simply that doing so would wrongly deny Canadians the self-determination to which they are entitled. In my view, Canadians have a right to order their internal affairs in a variety of suboptimal ways, and, as long as they treat neither their constituents nor foreigners unjustly, others have a duty to respect their right to self-determination. Thus, while others are not required to stand idly by if Canada should engage in activities such as ethnic cleansing or apartheid, Canadians do have a right to make choices such as whether or not to sign the North American Free Trade Agreement (NAFTA) regardless of what would maximize their well-being. And finally, if an external power unjustifiably forces Canada to sign NAFTA or to merge with the United States, for instance, the principal problem with this coercion is not that it fails to maximize overall happiness. Rather, the real crime is that it wrongs the Canadians; it wrongly disrespects their right to order their own affairs. Because any account that derives the value of group autonomy from its tendency to promote the welfare of the individuals within this group cannot capture this fact, it (like its individual counterpart) is ultimately unsatisfactory.

In the end, then, none of the three most obvious approaches to group autonomy is entirely satisfying: Espousing value-collectivism requires us to turn a blind eye to the morally significant differences between groups and individual persons; viewing group autonomy as an extension of individual autonomy leaves us unable to explain the right to self-determination of various groups, including just states; and deriving the value of group autonomy from its contribution to the welfare of the group's constituents fails to explain the deontological reasons to respect group self-determination. Given these difficulties, some might be tempted to affirm the importance of personal autonomy and yet deny that there are deontological reasons to respect the self-determination of groups. Elie Kedourie is a striking advocate of this position. When assessing a possible change in rulers, he suggests: "The only criterion capable of public defense is whether the new rulers are less corrupt or grasping, or more just and merciful, or whether there is no change at all, but the corruption, the greed, and the tyranny merely find victims other than those of the departed rulers."[13]

Although the foregoing survey of the problems with the three most salient accounts of group autonomy illustrates why people might be drawn to Kedourie's position, I ultimately reject it for two reasons. First, even if the value of group autonomy could not be squared with value-individualism, the implications of denying the deontological reasons to respect group self-determination are less palatable than denying value-individualism. Second, there is another value-individualist explanation of group self-determination that appeals to neither individual autonomy nor individual well-being. Let me explain each of these arguments in turn, beginning with the implausible implications of denying the noninstrumental value of group self-determination.

As emphasized earlier, one cannot adequately explain the reasons to respect a just state's sovereignty unless one posits the deontological value of group autonomy. And just as one could not satisfactorily explain why it is wrong to forcibly annex a perfectly legitimate state, one could not object to colonizing people against their collective will whenever the colonial power would do no worse a job of performing the political functions. Perhaps the most pressing reason to value group autonomy, though, is that the normative case for democracy seems adequate only if we grant the deontological reasons to respect group self-determination.

[13] Elie Kedourie, *Nationalism*, p. 140.

It is widely held that democracy brings about the best consequences, but most believe that the case for democracy does not depend solely, or even principally, upon its instrumental value. That is to say, the prevailing view is that people have a right to democratic governance even if better results could be achieved via undemocratic means. If Plato were right about philosophers being particularly bright and benevolent potential rulers who could be counted on to make much better decisions than the rulers who emerge from a democracy, for instance, most would insist that political subjects would nonetheless be wronged if forced to surrender their democratic governance. Because of the gap between individual autonomy and democratic decision making, however, this position is tenable only if there are deontological reasons to respect group self-determination. Thus, an additional (and very substantial) awkward implication of denying group autonomy would be that democracy would have only instrumental value, and thus citizens would be entitled to democracy only when it would generate the best results.[14]

To better appreciate this point, consider it in the context of Allen Buchanan's influential article "Democracy and Secession." In this essay, Buchanan takes Daniel Philpott and David Copp to task for arguing that the same values that support democracy also endorse rights to unilateral secession. In response to Philpott's proposal that individual autonomy grounds both democracy and a plebiscitary right of self-determination, Buchanan claims:

> ...it is simply false to say that an individual who participates in a democratic decision-making process is self-governing; he or she is governed by the majority. Unless one (unpersuasively) defines self-government as government by the majority (perhaps implausibly distinguishing between the individual's apparent will and her 'real' will, which the majority is said to express), an individual can be self-governing only if he or she dictates political decisions. Far from constituting self-government for individuals, majority rule, under conditions in which each individual's vote counts equally, excludes self-government for every individual.[15]

As should be clear from the arguments already canvassed, Buchanan is right: There is a gap between valuing individual autonomy and valuing the group autonomy necessary to justify secessionist rights. And, as I will explain in Chapter 7, similar problems emerge for those who seek to

---

[14] I will defend this claim further in Chapter 7, but I develop it most fully in my paper (coauthored with Andrew Altman) "Democracy and Group Self-Determination."

[15] Allen Buchanan, "Democracy and Secession," pp. 17–18.

ground democracy in individual equality. Thus, while Buchanan is on solid ground in highlighting the gap between individual autonomy and secessionist rights, Philpott and Copp are no less correct about the common support for democracy and political self-determination, because the very same gap exists between individual autonomy or equal respect for persons and democracy itself. Despite this gap (and the notorious difficulties it presents for those who seek to offer a noninstrumental defense of democracy), most of us remain committed to the view that one cannot deprive people of democracy without wronging them. Thus, while Buchanan rightly exposes a gap in existing value-individualist arguments for secession, it is the very same gap that continues to vex proponents of democracy. As a consequence, we cannot consistently cite this problem as a decisive argument against secessionist rights unless we similarly indict the case for democracy.

On reflection, it should come as no surprise that the arguments on behalf of democracy and secession share a common lacuna because, in the end, plebiscitary rights to secede are merely an extension of the principles of democratic governance to the issue of territorial boundaries. As John Stuart Mill put it: "One hardly knows what any division of the human race should be free to do, if not to determine with which of the various collective bodies of human beings they choose to associate themselves."[16] On this score, one might protest that not all matters should be up for democratic grabs; as Buchanan explains, "it shows no disrespect to anyone that certain issues are excluded altogether from democratic decision-making by a doctrine of constitutional rights."[17] Buchanan is once again right on target: Our basic rights place limits upon democracy's sphere; we would never allow a majority to vote to enslave or disenfranchise a minority, for instance. But this observation is entirely compatible with the theory of secession advanced here. As I have suggested, citizens should be prohibited from redrawing political boundaries in a fashion that would violate each person's right to a secure political environment, but within those limitations democratic decision making should prevail. Put in terms of the American context, one might recommend amending the Bill of Rights to include something like an immunity right against territorial boundaries being redrawn in a fashion that would preclude one's state from performing its requisite functions. Beyond that (as in other matters), it seems appropriate to let democracy run its course.

[16] John Stuart Mill, *Considerations on Representative Government*, p. 392.
[17] Buchanan, "Democracy and Secession," p. 21.

In conclusion, the value of group autonomy is an admittedly substantial assumption necessary for the argument in favor of secessionist rights, but it is an assumption that can be denied only by those willing to concede that we do no necessary injustice to groups of people when we colonize them, annex their legitimate states, or dismantle their legitimate democracies. Of course, virtually everyone now acknowledges the injustice of colonizing a foreign population, but the pivotal lesson of this chapter is that one cannot consistently invoke group autonomy to explain the impermissibility of colonization without also acknowledging the legitimacy of the secessionist claims to self-determination. Charles Beitz is no staunch supporter of self-determination, but even he appreciates that "it is not clear why the groups eligible to claim a right of self-determination should be limited to those, like colonial populations, that are already recognized as territorially distinct."[18] Put simply, if I am right about the implications for state breaking that follow from properly valuing group autonomy, then the only way to question the primary right to secede defended here is to deny (1) that there are nonconsequential reasons against forcibly colonizing others, (2) that legitimate states are entitled to an appropriate degree of sovereignty, and (3) that there are deontological reasons to support democratic governance.

Given these awkward implications of denying the deontological reasons to respect group self-determination, clearly we have reasons to posit the basic value of group autonomy even if we know of no straightforward way to square it with value-individualism. To put this point in terms of the quotation from Michael Hartney with which we began this section: Value-collectivism is admittedly counterintuitive, and the burden of argument therefore falls on anyone who would invoke considerations in tension with it, but the implications for democracy, colonization, and the forcible annexation of legitimate states provide the requisite argument. In other words, because the implications of denying the deontological value of group self-determination are less palatable than embracing a premise that may conflict with value-individualism, these implications enable one to shoulder the burden of argument that Hartney rightly claims value-collectivists must bear.

Let me emphasize, though, that I am not defending value-collectivism. Rather, I am suggesting that the deontological reasons to respect group autonomy should be affirmed even if it were unclear how this position could be fleshed out within a wholly value-individualist framework. The

---

[18] Beitz, *Political Theory and International Relations*, p. 105.

view I advocate here stops short of embracing value-collectivism because I do not claim that a *group* is wronged when its self-determination is violated. I propose instead that (even though the group as a whole exercises the right to self-determination) it is the *individuals*, qua members of this group, who are wronged when the right is violated. The challenge I face, then, is to explain how an individual can be wronged when her group's self-determination is disrespected. Put bluntly, if I was right earlier to argue that suspending political self-determination does not violate the individual autonomy of those in the group, then how can I assert that individuals are wronged when their group's self-determination is violated?

The key to answering this question lies in understanding how individuals are disrespected when their group is denied self-determination.[19] This understanding in turn requires me to show how an individual can be wrongfully disrespected when neither her individual autonomy has been violated nor her equality undermined. It is true that violations of autonomy and equality are central forms of moral disrespect, but not all respect is due to people in virtue of their standing as free and equal persons. In many cases, people are owed various types and levels of respect because of their special roles, standing, or achievements. A student could be culpably disrespectful to Amartya Sen, for instance, if she did not exhibit the type of deference to which Sen is entitled because of his remarkable accomplishments. Imagine that, upon seeing Sen walking across campus, a sophomore who had not yet met Professor Sen shouts, "Hey Amartya, wait up! I want to tell you about some problems with your views on famine!" Alternatively imagine that, convinced that children should be drinking only skim milk, a kindergarten teacher confiscates the carton of whole milk that a child's parent had packed for her child. Both actions are disrespectful in a way that is morally objectionable, but neither is disrespectful of Amartya Sen or the parent as a free and equal person. Without violating the autonomy or denying the fundamental equality of Sen or the parent, these actions are disrespectful because they fail properly to respect the special standing of the two. The student's behavior does not exhibit the appropriate deference owed to someone as accomplished as Professor Sen, and the teacher's behavior wrongly fails to defer to the mother's authority, an authority to which the mother is entitled in virtue of her satisfactory care for her child.

---

[19] I developed the following account in tandem with Andrew Altman while working with him on our coauthored paper "Democracy and Group Self-Determination."

As these examples illustrate, some forms of moral respect are owed to people because of the particular roles they occupy or for the things they achieve or accomplish. In this vein, I suggest that legitimate states are owed respect in virtue of their ability and willingness to perform the requisite political functions. And because a political community's ability and willingness to govern in a satisfactory fashion is a collective achievement possible only because of the individuals within the group, it makes perfect sense that the respect is ultimately owed to these individuals, qua members of this group. Thus, there is nothing mysterious about claiming that a group's members are disrespected when their group's right to self-determination is violated; the group is entitled to dominion over its self-regarding affairs only because it has obtained a certain status, a status achieved by the collective efforts of the individual group members. Just as parents who competently and conscientiously care for their children are entitled to raise these children as they see fit, a group of citizens who are able and willing to perform the requisite political functions have a right to group self-determination.

As for the colonization cases, the respect is not owed for something already achieved but for something within the capabilities of the group to achieve. Aside from exploitation and unjust policies, colonization is an affront to the colonized in the form of an attitude that says, "You cannot govern yourselves properly, and so we must govern you." No less than annexation, this affront cuts deeply and constitutes a serious wrong against the individuals who constitute the colonized group. To appreciate this key point, consider the following analogy. Imagine that a legal system did not allow women to apply for driver's licenses because the legislators assumed that women could not be safe drivers. Such a law would wrongly disrespect those women able and willing to drive in a safe fashion, as it would fail to acknowledge their capacities as competent drivers. I contend that a metropolitan power similarly disrespects those colonists who could adequately perform the requisite political functions; the only difference is that the women are disrespected qua individual competent drivers and the colonists are disrespected qua members of a group that collectively could secure a stable and just political environment. Whether people are wrongly treated as incapable of performing individual or collective chores, however, the disrespect is equally pernicious.

This sketch has admittedly been brief, but it is enough to show several advantages to grounding group self-determination in this fashion. Not only is this account constructed wholly from value-individualist components, it squares with the widespread conviction that one wrongly disrespects the members of a group when one interferes with that group's self-regarding affairs. What is more, this approach explains why some groups are entitled to group autonomy while others are not. In particular, by fastening on a group's ability and willingness to perform the requisite political functions, this account distinguishes between legitimate and illegitimate regimes in a manner that accords with the considered judgment that countries such as Australia and Belgium are entitled to group self-determination, whereas Somalia in the early 1990s and Milosevic's Yugoslavia were not. Finally, it is worth noting that this account appropriately focuses on the *political* capacities of a group to explain why it is entitled specifically to political self-determination.

If the preceding is on target, then the case for the deontological value of group self-determination is ultimately two-pronged. First, there are principled reasons to respect the autonomy of certain groups because denying them self-determination thereby disrespects their individual members. Second, even if the value of group self-determination could not be explained in wholly value-individualist terms, the implications that follow from denying the deontological reasons to respect group autonomy are less palatable than those of value-collectivism.

Who Has the Right to Secede?

I will have the opportunity to respond to various objections to my theory of secession in the course of next chapter's critical review of Abraham Lincoln's doubts about the Confederacy's right to political divorce, so let me close this chapter by merely saying something more about who has a moral right to secede.

The first point worth emphasizing is that there is no reason to suppose that political divisions must occur neatly along the lines of existing administrative units. If a majority of Texans sought to form their own country, for instance, their territory need not include all and only the state of Texas. As Margaret Moore explains:

In many cases, national minorities are correct to point out that administrative boundaries frequently have no moral basis themselves, or that they were often drawn in accordance with a moral or political conception that is irrelevant in the current political situation, or drawn by the central state in order to facilitate assimilation of the minority or its control by the dominant group. It is therefore hard to see why these boundaries should be cast in stone, as the only unit in which self-determination can take place.[20]

[20] Margaret Moore, *The Ethics of Nationalism*, p. 159.

Extending Moore's point a bit, I would add that the separatists' territory not only need not coincide perfectly with an administrative unit, it also need not be contained within only one host state. Thus, not only might a mere portion of Texas secede from the United States, a contiguous portion of Mexico might secede along with the separatist Texans. (A more realistic scenario might involve a contiguous group of Kurds seceding from Iraq, Iran, and Turkey in order to create a single, newly sovereign Kurdistan.) Of course, the international community was faced with this very question recently with the disintegration of the former Yugoslavia. As Moore notes:

> The question of whether the right to self-determination could be used to change republican boundaries – the republic being the internal administrative unit in this case – was posed by Serbia to the Badinter Arbitration Committee on the former Yugoslavia, a committee set up by the EU. The Serb minorities wanted to change the borders that had been drawn for administrative reasons at the end of the Second World War to ensure that most Serbs could be kept in one country.
>
> Much of the international community – the UN and the EU in particular – sought to recognize the self-determination of peoples as members of specific republics, but not as national groups.[21]

I am glad that the international community was finally willing to allow for state breaking, but, like Moore, I am not convinced that the political divisions had to occur along existing internal boundaries. Admittedly, there may be cases in which secession should occur along administrative lines (as when there are considerable political advantages to keeping the borders intact or – as with General Lee and his affection for the state of Virginia – when there happens to be substantial and widespread personal identification with the subfederal unit), but the paramount objective must be to create boundaries that are maximally consistent with the constituents' preferences. Political practicality will inevitably force us to design the secessionist region in a way that includes some unionists and excludes some separatists, but our goal must be to construct politically viable states that include as many separatists and as few unionists as possible.

I suspect that people have traditionally shied away from this approach for fear that it is at best messy, and at worst utterly confused. Critics delight in quoting W. Ivor Jennings's clever response: "On the surface (self-determination) seemed reasonable: let the people decide. It was in fact ridiculous because the people cannot decide until somebody decides

[21] Ibid., p. 140.

who are the people."[22] As Beitz notes, however, there is no reason to think the problem is in any way intractable: "One advantage of the view that the right of self-determination is derived from freedom of association is that it supplies a straightforward solution to this problem: the people should decide who the people are."[23] Harry Beran offers a blueprint for how this might be accomplished:

> If the issue of changing political borders arises in a polity, there is usually disagreement as to whether a change should be made. At the time of the breakup of the former Yugoslavia there was a majority in favour of secession from Yugoslavia in Croatia; but in the portion of Croatia known as Krajina, inhabited mostly by Serbs, there was a majority against secession. The reiterated use of the majority principle seems to be the only method of resolving such conflicts that is consistent with the voluntary association principle. According to this method, a separatist movement can call for a referendum, within a territory specified by it, to determine whether there should be a change in this territory's political status, e.g. whether it should secede from its state. If there is a majority in the territory as a whole for secession, then the territory's people may exercise its right of self-determination and secede. But there may be people within this territory who do not wish to be part of the newly independent state. They could show, by majority vote within their territory, that this is so, and then become independent in turn, or remain within the state from which the others wish to secede. This use of the majority principle may be continued until it is applied to a single community (i.e. a community which is not composed of a number of communities) to determine its political status.
>
> The reiterated use of the majority principle to settle disputes about political borders always yields a determinate result. It therefore provides an adequate response to Ivor Jennings' quip that 'the people cannot decide [issues of political borders] until someone decides who are the people'. It also maximizes the number of individuals who live in mutually desired political association, an ideal implicit in the right of freedom of association.[24]

As long as one takes care not to divide political states into units that are subsequently incapable of performing the requisite political functions, I think Beran's suggestion is right on target.

Many critics of secession fasten on the undeniable fact that, even if every effort is made to draw the new territorial lines in a manner that maximally excludes those who oppose secession, there will inevitably be a minority of people (which, in theory, could be as high as 49.9 percent) who are forced against their will into a new state. It is tempting

---

[22] W. Ivor Jennings, *The Approach to Self-Government*, p. 56.

[23] Beitz, *Political Theory and International Relations*, p. 106.

[24] Beran, "A Democratic Theory of Political Self-Determination for a New World Order," pp. 38–39.

to conclude that this makes the secession unjust; after all, surely people have a right not to be deprived of citizenship by a vote of others, no matter whether the result leaves them in peril or not. I disagree. As long as political states remain territorially rather than consensually defined (as they must, if they are satisfactorily to perform the functions that justify their coercive presence), it will simply not be possible for all citizens to enjoy complete discretion regarding their compatriots. (As we saw in the last chapter, the price of allowing everyone unlimited freedom of association in the political realm would be a perilous anarchy.) The best that we can reasonably hope for, then, must be the more modest goal of giving citizens the maximal say in drawing political borders consistent with maintaining viable, territorially defined states. The way to do this is to allow all and only those secessions that leave the separatists and the divorced party politically viable. Finally, to those who protest that this would allow a majority to place a minority in a dispreferred political situation, I counter that prohibiting political self-determination allows a minority to force a majority to remain in a dispreferred political arrangement. Indeed, notice that whereas my proposal admittedly could allow 51 percent of the population to force an unhappy 49 percent into a new state, denying unilateral secession could allow 1 percent to force an unhappy 99 percent to remain in their current state. Thus, the concern that we exercise maximal control over our citizenship actually *motivates*, rather than *undermines*, the case for secessionist rights.

At this point, one might object that my expression "dispreferred political arrangement" misses the point. The key, this critic suggests, is not merely that one would prefer a different arrangement; the real problem with secession is that it forces a minority of people to *change* their political affiliation. This objection is misguided, however, because if it were impermissible to change people's political arrangement without unanimous consent, then mergers like that between East and West Germany would be permitted only if every single one of the citizens in both independent states unanimously agreed to the union. Clearly, this is too strict a requirement. Against this, one might suggest that, unlike secessions, political mergers are permissible in the absence of unanimity because they *add* to the territory over which one's federal government presides, whereas state breaking *restricts* one's government's area of jurisdiction. This qualification helps some, but it remains too restrictive because it would also prohibit mutual divisions. What if 90 percent of the Norwegians *and* 90 percent of the Swedes had favored political divorce, for instance?[25] Or imagine that the vast majority of Germans later decided that the merger was a mistake and 90 percent of them voted to divide once again into East and West Germany. Would we object to either of these divisions on the grounds that a 10 percent minority would be forced to belong to smaller states? Presumably not. And if a minority does not have a right to block either political mergers or mutual divisions, it is not clear why they should have a right to contest unilateral divisions.

Here it is worth responding to the increasingly common suggestion that decisions regarding secession should not be reached only via a simple majority in a single plebiscite. Because political divorce is such a momentous step, many allege, secession should be allowed only after some sort of super-majority has voted in favor of secession in a series of plebiscites spanning a period of several years. After all, what if a mere simply majority of 51 percent votes to secede and then everyone later regrets it?

In principle, it is not clear to me that a simple majority vote on a single plebiscite should not be taken as decisive. I appreciate that the decision to secede is a grave one, but presumably its gravity would inhibit people from recklessly or nonchalantly voting in favor of division. Moreover, when one bears in mind that the existing government typically has (and uses) extensive tools of propaganda to inspire affection for and loyalty to the state, it seems that people would be more likely to err on the side of union than division. Finally, the fact that being stuck in a dispreferred political arrangement is a substantial matter cuts both ways: Just as we worry about dragging a reluctant minority along in a frivolous or otherwise ill-conceived political divorce, we should equally be concerned not to force an unhappy majority to stay in an unfortunate union. Thus – in principle, at least – it is far from obvious that there would be anything unjust or perhaps even unwise about allowing a simple majority to sanction a political divorce on the basis of a single plebiscite.

In practice, on the other hand, I have no strong objection to designing institutional safeguards to ensure that unilateral secession occurs only when a clear majority demonstrates an informed and enduring preference for political independence. Indeed, inspired by analogous considerations, many municipalities require a waiting period before a couple can get married or divorced, for instance, and these regulations have never struck me as intolerable limitations of individual liberty. (Though perhaps

---

[25] I do not know what the Swedish population thought of the divorce, but in the August 1905 referendum, 368,392 Norwegians voted to end the union, and only 184 voted against secession. Thus, more than 99 percent of Norwegians favored independence.

this only is because I have never felt a spontaneous and irresistible urge to rush to the altar.) I should add, though, that I am much more comfortable requiring a majority vote over a series of elections than insisting upon a super-majority. Because an emerging sovereign state will typically require years before it is in a position to assume its role, there is nothing wrong with intermittently confirming that the majority's preference for separation is an enduring one, especially since it is not unthinkable that a group's passion for independence might wane as it increasingly becomes aware of the real-world problems it must negotiate en route to establishing a sovereign state. On this score, David Copp has offered what I take to be a particularly sensible proposal. He recommends two plebiscites, the first to initiate the political divorce, and a follow-up referendum that takes place after the separation settlement with the potential remainder state has been reached "to determine whether the group still wants to secede, given the negotiated terms, and to determine whether it does in fact have a stable desire to form a state."[26] I am much less comfortable, however, with requirements that a super-majority must approve the political divorce. I recognize that it is not uncommon for governments to require super-majority votes over matters where stability is paramount (the U.S. Constitution cannot be amended with a simple majority, for instance), but it has always struck me as undemocratic to allow a minority to dictate how the majority must live. I understand that there are features of governments that should not be changed without good reason, but I would prefer other measures to ensure stability (like a series of votes over time) that seem more in keeping with majority rule.

Conclusion

The prevailing view regarding parental rights is that parents enjoy a general but defeasible position of dominion over their young children. As long as a parent is neither negligent nor abusive, she may raise her children more or less as she sees fit. If a parent is either grossly incompetent or sufficiently malicious, however, then the appropriate authorities have not only a right but a duty to interfere on behalf of the vulnerable children. The emerging consensus on state sovereignty is analogous. After a long period in which governments were given virtually unlimited discretion as to how to treat their own constituents, it is fast becoming standard to presume that states enjoy a privileged position of moral dominion over

---

[26] David Copp, "International Law and Morality in the Theory of Secession," p. 234.

their own affairs just in case they govern in a reasonably just manner. That is to say, it is now widely accepted that the international community has a right (and perhaps a duty, where it is not unreasonably costly) to interfere on behalf of another country's citizens when that country's government is either unable or unwilling to protect its constituents' basic moral rights. Thus, while everyone agrees that it would be impermissible to forcibly interfere with the internal affairs of a country like France, for instance, most now believe that the international community was justified in intervening in the internal affairs of Somalia and Kosovo.

The account of political self-determination I advance in this chapter, which combines an appreciation for the value of self-determination with a functional account of political legitimacy, is best able to accommodate the foregoing conclusions regarding state sovereignty and international intervention. In particular, we see that France's moral immunity against interference stems from the fact that its government is satisfactorily performing the requisite political functions for all those within its territory. Somalia in the early 1990s and Milosevic's Yugoslavia could not similarly appeal to self-determination, on the other hand, because the former was unable and the latter was unwilling to provide a secure political environment in which basic human rights were respected. I take it that these conclusions are neither mysterious nor provocative. What are controversial, on the other hand, are the strikingly permissive implications for secessionist rights that stem from these very same principles. As the arguments of this chapter establish, though, the value of self-determination not only applies to states, it also empowers all groups able and willing to perform the requisite political functions. In short, a consistent application of those principles necessary to explain our intuitions about the importance (and limits) of state sovereignty also demonstrate that unilateral rights to secede exist whenever both the separatist group and the remainder state would be able and willing to perform the requisite political functions.

4

Lincoln on Secession

A theory of secession as permissive as that which I advanced in the previous chapter is bound to be met with various objections as well as with
questions about its implications for actual, real-world secessionist conflicts. Both of these issues can in large measure be addressed by critically
reviewing Abraham Lincoln's arguments against the South's bid for independence. Lincoln is not typically heralded for his political theory, but his
arguments on secession deserve careful attention not only because he was
an exceptionally reflective principal in what was arguably history's most
spectacular, protracted secessionist conflict, but also because (descen-
dents of) his arguments continue to be influential.[1] With this in mind,
I divide this chapter into four sections. First I review Lincoln's ten arguments against secession. Next, I explain why none of these arguments
is adequate. In the third section, I illustrate how the functional theory
of secession actually points the way toward a better justification for
Lincoln's Unionist stance. Finally, I quickly sketch how the functional
account would adjudicate several other prominent secessionist conflicts.

Lincoln's Case against State Breaking

History records Lincoln as one of America's great political figures.
He is commonly not, however, listed among the pantheon of leading

---

[1] Allen Buchanan credits Lincoln as the originator of many of the arguments against secession that he surveys in *Secession: The Morality of Political Divorce from Fort Sumter to Lithuania
and Quebec*, and Philip Abbott reflects upon how contemporary liberals and communitarians might utilize Lincoln's various arguments in his article "The Lincoln Propositions
and the Spirit of Secession."

philosophical lights. Although he arguably gave an unprecedented amount of sustained attention to the ethics of state breaking, his public arguments on the topic make no strong case for revising history's assessment of him. While it is tempting to speculate about what arguments Lincoln might have advanced had he not been in office during this epic struggle, I will not indulge this temptation here. My principal aim is not to place his arguments in what would undoubtedly be a more forgiving political context but simply to review Lincoln's many arguments as he presented them.

Before examining these positions, however, two historical points need to be made. First, while Lincoln's writings span four decades, the great majority of his thinking about secession comes from a fairly short period of time; most of the documents to which I refer were written between the end of 1860 and the middle of 1861. Two documents, in particular, play a prominent role: his First Inaugural Address, delivered on March 4, 1861 (a month after the outbreak of the war), and his "Message to Congress in Special Session," delivered on July 4 of that year.

The second point is related. Because Lincoln did not take an active stand against Southern slavery until well after the war had begun (and then, in all probability, only in response to the South's dogged military resistance), the issue is conspicuously absent from the discussion of secession. Four months before taking office, Lincoln proclaimed:

I have labored in, and for, the Republican organization with entire confidence that whenever it shall be in power, each and all of the States will be left in as complete control of their own affairs respectively, and at as perfect liberty to choose, and employ, their own means of protecting property, and preserving peace and order within their respective limits, as they have ever been under my administration. (IV, 141)[2]

At his inauguration in March 1861, he put the point more directly: "I have no purpose, directly or indirectly, to interfere with the institution of slavery in the States where it exists. I believe I have no right to do so, and I have no inclination to do so." (IV, 250) The well-known irony is that, while slavery seemed to be in the forefront of the minds of Southern leaders, it was not the issue with which Lincoln was most directly concerned. Far from being a matter of principle, the omission more likely reflected Lincoln's understanding that any hint at abolition would surely lose the South. As I shall argue below, this tactic was not without moral costs.

[2] All citations from Lincoln are from *The Collected Works*, with the volume and page number shown in parentheses.

With these historical notes in mind, let us turn our attention to Lincoln's arguments, which are ten in number: two against secession of any stripe, one against withdrawing from a republic, and seven directed specifically against the South's claim to independence. The most sweeping objection to secession (argument #1) was made in the following terms: "If a minority... will secede rather than submit, they make a precedent which, in turn, will divide and ruin them; for a minority of their own number will secede from them whenever a majority refuses to be controlled by such minority." (IV, 256) Relating this point to the Confederacy, Lincoln writes:

For instance, why may not South Carolina, a year or two hence, arbitrarily, secede from a new Southern Confederacy, just as she now claims to secede from the present Union? Her people, and, indeed, all secession people, are now being educated to the precise temper of doing this. Is there such perfect identity of interests among the States to compose a Southern Union, as to produce harmony only, and prevent renewed secession? Will South Carolina be found lacking in either the restlessness or the ingenuity to pick a quarrel with Kentucky? (IV, 256)

The argument is straightforward: Allow one region to secede and you create an environment in which secession is increasingly seen as the answer to political problems. Presuming this outcome to be unacceptable, Lincoln here effectively ruled out any and all secession.

Lincoln's second objection to all secession (argument #2) was a reductio that compared secession to exclusion:

If all the States, save one, should assert the power to drive that one out of the Union, it is presumed the whole class of seceder politicians would at once deny the power, and denounce the act as the greatest outrage upon the State rights. But suppose that precisely the same act, instead of being called "driving the one out," should be called "the seceding of the others from the one," it would be exactly what the seceders claim to do; unless, indeed, they make the point, that the one, because it is a minority, may rightfully do, what the others, because they are a majority, may not rightfully do. (IV, 436)

Here Lincoln noted that there is no morally significant difference between minority and majority secessions. Would things be any different if the South constituted 49 or 51 percent of the Union, for instance? Presumably not, and thus there is no real difference between minority secession and majority secession, which is sometimes called "exclusion." However, exclusion is clearly impermissible: Surely everyone would agree that it would be wrong for all of the states to exclude South Carolina from the United States, for instance. But if exclusion is wrong and there is no morally relevant difference between minority and majority secessions, then minority secession is also wrong, because it is simply exclusion by another name.

A third argument was less sweeping. Rather than barring all secession, Lincoln argued that, at a minimum, it is incompatible with, or at least unnecessary within, a democracy, what he called a "republican form of government." The claim here is that the institutions of change in such a government – elections,[3] constitutional amendments,[4] and even provisions for revolution[5] (as well as "intelligence, patriotism, Christianity, and a firm reliance on Him" [IV, 261]) – are adequate to address all conceivable grievances. Indeed, such ability to accommodate is what, for Lincoln, gave republicanism its moral stature.

Beyond these three general arguments, Lincoln cast a much narrower net, catching only the difficulties inherent in the Confederacy's secessionist claims. In his July 4, 1861, message to Congress (three months after the attack on Fort Sumter), he stated that:

[o]ur adversaries have adopted some Declarations of Independence; in which, unlike the good old one, penned by Jefferson, they omit the words "all men are created equal." Why? They have adopted a temporary national constitution, in the preamble of which, unlike the good old one, signed by Washington, they omit "We, the People," and substitute "We the deputies of the sovereign and independent States," Why? Why this deliberate pressing out of view, the rights of men, and the authority of the people? (IV, 438)

With this concern over the South's political philosophy in mind, Lincoln addressed the issue of secession:

The Constitution provides, and all the States have accepted the provision, that "The United States shall guarantee to every State in this Union a republican form of government." But, if a State may lawfully go out of the Union, having done so, it may also discard the republican form of government; so that to prevent its going out, is an indispensable *means*, to the *end*, of maintaining the guaranty mentioned. (IV, 440)

---

[3] "I do not deny the possibility that the people may err in an election; but if they do, the true cure is in the next election; and not in the treachery of the party elected." (IV, 259) The point is perhaps more elegantly put in his July 4 (1861) "Message to Congress in Special Session," where he suggests that the United States system teaches "men that what they cannot take by an election, neither can they take it by a war." (IV, 439)

[4] "Whenever [the people] shall grow weary of the existing government, they can exercise their *constitutional* right of amending it, or their *revolutionary* right to dismember it." (IV, 260)

[5] See the preceding note. By "revolutionary right" Lincoln undoubtedly meant that right referred to in the Declaration of Independence. Notice the contradiction with the argument mentioned earlier that "no government proper, ever had a provision in its organic law for its own termination ..." (IV, 252)

Here Lincoln made no blanket objection to secession, only a plea to protect that ("republican government") which secession threatens. That threat was, in his mind, evident not just in the words of Southern political philosophy; it could also be seen in the way in which contemporary political decisions were being made: "It may well be questioned whether there is, to-day, a majority of the legally qualified voters of any State, except perhaps South Carolina, in favor of disunion. There is much reason to believe that the Union men are the majority in many, if not in every other one, of the so-called seceded States." (IV, 437) He goes on to cite the elections in Virginia and Tennessee that, given the strong element of coercion involved, could "scarcely be considered as demonstrating popular sentiment."[6] (IV, 437)

Two distinct arguments can be seen in these remarks. One (argument #4) is that the secession was, far from a popular uprising, a movement co-opted by elites and therefore illegitimate from a republican (to continue in Lincoln's vernacular) standpoint. Lincoln is here emphasizing that the legitimacy of secession requires, among other things, that a majority of those in the seceding region freely support the separatist movement.

The second argument (argument #5) concerned the ultimate outcome of the separation. In light of the wording of the Confederacy's documents, Lincoln worried that the Confederacy was poised to create an unjust (because nonrepublican) form of government that would thereby violate the rights of its free (i.e., nonslave) constituents.

Lincoln's third objection to the South's separation (argument #6) was that the Confederacy was contractually obligated to remain in the Union. Lincoln himself did not believe that the United States should be thought of as merely a contract. For the sake of argument, however, he was willing to think of it as just that. In his mind, this raised the following question: "[I]f the United States be not a government proper, but an association of States in the nature of a contract merely, can it, as a contract, be peacefully unmade, by less than all the parties who made it?" His answer was unequivocal: "[O]ne party to a contract may violate it – break it, so to speak; but does it not require all to rescind it?" (IV, 253) Just as Jones may not permissibly fail to deliver widgets to Smith if Smith has not released him from his contractual obligation to do so, the South, so Lincoln argued, may not permissibly withdraw from the contractual Union unless the North has agreed to release it. In short, even if the

---

[6] "At such an election, all that large class who are, at once *for* the Union and *against* coercion, would be coerced to vote against the Union." (IV, 437)

United States were a "mere" contract, unilateral secession would not be permissible.

A fourth objection (argument #7) to the South's secession was related. In Lincoln's mind, the Southern position rested on an "ingenious sophism," namely, that "any state of the Union may, *consistently* with the national Constitution, and therefore *lawfully*, and *peacefully*, withdraw from the Union, without the consent of the Union, or of any other state." (IV, 433) For Lincoln, the heart of the sophism lay with the assumption that "there is some omnipotent, and sacred supremacy, pertaining to a *State*." (IV, 433) He denied this out of hand: "[O]ur States have neither more, nor less power, than that reserved to them, in the Union, by the Constitution – no one of them ever having been a State *out* of the Union." (IV, 433) The conclusion, which he drew rhetorically, was clear: "[H]aving never been States, either in substance, or in name, outside of the Union, whence this magical omnipotence of 'State rights,' asserting a claim of power to lawfully destroy the Union itself?" (IV, 434) The central idea seems to be that since neither the Confederacy nor its constituent States enjoyed sovereign status prior to their inclusion in the United States, neither could be in a position to subsequently (re)claim it.[7]

The remaining three arguments employ a strategy already suggested with his concern for the Confederacy's republican credentials – namely, an emphasis not on the status of the seceding region, but rather on the consequences of state breaking. First (argument #8), Lincoln wondered what economic harm might come to the "plain people," claiming that "[t]hey understand, without argument, that destroying the government, which was made by Washington, means no good to them." (IV, 439) The concern, of course, was not without merit. With the loss of the North's industrial base, and the reticence of European countries to offer support to its cause, the South would face very real economic challenges.

---

[7] This was not the first time Lincoln had emphasized the temporal issues surrounding statehood and sovereignty. In attempting to establish the legal status of the Union's perpetual nature, he argued in the First Inaugural Address that the "Union is much older than the Constitution." (IV, 253) In fact, he went on, "[i]t was formed...by the Articles of Association in 1774...[and] matured and continued by the Declaration of Independence in 1776...[and] further matured and expressly declared and pledged, to be perpetual, by the Articles of Confederation in 1778." As Philip Abbott explains in "The Lincoln Propositions and the Spirit of Secession," dating the Union back to the period prior to the Constitution bolstered his claim that the states could in no way be seen as having enjoyed sovereign status prior to their inclusion in the United States.

A second consequence (argument #9) was related: Even if the South's economy made the transition unscathed, would it use its wealth in a manner to which it was obligated? As Lincoln explained:

> ...nothing should ever be implied as law, which leads to unjust, or absurd consequences. The nation purchased, with money, the countries out of which several of these States were formed. Is it just that they shall go off without leave, and without refunding? The nation paid very large sums...to relieve Florida of the aboriginal tribes. Is it just that she shall now be off without consent, or without making any return? The nation is now in debt for money applied to the benefit of these so-called seceding States, in common with the rest. Is it just, either that creditors shall go unpaid, or the remaining State pay the whole? A part of the present national debt was contracted to pay the old debts of Texas. Is it just that she shall leave, and pay no part of this herself?...Again, if one State may secede, so may another; and when all shall have seceded, none is left to pay the debts. Is this quite just to creditors? Did we notify them of this sage view of ours, when we borrowed the money? (IV, 435–6)

Thus, Lincoln objected that the South's secession would allow them to skip out on their share of the national debt.

Finally (argument #10), there were consequences not just to the North and South, but to all of humanity. Lincoln expressed this concern most clearly in the Gettysburg Address, when he spoke of the war as "testing whether that nation, or any nation so conceived and so dedicated, can long endure." The Union goal, he argued, is thus to insure that "government of the people, by the people, for the people, shall not perish from the earth." (VII, 23) As Allen Buchanan records: "Lincoln was convinced that the fate of democracy in the world depended on the success of the American experiment, that if the Union dissolved, political freedom and all its fruits might 'perish from the earth.'"[8]

Assessing Lincoln's Arguments

In this section, I explain why none of Lincoln's ten arguments is adequate. Reviewing them in the order I introduced them earlier, let us begin with what might be dubbed his "Russian Doll" argument (argument #1), which purports to establish the impermissibility of all secession. According to this argument, no right to secede can exist because, were any secession allowed, there would be no justification for denying subsequent separatist movements that in turn seek independence from the newly sovereign states. As it stands, this argument may not appear very compelling. In

---

[8] Buchanan, *Secession*, p. 97.

general, it does no good to suggest that one can never permit X on the grounds that permitting X once will lead to many reiterations of X *unless one also explains why the proliferation of X is problematic.* Imagine, for instance, protesting that we can never allow anyone to put her pants on one leg at a time because this might lead to *everyone* putting their pants on one leg at a time. Since there is nothing wrong with everyone putting their pants on one leg at a time, clearly we have no reason to fear the precedent set by the first person doing so.

In fairness to Lincoln, it seems reasonable to construe his first argument as a slippery slope argument that includes the (plausible) implicit premise that the proliferation of state breaking could be extremely harmful. Understood in this manner, Lincoln's first argument is probably the most common objection to allowing secession. As Lee Buchheit says:

> By far the most frequent cry raised against the principle of secessionist self-determination is that it will result in a multiplicity of small, squabbling States, especially in areas where tribal or clannish divisions are still pervasive. It would, so the argument goes, give free rein to the parochial instincts of the countless insular groups around the world, resulting in an unhealthy fractionalization of previously unified States. Many of the resulting smaller units might then lack a viable economic base, strong political structure, and adequate military defense. It is assumed that this process, often terms Balkanization, would inevitably result in injury both to the internal social harmony of these territories and the general international order.[9]

Put plainly, once one starts the secessionist ball rolling, there would be no stopping it short of anarchy.[10] Thus, we cannot allow any secessionist rights, because doing so would lead to subsequent, clearly harmful reiterations.

The first thing to note about Lincoln's blanket denial of the right to secede is that it saddles him with the awkward conclusion that the American Revolution, itself an act of secession, was unjustified. Of course, Lincoln is not logically barred from claiming that the American colonists had no right to secede, but I suspect that he would not want to endorse

---

[9] Lee C. Buchheit, *Secession: The Legitimacy of Self-Determination*, p. 28.

[10] Russell Muirhead has suggested to me that Lincoln's real fear of the Confederacy's leaving was that it would initiate a series of secessions that would ultimately destroy any chance of the United States serving as the world's example of a well-ordered republic. I do not explore this more nuanced version of the Russian Doll argument here because it depends upon the implicit premise that it is permissible to restrict political self-determination in order to complete the "Great American Experiment," and I will later contest this premise.

such a conclusion and thus might refrain from condemning secession per se.

Even if Lincoln were prepared to condemn George Washington and the others, there are additional problems with his Russian Doll argument. To appreciate these difficulties, notice that his argument requires two implicit premises: (1) Unlimited state breaking would result in unpalatable circumstances, and (2) one cannot permit some political divisions without licensing all of them. As should be clear from my discussion of political legitimacy in Chapter 2, I share Lincoln's fear of political instability, and thus I accept his first premise. I deny his second premise, however, because there is nothing to prevent one from distinguishing between harmless versus harmful secessions and disallowing only the latter. If one wants to avoid political instability, then one should prohibit only those political divorces liable to cause such instability. The key is that if one is worried about political instability rather than secession, then one should prohibit only the former. Of course, avoiding this instability might require disallowing *some* state breaking, but it does not follow from this that secession can *never* be permissible. In short, just as one would not outlaw all driving merely because driving while drunk is dangerous, we should not outlaw all state breaking merely because there are circumstances in which secession would prove dangerous. Thus, in the absence of an explanation as to why one could not allow harmless political divorces without also allowing subsequent harmful ones, I deny that the slope from permitting any secession to anarchic chaos is as slippery as Lincoln's Russian Doll argument presumes.[11]

---

[11] Here a defender of Lincoln might protest that I have oversimplified the matter. In particular, one might worry that it is not so easy to prohibit only those secessions liable to cause political instability; difficult questions must be answered regarding who should make this determination and by what criteria. Both because there are bound to be controversial cases, and because the separatists and the unionists are each interested parties whose impartiality cannot be relied upon, contemporary theorists increasingly suggest that international bodies be established to adjudicate these disputes according to clear and promulgated rules.

As will become plain in Chapter 7, I am receptive to this suggestion, but the fact remains that political leaders will be forced to make their decisions in an institutional vacuum until such effective international courts are established. Moreover, because it was clear that the division between the North and the South would not have resulted in anarchic chaos, Lincoln could not invoke such concerns to justify resisting this particular secession. Thus, while I agree that we should work toward a future where leaders like Lincoln will not effectively preside over secessionist conflicts, this does nothing to diminish my concerns about Lincoln's first argument.

Lincoln's second general argument (argument #2) was a simple one involving only two premises: (1) There is no morally relevant difference between minority and majority secessions, and (2) majority secessions (otherwise known as "exclusions") are obviously wrong. Discussing this argument in the context of international law, Buchheit writes: "... if the majority or dominant group is hindered by international law in its ability to cast out the minority, then the minority should be similarly fettered to the majority in its implementation of a secessionist demand."[12] I resist Lincoln's second argument because I disagree that all exclusions are necessarily impermissible. Admittedly, it would be wrong for an overwhelming majority to exclude a tiny, fragile minority who could not form a viable country on their own, but what makes this particular case of majority secession worrisome is not that the majority leaves the minority but that a majority leaves a group in perilous circumstances where it cannot secure political stability. In short, it is the excluded group's political incapacity rather than its minority status that is worrisome. If this is correct, then there is nothing wrong with majority secession per se; rather, there is something problematic only about excluding vulnerable groups.[13]

From this, we can draw two conclusions: First, even if Lincoln was right (as I think he was) that there is no morally relevant difference between minority and majority secessions, Lincoln's argument fails for its reliance upon the false premise that no majority secession is permissible. Second, if Lincoln were to retreat to the more plausible premise that no party may secede from a politically unviable group, this would render his argument impotent against the South's bid to secede, because the North clearly would have been able to perform the requisite political functions on its own. Thus, while I applaud Lincoln's insight that minority and majority

---

[12] Buchheit, *Secession: The Legitimacy of Self-Determination*, p. 27.

[13] One might contest my claim that exclusion is permissible unless it leaves the excluded group in a politically unviable position. After all, surely people have a right not to be deprived of citizenship by a vote of others, no matter whether the result leaves them in peril or not. I disagree. As I explained in the previous chapter's defense of political self-determination, as long as political states remain territorially rather than consensually defined (as they must, if they are satisfactorily to perform the functions that justify their existence), not all citizens will have complete discretion to choose their compatriots. The more modest goal, then, must be to give citizens the maximal say in drawing political borders consistent with maintaining viable, territorially defined states. The way to do this is to allow all and only those secessions/exclusions that leave the separatists and the divorced party politically viable. Thus, the concern that we exercise maximal control over our citizenship actually buttresses my recommendation.

secessions are not as different as one might initially suspect, I deny that any blanket rejection of secession follows from this.

Lincoln's next argument (argument #3) is more restricted; it applies only to democracies (or, in Lincoln's terms, "republican" forms of government). In Lincoln's mind, democracy requires accepting defeat at the polls, and it was ridiculous for the Confederates to secede merely because they preferred a different presidential candidate. As he put it:

Prior to my instalation here it had been inculcated that any State had a lawful right to secede from the national Union; and that it would be expedient to exercise the right, whenever the devotees of the doctrine should fail to elect a President to their own liking. I was elected contrary to their liking; and accordingly, so far as it was legally possible, they had taken seven states out of the Union. (VI, 263)

In short, Lincoln maintained that democracy makes secession unnecessary and impermissible. Secession from a democracy is impermissible because voting makes sense only if one presumes that all voters will be bound by the results, and it is unnecessary because democracy offers citizens alternative (nonseparatist) means of voicing concerns and expressing preferences.

Clearly, Lincoln was right to suggest that democracy requires accepting defeat at the polls – one might even say that democracy is defined by the losers' continued embrace of the system.[14] But while I appreciate that democracy would be unintelligible if its results were never respected, it does not follow from this that secession from a democracy must be both unnecessary and impermissible. To see this, consider the following scenario.

Imagine that Germany wished to annex Poland. Rather than merely impose themselves on the Poles, however, the Germans sponsored a plebiscite in both countries. Suppose further than an overwhelming majority of Germans favored the merger; virtually all of the Poles voted against the proposal; and (because Germany has a substantially larger population) a clear majority of the whole favored the creation of the new larger state. Would the Poles be morally prohibited from resisting the merger merely because they were allowed a vote in whether or not they would be annexed? Presumably not. In the absence of some other

[14] While Lincoln might not agree with Rousseau that "when...the opinion contrary to mine prevails, this proves merely that I was in error," (*The Social Contract*, p. 206) he likely appreciated Tocqueville's assessment that "every American feels a sort of personal interest in obeying the laws, for a man who is not today one of the majority party may be so tomorrow." (*Democracy in America*, p. 240)

consideration that explains Poland's obligation to accept the results, there is no reason to suppose that their participation in the vote morally binds the Poles to accept the merger. As this scenario illustrates, the mere fact that a government reaches its decisions democratically cannot be enough to establish that all parties are thereby bound to it.

Here a defender of Lincoln's position might protest that my thought experiment is inapt because of the disanalogy between the Poles and the Southerners. In particular, unlike the Southerners, the Poles clearly have a right to political self-determination that entitles them to ignore the preferences of the Germans. Notice, however, that it simply begs the crucial question to assume that the Southerners have any less right to self-determination than the Poles. As my arguments in the previous chapter were designed to show, one cannot without inconsistency suggest that existing states and colonies have a right to determine their own affairs and simultaneously assume that no internal separatist groups do. Secondly, even if there are specific reasons that explain why the Southerners, unlike the Polish, had no right to self-determination, this would not vindicate the argument from democracy, because it would then be these additional considerations, rather than the democracy itself, that explains the duty to remain.

At this point, a critic might contend that my thought experiment misses the mark because Germany and Poland are not currently within a democracy. In other words, my argument fails not because there is a disanalogy between the Southerners and the Poles, but because there is a morally relevant difference between the existing political relationship between the North and the South versus that shared by Germany and Poland. Specifically, unlike Germany and Poland, the North and the South were already in an existing union, a union within which the North had made its share of the democratically required sacrifices. Thus, given that the North had routinely respected the political process even when it lost out to the South, it was patently unfair for the South to defect when it lost out to the North.

I think that there is an important kernel of truth to this last version of the argument, but it can be appreciated without denying the permissibility of secession. To see why, notice that there are two distinct ways in which one might defect from a collective decision. First, as the Confederates sought to, one might leave the democracy. Second, one might remain in the political union, expect others to respect all democratically derived decisions, and yet personally ignore those political results with which one disagreed. The latter would clearly be impermissible because it involves unfairly free riding on the political sacrifices of others, but that is not what the Confederates sought to do. Rather, they believed that the costs of political membership had become prohibitive, and thus they suggested that both they and the North should no longer be bound by each other's will. In short, the Confederates were not trying to unfairly pick and choose which democratically enacted laws to follow while simultaneously expecting the North to follow all such laws; rather, they merely sought to exit the cooperative. Thus, unless the South had in the past refused to let the North secede when it had wanted to, it is hard to see what would be unfair about the South's doing so.

Finally, for those who remain convinced that my thought experiment misses the mark because there is something important about being in an existing democracy, we need only tweak the initial example a bit. According to the second version, imagine that Germany and Poland are united (perhaps as a result of some postwar agreement) as "Gerland," where all major political decisions are made democratically. Although each former Pole is accorded the same political voice as her formerly German counterparts, Gerland's laws are consistently decided by the former Germans outvoting the former Poles. The former Poles are allowed to run for office and argue publicly for their various favored positions and candidates, but they continue to lose elections. This second set of circumstances reveals not only that secession from an existing democracy might be permissible, but also that Lincoln was too quick to assume that democracy makes political divorce unnecessary. I shall address this issue at greater length in Chapter 5; for now, let me suggest that reflecting on this hypothetical Gerland illustrates that secession can be necessary, even from democracies, as an effective remedy to the otherwise intractable problem of persistent minorities.

If my reasoning to this point has been on target, then Lincoln was wrong to suggest either that secession must always be impermissible or that political divorce from democracies can never be legitimate. The arguments on which Lincoln placed the greatest emphasis, however, were those directed specifically against the South's claim to independence, so let us now examine those seven arguments.

Lincoln's first objection to the South's separatist movement (argument #4) was that it lacked popular support. On his view, the Confederacy's Declaration of Independence was the initiative of an elite few who lacked democratic authorization and whose views were unrepresentative of the wishes of most Southerners. I would take this argument very seriously if I were convinced of the accuracy of this descriptive claim, but I lack

Lincoln's conviction that the majority of Southerners preferred to remain in the union. Lincoln correctly noted that not every state had a free plebiscite on the matter, but, given the nature of political representation at the time, I am unimpressed with this fact. It might strike some as awkward to contextualize the need for plebiscites, but consider the American Revolution, or the division of the former Czechoslovakia into the Czech and Slovak Republics: in neither instance was a free plebiscite held on the issue of political divorce. In the case of the American Revolution, it strikes me as objectionably anachronistic to condemn the colonists for not having taken a plebiscite. Let me be clear here: I agree that political elites ought not to have started the war if they knew that the majority of their fellow colonists preferred to maintain their affiliation with Britain, but it does not follow from this that these same elites should not have declared independence without first polling those they sought to represent. In the case of Czechoslovakia, on the other hand, it seems right to question why no plebiscite was held. Because the democratic institutions and technological machinery necessary to perform the plebiscite were readily available in the latter case, it does not seem too much to demand. (As John McGarry records: "Slovakia's secession from Czechoslovakia in 1993 ... was largely an elite project, which the majority of Slovaks – quite apart from the Magyar minority – did not share. An opinion poll in 1990 indicated that only 8 per cent of Slovakia's population desired secession.")[15] Thus, I am not suggesting that the people's preferences are morally insignificant; rather, I am making the less contentious descriptive claim that the mere absence of a free plebiscite in the Confederate case does not necessarily imply a lack of popular will. Given the standards of political representation at the time, it strikes me that the general behavior of Southerners is the best indication of their preferences, and I take their willingness to engage in such a horrendously long and costly war as at least prima facie evidence that there was ample popular interest in independence.

Lincoln's second concern about the South's separatist movement (argument #5) was that its subsequent sovereign state would not be republican. I agree with what must be seen as the general principle here: A group has no right to secede in order to form a substantially less just state than the one in which it currently resides. My only question concerns Lincoln's evidence that such an argument applies to the Southern case.

[15] John McGarry, " 'Orphans of Secession': National Pluralism in Secessionist Regions and Post-Secession States," p. 220.

Lincoln inferred the injustice of the Confederacy from two observations: (1) The secession was not popularly supported in the South, and (2) the Confederacy's Declaration of Independence included neither the phrase "all men are created equal" nor "We, the People" (instead, it substituted "We the deputies of the sovereign and independent States"). While an independent South may indeed have presented a shaky moral vision (by contemporary standards especially), I nonetheless find neither of Lincoln's inferences of injustice sound.

Having just addressed (1) above, let me explain my doubts about (2). Lincoln alleged that the substitution of "We the deputies of the sovereign and independent States" for "We, the People" signaled a departure from republican principles. In my view, however, a more plausible interpretation of this substitution is that it is an attempt to claim the status thought necessary to demand independence. That is, the Confederates sought to emphasize their standing as sovereign and independent states in order to buttress their moral claim to political self-determination, not to signal their reluctance to govern democratically. Whether or not my reading of the Confederacy's Declaration of Independence is more accurate is, in the end, a question best left to more qualified historians. What is paramount here is simply that speculation about the South's political future drawn from questionable textual interpretation hardly constitutes the sort of empirical support necessary for rejecting secession on justice grounds.

On the other hand, if Lincoln had objected to the South's intention to create a state that condoned slavery, then (as I will emphasize later) he would have been on solid footing in resisting their creation of an objectionably unjust state. Of course, Lincoln explicitly refused to criticize the Confederacy on these grounds.[16] Thus, although Lincoln was right to insist that the South should not be permitted to form a substantially less just government, the contestable textual evidence he offered in support of his claim is clearly insufficient, and, as a consequence, his version of this argument should be rejected.

Lincoln's third argument against the South's right to secede (argument #6) was that even if the Union were merely a contract (which he did not believe), the South would be contractually obligated to remain in

---

[16] This may be an instance in which Lincoln's political position and motives inhibited him from making a more philosophically sound argument. I cannot make the case here, but it seems reasonable to speculate that Lincoln believed that the South's perpetuation of slavery should count against its claim to sovereignty. If so, perhaps Lincoln eschewed this (clearly more compelling) objection only because it was politically problematic.

it. This argument rests on two claims, one historical and one philosophical. The historical claim is that *if it were* a contract, there is substantial legal precedent to show that it would have entailed a perpetual Union. The philosophical claim is that, *given the nature of contracts*, the Southern secession would thereby be ruled out.

For the sake of argument, let us presume that the Union *was* formed by a contract purporting to bind all parties in perpetuity. Does it follow from that fact that the parties *would be* thus bound? Does the philosophical claim hold? For two reasons I argue that it does not. First, even if we grant *arguendo* that the representatives were capable of binding all of their constituents at the time, it is problematic to suppose that future generations can be bound by an agreement made by their forebears.[17] As Rousseau observed: "Even if each person can alienate himself, he cannot alienate his children."[18] I take this point to be commonsensical: If Peter's grandmother promised someone in her church that Peter would become a monk, for instance, no one would think that he had a moral duty to do so.[19]

Moreover, even if the Southerners could inherit political obligations from a contract entered into generations earlier, we must not assume without argument that the obligation would be to remain in the Union; it seems more plausible to suppose that they would have only the more modest responsibility to secede in a fair fashion. In support of this, notice what obligations we ascribe to married individuals. Even though the contract between spouses is much less problematic (insofar as it is explicit, consensual, and personal rather than intergenerational), we still do not insist that couples must stay together as promised; instead, we claim only that they are obligated to divorce under certain terms. (We insist that their collective assets be divided fairly, for instance, and we sometimes arrange for the provision of children and/or for continued transfers.) Along these

---

[17] One might resist my contention that future generations cannot be bound by their forbears on the grounds that this would seem to undermine the very idea of a constitution. In response, consider two points: First, I mean to suggest only that future generations cannot be *morally*, as opposed to *legally*, bound. Second, even legal constitutions typically provide means for future generations to amend them, so that future citizens will not be irreparably bound by their ancestors' vision.

[18] Jean Jacques Rousseau, *The Social Contract*, p. 144.

[19] Of course, one might object that there is a morally relevant difference between the person to whom Peter's grandmother made a promise and our political partners because the latter have reasonable expectations of continued cooperation based upon the years of cooperation. This difference may indeed be morally relevant, but if so, it indicates that whatever political duties the South had to the Union were based on this ongoing cooperation rather than on some contract purportedly entered into in either 1776 or 1789.

same lines (and because the marriage contract seems a more apt basis of comparison than a commercial contract), whatever residual obligation the South had to the larger union would require them only to secede under fair terms (by agreeing to pay a fair portion of the national debt, for instance) rather than to remain in the political union indefinitely.

Lincoln's fourth concern (argument #7) was that the Confederacy (and/or the seceding states) lacked the proper pre-union status. He insisted that, because the Southern states were not sovereign political units prior to the formation of the United States, they had no right to withdraw from the Union. In my view, this is among the weakest of Lincoln's arguments. I appreciate that there was considerable controversy at the time regarding the pre-union status of the Southern states, but I think that this entire issue can be safely side-stepped, since it is implausible to suppose that only previously autonomous regions can qualify for the right to secede. For instance, would one really want to deny the Kurds a right to secede from Iraq *on these grounds?* In light of the fact that political boundaries are so often the result of fraud, force, and historical contingencies, it seems wrong to place so much moral weight on a party's political pedigree. Given that so many Southerners at the time were arguing that their right to secede stemmed from the nature of the agreement into which these states had entered, it is understandable that Lincoln would have been attracted to this politically expedient position; the problem is that he offered no decent argument to support his counterintuitive premise that only previously autonomous units could claim the right to sovereignty. Finally, notice that the original thirteen colonies clearly lacked this status vis-à-vis Britain, so even if Lincoln could manufacture the requisite arguments on this issue, it would leave him with the awkward implication that the United States had no right to its own independence.

Lincoln's fifth argument against the political division (argument #8) was that individuals in the South would suffer economically. I believe that this argument too can be rejected even if its principal descriptive claim is true. That is to say, even if Lincoln was right that the South's economy would do less well on its own, it seems that the Southerners enjoyed the moral dominion to decide whether the benefits of independence are worth the economic costs.[20] By analogy, I would presumably

---

[20] As Lee Buchheit notes: "It appears that many groups would gladly embrace an impoverished, defenseless existence in return for the emotional satisfaction of self-government. There were many expressions of this heroic sentiment in the colonial context, such as the splendidly Miltonic statement of a Filipino senator during the 1920s that "[W]e would prefer a government run like hell by Filipinos to one run like heaven by Americans." (*Secession: The Legitimacy of Self-Determination*, p. 8)

earn considerably more as an investment broker than I currently do as a professor, but no one would claim that I am therefore obligated to leave my post at the university in order to maximize my economic prospects. It is up to me to decide how important financial success is, and – regardless of whether others think I am wise to forego the economic opportunities I do – it is my right to make these choices. (By the same token, it is not surprising that few objected to the political division of the former Czechoslovakia even though it was widely taken for granted that the newly sovereign Slovak Republic would subsequently suffer economically.) Thus, whether or not Lincoln's economic predictions were on target, I am unmoved by this argument.[21]

Lincoln's sixth argument in favor of forcibly preserving the union (argument #9) was his fear that the South would default on its debts to the North after the secession. In particular, Lincoln expressed concern about the South not paying its fair share of the national debt, much of which was assumed when the United States purchased portions of the Southern territory. Certainly it is appropriate to hold the South responsible for its portion of the country's expenses, but I deny that this undermines the South's right to secede. In my view, the Confederacy's secession is consistent with its paying its portion of the national bills, just as marital divorce is compatible with each of the individuals exiting with his or her fair share of the couple's assets and debts. Thus, if Lincoln were genuinely concerned only about the national debt, his appropriate action would have been to insist that the South could secede only on the condition that it leave with its portion of the overall debt. Of course, Lincoln might object to this proposal on the grounds that there would be little the North could do to ensure that the South would honor this debt after the separation. (After all, there is an important disanalogy between marital and political divorces in that the former occur under the supervision of

---

[21] There is a more sophisticated version of this argument that would be more compelling, but it requires an implausible descriptive premise. Specifically, one might suggest that, while no one can rightly demand that her country be maximally economically efficient, each of us has a right to a decent minimum. If one combines this claim with the observation that – unlike an individual choosing her own profession – state breaking raises moral issues insofar as it inevitably includes unwilling constituents who would prefer to remain in the existing union, one could plausibly suggest that secession is impermissible whenever it would cause such economic deprivation that unwilling individuals would have to endure extreme economic hardship. I do not worry about this more sophisticated variation on Lincoln's argument, though, because it is unreasonable to suppose that the South's independence would have had such a profound detrimental effect upon its economy.

effective legal systems capable of enforcing the terms of separation; there was no comparably powerful institution of international law at the time to ensure that sovereign states honor their exit agreements.) If Lincoln's worries were legitimate, then he would have been justified in insisting that the secession be incremental or provisional until the debt was paid off (or, at the very most, he might have suggested that the secession be delayed until the South had either paid its debt or, more reasonably, given sufficient collateral or assurances that it would do so). But none of this is sufficient to establish that the South's political divorce was illegitimate *simpliciter*. Rather, these considerations imply only that Lincoln might have permissibly placed conditions on the Confederacy's separation.

Finally, we come to the argument that apparently played the biggest role in motivating Lincoln's resistance to the division (argument #10), his desire to fulfill what has been called the "Great American Experiment." Few of us would be indifferent to having our countries partitioned, so it is more than understandable that Lincoln would be so uncomfortable with the United States' splitting in two on his watch. In Lincoln's view, however, it was especially important to preserve the United States, for he believed that America's republican form of government was a model for the future. As a consequence, Lincoln conceived of himself as duty-bound to do whatever was necessary to keep the country intact not just for future citizens, but for all of humankind.

Insofar as I am a fan of constitutional democracy who (with some reservations) is happy that the United States has served as an influential model of how governments might order their affairs, I am not without sympathy for this argument. The problem is that it is not clear why the remaining Northern states could not just as well have supplied the world with such a paradigm after the political division. As Philip Abbott observes: "... it is possible to argue, as some abolitionists did, that the American experiment was more likely to succeed should the South leave the union peacefully, and that the North would defeat the South eventually through peaceful economic competition."[22] (Indeed, it is not unreasonable to suppose that, unencumbered by the South, the remaining states would have enjoyed even more economic, political, and moral success.) Thus, unless there is some reason to believe that the rump state would have foundered, it appears that an alternative "Great American Experiment" could have continued without the South, and that, as a consequence, the

[22] Abbott, "The Lincoln Propositions and the Spirit of Secession," p. 198.

value of preserving a model government did not justify forcibly resisting the secession.

Moreover, problems remain even if we concede for the sake of argument that neither of the two post-secession countries would have provided a suitable model of government. The chief difficulty is that it is impermissible to treat the antebellum Southerners merely as a means to creating a greater good for future generations. To see this, consider the pyramids: Regardless of how happy we may be that these tremendously impressive structures were constructed, their magnificence cannot justify the institution of slavery used to build them. Or, put in more contemporary terms, no matter how confident we might be that humanity into the indefinite future would appreciate our completing, say, a huge space station for scientific exploration, these expected returns would not justify our using slave labor *even if the latter were necessary to finish this project.* For the same reasons, Lincoln could not permissibly limit the Southerners' political self-determination if his only justification for doing so was that it was necessary in order to secure dividends for future generations.

At this point, one might protest that, because the latter is so much less significant, it is inappropriate to compare preserving democracy to building pyramids. Whereas the pyramids supply little more than aesthetic value, the importance of political arrangements is in an entirely different league, both because they have such a profound effect upon those living under them and because they can be replicated in a manner that allows an unlimited number to benefit.

For two reasons, I resist this response. First, the twentieth century was sadly littered with despots who tragically miscalculated that self-determination may legitimately be disrespected in the name of "promising" political experiments. Indeed, it is difficult to think of a terrorist or totalitarian leader who could not defend treating humans merely as a means if permitted to do so in the name of the some putative benefit to humanity. Second and more importantly, there is something ironic about denying the South's political self-determination in the name of a republican form of government, as the principal virtue of, and justification for, democracy is its maximal promotion of political self-determination. As I explained in the last chapter, it is striking that it is not only defenders of secession like Harry Beran, David Copp, and Daniel Philpott who have argued that the best defense of state breaking grounded in self-determination is to be found in democratic theory; arch-defenders of democracy like Robert Dahl have independently concluded that secession is "perfectly consistent with democratic practice."[23] Thus, insofar as the very principles that demand that important social decisions be reached democratically also justify secession grounded in self-determination, it is awkward to deny the latter in the name of the former. As Lord Acton put it in a letter to Robert E. Lee after the war: "[S]ecession filled me with hope, not as the destruction but as the redemption of Democracy.... Therefore I deemed that you were fighting the battles of our liberty, our progress, our civilization; and I mourn for the stake which was lost at Richmond more deeply than I rejoice over that which was saved at Waterloo."[24] I conclude, therefore, that the "Great American Experiment" no more justified Lincoln's denial of the South's exercise of political self-determination than it would justify Canada's forcibly annexing the United States in an effort to conduct a "Great *North* American Experiment."

Taken as a whole, then, my response to Lincoln's arguments is reminiscent of Dax Cowart's attitude toward those who denied his right to die. Cowart was the victim of an explosion that killed his father and left him blind and horribly burned all over his body. The treatments he endured for his burns were such torture that he decided that the remainder of his life was clearly not worth these twice-a-day procedures (which involved peeling the bandages off of his skinless body, scraping away any potentially infectious material, and lowering him into a tub of liquid that was tantamount to acid). When he told the hospital staff of his desire to die, they ignored his wishes and removed the phone from his room so that he could not call a lawyer. Now, years after his recovery, Cowart is happy to be alive. Still, he insists that (1) he had a right to die; (2) the medical practitioners acted impermissibly in disrespecting his self-determination; (3) if faced with the choice again, he would again choose to die rather than face the horrific treatment; and finally, (4) though they acted wrongly, Cowart understands that the hospital staff meant well and acted with noble intentions. Similarly, despite the fact that I am happy that the Union was preserved, I believe that (1) none of Lincoln's arguments justified his denying the South's political self-determination; (2) if faced with a Southern secessionist movement today, the North would have no right to deny the South independence; and finally, (3) though his arguments were poor, Lincoln acted with noble intentions.

---

[23] Robert Dahl, *Democracy and Its Critics*, p. 196.
[24] Quoted in Donald W. Livingston, "The Very Idea of Secession," p. 43.

An Alternative Argument against Southern Secession

Although I reject each of Lincoln's ten arguments, I believe neither that the South had a right to secede nor that Lincoln acted impermissibly in forcibly resisting the secession. In this section, I first explain why the South had no right to secede and then comment briefly on what I take to be a defect of both the arguments Lincoln posits and those he omits.

Because I appreciate the value of self-determination, I do not insist that a group must have been treated unjustly in order to qualify for a right to secede. As I emphasized in the previous chapter, though, we should restrict the right to secede only to those parties not only able but also willing to form a state at least as just as the one from which they seek to secede. Applying this reasoning to the Confederates, their capacity to perform the requisite political functions qualified them for a right to independence as long as they were willing to do so in a just manner. As we have seen, Lincoln questioned whether the Confederacy was in fact willing to govern in a just manner. In my assessment he missed the mark, though, by focusing on the Confederacy's republican credentials rather than on the institution that most discredited the South's claim to legitimacy. Insofar as Southern leaders sought to continue slavery, any professed intention on their part to form a just state, and thus any right of secession, may be soundly rejected.

Before moving on, it is important to spell out the conditional nature of this argument. Specifically, I submit that Lincoln was justified in forcibly resisting the separatist movement *if this was the only way to end slavery*. Taking seriously the hypothetical nature of this conclusion reveals that this justification did not license Lincoln to fight the division no matter what; it authorized him only to place a condition on the political divorce. In particular, since Lincoln's only legitimate grievance about the secession was that the subsequent sovereign state would be unjust, Lincoln should have extended the Southern states the following offer: "If you agree to permanently abolish slavery, then I will not contest your departure. If you plan to maintain slavery, on the other hand, then you leave me no choice but to forcibly resist the secession so that I can eradicate that horribly unjust institution." In the end, then, I contend that Lincoln might have had a right to deny the South's bid for independence, but because he would be justified in doing so only if it were necessary to end slavery, he was required first to offer the South the option of seceding without slavery. In other words, since it was the *slavery* rather than the *secession* to which Lincoln could righteously object, this justification permitted him only to place a condition on the terms of the political divorce. However, because the Southern states were adamant about maintaining slavery, this condition, unlike those discussed earlier, is pivotal. Putting this point in terms of liberalism, Daniel Philpott insists:

This was the problem with the Confederacy, and why it was morally impermissible for it to secede from the relatively liberal North. Not only did the Confederacy have no intention of outlawing slavery, but it seceded largely for the purpose of perpetuating slavery, and precisely this secession would have made it possible. Secession could not have been allowed, however, if liberalism means anything at all."[25]

If my analysis is on target, it highlights that there are two distinct issues: the eradication of slavery and the preservation of the union. It is striking that Lincoln explicitly recognized that these concerns posed two distinct questions. When discussing the issue of slavery, Lincoln explained:

[M]y paramount object in this struggle *is* to save the Union, and is *not* either to save or to destroy slavery. If I could save the Union without freeing *any* slave I would do it, and if I could save it by freeing *all* the slaves I would do it; and if I could save the Union by freeing some and leaving others alone I would also do that. What I do about slavery, and the colored race, I do because I believe it helps to save the Union. (V, 388)

But, while Lincoln is to be applauded for distinguishing clearly between the separate issues of slavery and secession, he can be criticized for his positions on each of the two distinct matters. Whereas Lincoln asserted (1) that the South had no right to secede, (2) that continuing the practice of slavery was, if expedient, an acceptable option, and (3) that the correct stance to take regarding slavery was determined by the more important issue of preserving the Union, I would submit (1A) that the Southerners had a right to secede if they would abolish slavery, (2A) that under no circumstances was slavery an acceptable option, and (3A) that the only justification for denying the South's political self-determination was as a necessary means to eliminating the (more important) institution of slavery. In fact, I maintain that slavery is such a grave injustice that it not only permitted Lincoln to do what was necessary to extinguish it, it *obligated* him to do so. As a result, not only do I contend that Lincoln would have been justified in denying the South's independence if this had been the only way to eradicate slavery, I assert that, if the North had wanted to secede from the South, the North would have been obligated to

[25] Daniel Philpott, "In Defense of Self-Determination," p. 375.

remain in the Union if this had been the only way to put an end to slavery. Thus (as should be clear from both the theory of political legitimacy I developed in Chapter 2 and the corresponding theory of secession I defended in the last chapter), my stance does not stem from a failure to respect the autonomy of the South in particular; it springs instead from my more general conviction that when injustice is sufficiently grave, its urgency can outweigh the pressing moral reasons to respect political self-determination.

Before concluding, it is worth noting that my criticism of Lincoln's position on the South's independence and my concern about his stance on slavery both stem from a dissatisfaction with the value he places on self-determination. In the case of the political divorce, Lincoln's arguments insufficiently appreciate the South's right to political self-determination, and regarding slavery, he failed to respect the slaves' rights to personal self-determination. Thus, while he might have had a general regard for the importance of autonomy, he did not recognize key parties (i.e., black slaves and nonsovereign groups) who qualify for moral rights to self-determination. In the end, then, his ten arguments against the South's bid for independence all fail for their incompatibility with the South's moral dominion over its own affairs, and he failed to make the one argument against the political divorce that I believe would have been compelling because he did not appreciate the importance of a slave's right to self-determination.

In closing, let me reiterate that my criticism is directed exclusively toward Lincoln's *arguments*, not toward Lincoln as a person or statesperson. Without retreating from my objection that Lincoln's arguments consistently give insufficient weight to the value of self-determination, I want to emphasize that I appreciate that his cultural era and political position placed enormous constraints on what he might reasonably be expected to believe, much less to endorse publicly. Thus, my relatively low estimation of his stated arguments against the South's bid to secede in no way dampens my profound admiration for Lincoln as a statesperson. In short, nothing in this chapter is meant to deny that the United States was exceedingly fortunate to have such an extraordinarily wise, virtuous, and politically savvy leader at the helm during its greatest crisis.

Implications for Other Cases

Although I obviously cannot discuss them in as great detail, let me briefly explain how my theory of secession would adjudicate several other prominent secessionist conflicts: the American Revolution, Norway's divorce from Sweden, the Lithuanian secession from the Soviet Union, the break-up of Yugoslavia, the division of Czechoslovakia, Chechnya's bid for sovereignty, and Quebec's separatist movement. Such a survey promises to be doubly instructive: Not only will it reveal how the functional theory of secession can generate clear and systematically derived answers to actual political controversies, it might also illustrate how previous discussions of political self-determination have been led astray by focusing on peripheral rather than central issues.

Despite its revolutionary character, the American "Revolution" was actually a secession, because the colonists never sought to overthrow the British government; they contested only the latter's authority to govern a portion of its existing territory. Under the banner "No Taxation without Representation!" the colonists demanded that the British Empire either treat them as equal citizens or grant them political independence. Because virtually everyone appreciates that the importance of self-determination prohibits a country from forcibly maintaining a colony, it is now generally accepted that the American colonies had the right to secede. On my view, though, a separatist group need not be the victim of colonization to qualify for a right political self-determination. To appreciate the difference between the traditional account and my own analysis, imagine that the British had responded to the cry of "No Taxation without Representation!" first by extending full rights of citizenship to the American colonists and then by creating a more equitable flow of taxes and services between England and America. On the traditional thinking, those citizens in America would no longer be the victims of injustice and, as a consequence, would no longer have a right to independence. According to the functional theory of secession, though, the question of colonization is beside the point, because a group need not be treated unjustly in order to have a right to secede. Daniel Philpott puts this point nicely: "The group's economic grievance, if it is valid, may be an accessory justification for self-determination and may enhance its claim to a form of self-determination that remedies the injustice (at least economic independence), but it is not necessary."[26] What is singularly important, I suggest, is the capacity to perform the requisite political functions. And since those in America were able to govern themselves satisfactorily, they had a right to secede and form their own state regardless of whether or not the British were willing to treat them as equals. Finally,

[26] Ibid., p. 377.

even if the British deserved some form of compensation in return for their initial investment in the colonies, this does not justify their denying the colonists' political liberty; at most, it can set limiting conditions upon the political divorce.

It is difficult to find fault with Norway's secession from Sweden in 1905. Given (1) that Norway and Sweden were both able to perform the requisite political functions, (2) that there was no indication that either sought to govern in an unjust fashion, and (3) that both parties preferred to peacefully go their separate ways, there was little reason for the international community to protest the division. The key to avoiding controversy was undoubtedly the fact that the divorce was mutual; very likely there would have been much greater consternation if Sweden had vigorously contested the separation. But just as no one would deny that a spouse has a right to unilateral divorce, we should not require that political divisions be bilateral. The functional theory of secession captures this fact, and thus, while mutual divisions are unquestionably easier, I insist that Norway's right to secede did not depend upon Sweden's willingness to allow the separation.

Lithuania's recent secession from the Soviet Union provides another example of how my analysis of political self-determination diverges from more traditional accounts. Lithuanians alleged that, because they had been forcibly annexed fifty years earlier, their independence amounted merely to reclaiming territory that had been unjustly occupied for half of a century. Virtually everyone accepts that the importance of political self-determination renders forcible annexation impermissible, but many believe that a state can acquire legitimacy over seized territory after a sufficient period of effective rule. (As Lee Buchheit explains: "International law is thus asked to perceive a distinction between the historical subjugation of an alien population living in a different part of the globe and the historical subjugation of an alien population living on a piece of land abutting that of its oppressors. The former can apparently never be legitimated by the mere passage of time, whereas the latter is eventually transformed into a protected status quo.")[27] As a consequence, many supposed that the pivotal question regarding Lithuania was whether the Soviet Union had governed the region long enough to gain legitimate title to this territory.[28] Once again, I conceive of the conflict differently. I insist that the Lithuanians should be required to give credible assurances

---

[27] Buchheit, *Secession: The Legitimacy of Self-Determination*, p. 18.
[28] For an example of this type of analysis, see Allen Buchanan's discussion in *Secession*, pp. 87–88.

that Russians living in a newly sovereign Lithuania would be treated justly. Presuming their willingness to do so, however, the crucial issue was Lithuania's capacity to function as a sovereign state. If Lithuania had the requisite capacity, the Soviet Union could not legitimately limit its liberty even if the Soviet Union had effectively governed that territory for a hundred years. If Lithuania lacked the relevant political abilities (as well as the potential to regain them), on the other hand, then it would have had no claim to sovereignty even if it had been forcibly annexed only ten years earlier.

Many onlookers marveled at Marshal Tito's ability to unite politically the different peoples of Yugoslavia. Initially, Tito rallied the Serbs, Croats, Slovenians, and others against a common military enemy, but once this threat had been neutralized, it became an open question whether they would remain united. Tito's immense presence among all the groups was a significant factor in cementing the union. More recently – a surprisingly long time after Tito's death – the Croats and Slovenians initiated viable secessionist movements. Clearly, I cannot do justice to the immensely complicated problem that these secessionist movements created for Yugoslavia and the international community, but I would be remiss if I did not at least offer some (admittedly simplified) remarks on how the functional theory would approach this conflict.

To begin, my impression is that, in addition to the usual aversion to having one's country dismantled, many Serbs feared this political divorce because they were less wealthy and economically advanced than those who sought independence. Although the Serbs controlled most of the country's political and military power, they were in many ways economically less well off than the Croats and Slovenians. If this is right, then a chief motivation for resisting the political division was fear of how a Serbian remainder state would fare economically. Even if this fear was justified, two questions emerge. First, did the Serbs have a right to, or merely an interest in, economic assistance from and cooperation with the other peoples of Yugoslavia? If the Serbs had no economic right to (but instead only an interest in) this union, then certainly their concern could not justify resisting the break-up. But even if the Croats and/or the Slovenians had economic duties to the Serbs, the former would have had a right to secede; they could have seceded on the condition that they continue as economic partners. (As the European Union amply demonstrates, there is nothing inconsistent about sovereign states cooperating intimately and extensively on economic matters.) According to the functional theory, the only type of dependence that can block secession *simpliciter* (as opposed to setting limiting conditions upon independence) is *political* dependence.

If the Serbs had been unable to perform the essential functions of a government without the Croats and/or the Slovenians, then the latter would have been bound to remain in the union. I assume that the Serbs were politically self-sufficient, and thus that they had at most economic rights against the Croats and Slovenians.

The functional theory's permissive stance on the division of Yugoslavia might not seem so radical now, but it is important both to recall how resistant the international community was to Yugoslavia's division and to appreciate how horribly costly this resistance proved to be. Indeed, in *The Balkan Odyssey*, David Owen concludes that, in retrospect, the European community's "biggest mistake" was refusing to consider secession as a solution earlier in the peace process. He writes:

> If the EC had launched a political initiative in August 1991 to address the key problem facing the parties to the dispute, namely the republics' borders, and had openly been ready to see an orderly and agreed secession of separate states in revised borders, then in conjunction with NATO a credible call could have been made for an immediate ceasefire.... It is in the first few days and weeks of a conflict developing that conflict resolution has its greatest chance of success. In July 1991 there was such an opportunity; once missed, it took until 1995 for war exhaustion to become the determining factor.[29]

It is tempting to suppose that the international community was so reluctant to consider secession principally for fear of the precedent it would set, but, in all fairness, there were legitimate concerns about how safe the various minorities would be in the newly created nation-states. For several reasons, though, the problem of minority rights was less decisive than those who were attempting to broker the peace imagined. First of all, as I argued in Chapter 3, there is no reason why the existing administrative boundaries could not have been abandoned in favor of boundaries drawn specifically to minimize the number of minorities. Again, David Owen puts the point nicely: "The unwarranted insistence on ruling out changes to what had been internal administrative boundaries within a sovereign state was a fatal flaw in the attempted peacemaking in Yugoslavia.... Of course the world has to be aware of the dangers of drawing state borders along ethnic lines; but the world also has to recognize the dangers of ignoring ethnic and national voices."[30] Second, it seems

---

[29] David Owen, *The Balkan Odyssey*, p. 342.

[30] Ibid., pp. 342–343. (Margaret Moore also makes this point in *The Ethics of Nationalism*.) Owen has reflected in personal conversation with the author that the lesson of Yugoslavia is that "you simply cannot force people to live together."

almost perverse to object to secession on the grounds that minority rights might be disrespected *when minorities are already suffering widespread and systematic abuse in the existing state.* This is especially so because the international community would clearly have more de facto control over the emerging nation-states than it had over Yugoslavia as a whole.[31] Finally, it seems clear that the problems of minorities in the seceding states were made immeasurably worse principally because the abuses escalated to such a horrific scale and gravity while the international community kept all the groups together in Yugoslavia. In sum, it appears not only that the Croatians and Slovenians had a right to secede but that the international community might have done considerable damage by being so reluctant to honor their claims to independence.

Consider now Slovakia's secession from Czechoslovakia. At first blush, the division of Czechoslovakia into the Czech and Slovak Republics appears morally identical to Norway's break from Sweden insofar as both were mutual political divorces. I have reservations about the morality of the Czechoslovakian break-up, though, because of how the decision to separate was reached. The motivation behind my theory of secession is that citizens should have the maximal say in determining their territorial boundaries, and thus I find the dissolution of Czechoslovakia problematic because Slovakia held no plebiscite on the issue. Instead, the Czech leaders offered little resistance when the newly elected Vladimir Meciar began pushing for Slovakia's political independence. (In fact, some observers were convinced that even Meciar never really wanted independence. Diane Orentlicher, for instance, suggests that Meciar's stated

---

[31] In "A Right to Secede?," Donald Horowitz questions why one should think that the international community would have any luck monitoring the conduct of newly seceded states. He writes:

> Proponents of the right to secession assure us that minority rights must be guaranteed in the secessionist states and that secession should be less favored if minority rights are unlikely to be respected, but the verbal facility of this formulation masks the difficulty of achieving any such results. If, after all, conditions on the exercise of an international-law right to secede can be enforced, why not enforce these conditions in the undivided state so as to forestall the need to secede? International law has been notoriously ineffective in insuring long-standing, internationally recognized minority rights, and proponents of secession have no new ideas to offer on this matter. (p. 54)

In his "Introduction" to the *Nomos* volume in which Horowitz's article appears, Allen Buchanan responds to Horowitz's challenge as follows: "... new entities created by secession are more amenable to international influence than existing states because they crave international recognition as legitimate states. Thus the international community has greater leverage over secessionist entities than over existing states and may be able to do a better job of protecting minorities in the former than the latter." (p. 5)

interest in secession was a bluff to gain more control over Czechoslovakia's economic policy, and that Klaus, determined to pursue capitalism, unexpectedly responded by allowing the political division.)[32] Certainly there are advantages to representative democracy, but it seems clear that a plebiscite is at least preferable, if not required, on any matter as important as the redrawing of territorial boundaries. Indeed, this is especially so with secession, where the local leaders often stand to gain the most from a region's gaining sovereignty. (As Donald Horowitz notes in explaining why groups will sometimes secede despite the economic costs of divorce, "Elite and mass economic interests . . . generally diverge at the moment of decision. Whereas the region as a whole stands to suffer if it opts for secession, educated elites stand to gain from the creation of new opportunities in a smaller, albeit poorer, state. . . . Secession creates new positions, while reducing the pool of competitors. Advanced segments of backward groups do not resist but generally lead the movement.")[33] Finally, even if one could make a general case for representatives handling questions pertaining to state breaking, it would be difficult to apply it to the Czechoslovakian secession because Meciar was elected in 1992 with less than 40 percent of the votes. Thus, even if one could somehow establish that all of those who voted for Meciar supported the separatist component of his platform, that still would not show that his push for sovereignty represented the will of the majority of Slovaks. In sum, while it might be objectionably anachronistic to demand plebiscites in the case of the American colonies or the Confederacy, this is certainly not too much to demand from secessionist movements as recent as the Slovakian case (especially when a 1990 poll indicated that only 8 percent of the Slovaks sought independence). Thus, the functional theory of secession need not give this political divorce the unqualified support that one might initially suspect.

Chechnya's bid for independence is an easy case, both politically and morally. Given Russia's geopolitical stature, their resolve not to lose this territory, and the fact that international law supports the status quo, the politically prudent course for virtually all international actors is clearly to look the other way as Russia deals with its own "internal matter." (This is especially true for the United States as it struggles mightily to marshal

---

[32] Diane Orentlicher, "International Responses to Separatist Claims: Are Democratic Principles Relevant?," p. 33.

[33] Donald L. Horowitz, *Ethnic Groups in Conflict*, p. 238.

international support for the ongoing "war on terror.") As politically relevant as these facts may be, none changes the ethics of the situation.
Indeed, even if international law still allows for unilateral secession only
when the separatists are a geographically distant colony, most political
theorists now appreciate that a group can have a right to secede when it
has been the victim of injustice. And given the twin facts that Chechnya
was forcibly annexed and has since been mistreated (to say nothing of the
brutal fashion in which Russia has tried to quash the secessionist uprising), even those who deny primary rights to secede acknowledge that
Chechnya is entitled to independence.[34] For those of us who value political self-determination, then, this case is morally analogous to Lithuania's.
The only real question is whether the Chechens can be trusted not to
mistreat the ethnic Russians who might remain in a sovereign Chechnya.
Thus, if the Chechens can give reliable assurances that they will govern
in a just fashion, there is no justification for denying them their political
self-determination.

Finally, consider Quebec's movement to secede from Canada. The
Quebecois have claimed a right to secede on a number of grounds, including discriminatory redistribution and forcible annexation (a portion of
what is now Quebec was initially seized by the British), but primarily
they cite the ways in which political independence would enable them
to preserve and strengthen their distinctive francophone culture. Without denying that, until very recently, liberals have egregiously neglected
a state's responsibility to support minority cultures, I suggest that the
Quebecois are wrong to focus upon this issue. If the functional theory of
secession is correct to insist that a state cannot justifiably restrict acts
of political liberty that are not excessively harmful, then contemporary
movements like the *Quebecois* should shift their concentration from arguments regarding the importance of culture and focus instead on defending the claim that both they and the remaining portion of Canada would
be able to perform the necessary political functions. This thesis is unlikely
to be welcomed by the many defenders of nationalism who have worked
in this area, but let me postpone a more extended defense of this position until the next chapter, when I critically examine the nationalist
principle.

---

[34] Allen Buchanan, for instance, concludes: "In my judgment a very strong case can be made
that the pattern of colonial injustice and the violation of autonomy agreements confers
on the Chechens a unilateral right to secede." (*Justice, Legitimacy, and Self-Determination,*
p. 211)

Conclusion

This discussion of Lincoln's objections to the South's bid for independence as well as the quick survey of other prominent secessionist conflicts clearly does not answer every possible objection to the functional theory, but hopefully it illustrates that many of the standard objections to respecting political self-determination miss the mark. The lesson of this chapter, taken as a whole, is perhaps that many of the common criticisms of secession show that we might legitimately put conditions on any given divorce, but that none establishes that secession itself cannot be permitted wherever it leaves neither the separatists nor the rump state politically incapacitated.

5

The Truth in Nationalism

The functional theory of secession runs counter to the dominant trends in the literature not only because it allows secession in the absence of injustice but also insofar as it focuses on the political capabilities rather than the cultural characteristics of the separatist party. This is striking because the majority of those receptive to political self-determination recommend redrawing political boundaries so as to better accommodate culturally defined nations. In this chapter, I argue that, although there is some truth in nationalism, any account of political self-determination that focuses principally on a group's status as a nation is misguided.

Thoroughgoing nationalists typically defend a threefold thesis: (1) There is nothing inappropriate about identifying with one's nation and conationals; (2) conationals have special obligations toward one another; and (3) each nation has a right to political self-determination. Although only the third prong of this tripartite thesis (the "nationalist principle") is directly relevant to secession, I will briefly examine the first two nationalist claims as well, because the three theses are generally taken to be mutually supporting. Thus, after an introductory section in which I explain my use of the term "nation," I divide this chapter into five main parts. First, I consider the appropriateness of identifying with one's nation and conationals. Next, I examine whether conationals have special obligations to one another. In the third section, I argue that a group's status as a nation can play at most a secondary role in establishing its right to secede. In the fourth section, I respond to possible objections that I underestimate the importance of nationality in a group's claim to its territory. Finally, I consider worries about the history of rights abuses perpetrated by national groups. In the end, I affirm that many nations have a right to secede, but I deny that their nationhood is their principal qualification for this right.

What Is a Nation?

The term "nation" is popularly used to designate both cultural groups and political units. Throughout this book, I follow many academic writers in restricting my use of "nation" only to cultural groups. (I refer to political units as either "states" or "countries.") Despite this specification, there is ample room for confusion. Much of this obscurity is unavoidable, but let me clarify matters some by briefly explaining how I understand the term. On my view, a nation is a cultural group of people who identify with one another and who either have or seek to have some degree of political self-determination. Understood in this way, nations have three types of features: cultural, psychological, and political. Consider each in turn.

Nations are cultural groups in that their members must share some combination of the following attributes: language, history, religion, dress, traditions, crafts, moral values, political institutions, art, music, holidays, etiquette, literature, popular culture, ethnicity, sense of destiny, ancestral or current territory, and military enemies and/or allies. This is not an exhaustive list, nor is any of these features either necessary or sufficient. As I understand it, a nation is a cluster concept, so that different groups may qualify as nations in virtue of sharing various configurations of these characteristics, and the same feature may be more or less important to different nations. While speaking French is paramount to the *Québecois*, no language is common to the Swiss, for instance.

It is not enough, however, merely objectively to share these attributes; these common characteristics must make a subjective difference. To qualify as a nation, a group's members must view themselves as belonging to the group in virtue of these common characteristics. Thus, the Basques might constitute a nation, whereas the collection of left-handed, hazel-eyed people would not, because only the former sufficiently identify with one another. Typically, this identification is such that a person will not only take pride in the successes (and be ashamed of the failures) of her fellow nationals, she will also likely regard herself as having special standing among her conationals, a standing to which additional rights and responsibilities attach. Any given Croatian, for example, is likely to feel personally motivated and morally obligated to assist another Croatian before she would be so inclined toward a similarly imperiled non-national.

Finally, a group must either have or seek to gain political self-determination. At its extreme, a nation might have or covet its own state, but this is not necessary. Less dramatically, a cultural group may merely have or seek special status within a larger multinational state.[1] Typically, nations lobby for special language, religious, or property rights. Native American groups in the United States and Canada are prime examples of groups that have distinctive political status.

Nations and Personal Identity

What is it for someone to identify with her nation and conationals, and is such identification both rational and morally appropriate? Kai Nielsen offers the following paradigmatic instance of nationalist identification:

When a Dane, for example, meets a fellow Dane abroad there is usually a spontaneous recognition of a common membership in a nation which is not the same when she meets, for example, a Chilean, though, if she is reflective and cosmopolitan, she will take an interest in the different life experiences, conceptions of things, and cultural attunements of people with nationalities different than her own. But normally there will be a sense of at-homeness and an affinity with her fellow Danes that is rooted in their having a common culture: the songs they sing, the structure of jokes, the memories of places, a sense of common history, literary references, political experiences, and the having of all kinds of common forms of intimate ways of living.[2]

Nationalists contend that it is fitting that we should seek the company of, value the approval of, strive to advance the causes of, and have special concern for our conationals. We are not all alike; there is a great diversity of ways to approach life, and it is natural and appropriate to feel most comfortable with, and interested in, those who share one's values, customs, and general view of life. In short, there is nothing curious about identifying with fellow nationals.

Nationalists often point to the great diversity of circumstances in which national sentiment flourishes as evidence that it is natural to identify with one's conationals. They typically suggest not only that there is nothing irrational about fastening upon one's national membership as a way to fix one's place in the world, but also that there would be something inappropriate about *not* taking pride in (and feeling ashamed of) the actions of conationals. The core idea is that we are fundamentally social

---

[1] For an excellent taxonomy of different types of minority culture rights, see Jacob Levy, *The Multiculturalism of Fear*, pp. 125–160.

[2] Kai Nielsen, "Liberal Nationalism and Secession," p. 109.

beings, and thus that it is altogether understandable that we should define ourselves at least partially in terms of our communal attachments.

Skeptics counter that nationalism's current prevalence does not show that nationalism is in any way ordained by human nature. To the contrary, authors such as Ernest Gellner maintain that it is a contingent phenomenon possible only within the linguistic, political, and economic conditions of modernity.[3] On this account, nationalism as we know it would not have emerged unless the socioeconomic environment had fostered occupational mobility, common educational systems, as well as the widespread literacy and mass media that this type of educational system allows. What is more, critics argue that nationalism is a regrettable phenomenon that we should strive to overcome. As Albert Einstein put it, nationalism is an "infantile disease" comparable to the "measles of mankind."[4] According to these detractors, national sentiment is an irrational, atavistic passion that involves wrongly treating the successes and failures of others as if they were one's own. There is nothing wrong with taking pride in one's successes and investing in one's future, but why should one take pride in the successes or invest in the futures of other people? If the accomplishments are someone else's, it just seems wrongheaded to treat them as if they were one's own. And since the future of someone else affects that person rather than oneself, it seems the very picture of irrationality to ignore one's own pursuits in favor of the aims of a large and anonymous nation.

Nationalists are seldom swayed by this objection, because it relies on what they regard as an excessively atomistic account of human rationality. A person who identified only with her own individualistic projects is conceivable, but she would strike most of us as both odd and unappealing. Imagine someone who felt no connection to her siblings and closest friends, for instance. What should we think of someone who was no more moved by her best friend's winning a Nobel Prize than if a stranger had won it? Indeed, just asking the question reveals that one cannot really be said to have close friends unless one is somehow personally invested in them. The fact is that we regularly and appropriately identify with various persons to whom we have personal attachments, and no theory should ask us to apologize for the connections we feel toward others. These considerations indicate that we should reject any account of rationality that requires us to be indifferent to all but our own individualistic pursuits.

---

[3] Ernest Gellner, *Nations and Nationalism.*
[4] David Baker (ed.), *Political Quotations* (Detroit: Gale Research, 1990), p. 144.

This alone, however, is not enough to exonerate nationalism. In order to defend national sentiments fully, one must explain why conationals are, like friends and family, *appropriate* objects of personal identification. The problem is that, whereas we have close personal relationships with our intimates, we do not even know the vast majority of those in our nation. Thus, it is open for a skeptic of nationalism to concede the appropriateness of identifying with, say, family members and still question the rationality of feeling connected to conationals. In other words, by acknowledging the importance of personal relationships in our lives, the critic of nationalism can avoid the charge of atomism without abandoning her attack.

Nationalists have responded to this more sophisticated objection in various ways, but one prominent approach is to admit that nations are "imagined" communities and then to suggest that they are nonetheless real communities and appropriate objects of personal identification.[5] The first thing to note is that most of us have numerous "imagined" connections; in other words, there are many people with whom we identify despite having no personal relationship with them. Recall how many people were poignantly moved by Princess Diana's death, for instance. All over the world, people who had never met Diana grieved when she passed. Alternatively, notice how excited spectators get about sporting events; we become invested in the outcome even though we have no personal connection to any of the participants. That is to say, we often root for a team and experience various degrees of joy or disappointment when "our" team wins or loses.

As these examples illustrate, there is nothing extraordinary or necessarily suspect about the "imagined" element of national communities. Margaret Moore puts this point nicely: "The fact that nations are socially constructed does not suggest that they are less real or are to be regarded with suspicion. Some people focus on the fact that they are 'imagined' communities to suggest that they may have no basis in 'reality.' Here it is important to distinguish between 'imagined' communities and 'imaginary' ones."[6] Still, a critic might insist that, despite being common, all imagined connections are irrational, so it is incumbent upon a nationalist to explain the appropriateness of identifying with conationals one has never met. Here I think the nationalist's most promising avenue is to explain why conationals share a relationship akin to that among

---

[5] See Benedict Anderson's landmark book, *Imagined Communities*.
[6] Margaret Moore, *The Ethics of Nationalism*, p. 13.

teammates. This analogy is helpful because few suppose that there is anything suspect about fellow feeling among teammates. Indeed, because of the personal relationships that emerge when people work together for a common goal, teammates typically form close friendships that transcend normally unbridgeable differences in social, economic, or cultural background.

Nationalists can invoke the relationship among teammates because there is a sense in which conationals are imagined "teammates in life." Conationals are teammates in life insofar as they share a common view of how one should live one's life. That is, nations regularly instruct one in a variety of subtle and not-so-subtle ways about how to live a good life. This common conception of the good life makes conationals like teammates because (since there are innumerable different ways to live one's life, many of which cannot be ranked according to objective criteria) ways of life are appealing to the extent that they enable their adherents to flourish. As a result, the extent to which my way of life strikes me as sensible and worthwhile depends upon the degree to which I *and those who live as I do* flourish. Thus, if I and all of those who embrace my way of being in the world are struggling to find meaning in our lives, then I am less likely to see this way of life as worthy of pursuit. If a great many of those who share my values are flourishing, on the other hand, then I can embrace this path with confidence that it is an appropriate (if not *the* appropriate) way of being in the world. Most of all, it is important to recognize that our self-esteem depends crucially on our confidence in our way of life. One does not choose among ways of life in the same manner that one shops for a candy bar. We typically mature into adulthood with a relatively well-defined and inelastic conception of the good life. Most of us spend the rest of our lives tinkering with patches in our quilt of values, but typically the design as a whole is a given that we are psychologically incapable of questioning, let alone changing. And because we base our whole lives around this pattern, our confidence in it is crucial to our self-esteem.

If the preceding is on target, then it is easy to see how conationals are like teammates in life. Very simply, (1) because our self-esteem is inextricably and crucially tied to our confidence in our way of being in the world, (2) because our confidence in this conception of the good life depends on the extent to which those who embrace it flourish, and (3) because our conationals are those who share our conception of our good life, it follows that (4) our self-esteem is fundamentally tied to whether our conationals flourish or founder. A conational's victory is a victory for me because it is evidence that our shared conception of how to be in the world is rewarding and worthwhile, and any such evidence buttresses my own self-esteem. Thus, conationals are teammates in life insofar as a goal scored by one is a goal scored for all, and a goal scored against any is a goal scored against all. And just as no one would question the joy I would feel were a close friend to win a Nobel Prize, no one should be suspicious when I take pride in a conational's winning such an honor. Given this, it is perfectly understandable that conationals should root for, invest in, seek the company of, value the approval of, and take pride and shame in one another. In short, it seems appropriate that conationals should identify with one another.

While I think this analogy between conationals and teammates is revealing, it is not enough to silence all critics. At least two potential problems remain. First, many contend that nations are importantly disanalogous to teams because national sentiment is often based on false histories and exaggerated conceptions of the commonalities among conationals and their distinctiveness from others. Thus, detractors allege that conationals are at least twice removed from teammates in that the former not only do not have personal relationships with one another, they also are prone to base their allegiance on fabrications. Second, critics object that these false stories inspire irrational violence between the imagined "teams." The problem is that there cannot be an "us" without a "them," and many nations have a terrible history of trying to elevate themselves by degrading others.

Each of these objections is important, but few defenders of nationalism take them to be decisive. In response to the first worry, nationalists suggest that, while some people undoubtedly cling to romanticized versions of their nation's history, this does not show that there is no distinct nation any more than an individual's self-deception entails that she is not a distinct person. (Indeed, team "histories" may also be distorted, but this does not make their members any less teammates.)[7] Moreover, authors such as David Miller have argued that the truth of a nation's story about itself is less important than how it inspires its members to behave. He writes: "Rather than dismissing nationality out of hand once we discover that national identities contain elements of myth, we should ask what part these myths play in building and sustaining nations. For it may not be rational to discard beliefs, even if they are, strictly speaking, false, when they can be shown to contribute significantly to the support

---

[7] I owe this point to Wayne Norman.

of valuable social relations."[8] If an exaggerated story about a nation's historical struggle inspires its members to be more civic-minded and to make greater sacrifices on each other's behalf, for instance, then it seems fetishistic about truth to demand that we should rid these nationals of their misconceptions.

And, while no one would claim that nations have never warred with one another, many nationalists assert that there is no necessary connection between supporting one's nation and attacking others. In fact, one of the most active movements in contemporary political theory is to argue that nationalism is perfectly compatible with – indeed, is a healthy supplement to – the universal rights of liberalism. Liberal nationalists allege that national sentiment can safely be added to a commitment to the traditional liberal rights, so that members of nations respect everyone and simply go above and beyond the minimum demands of universal morality to give special consideration and assistance to fellow nationals.[9] Not everyone is convinced that nationalism is fully compatible with the liberal ideals of equality and liberty, but the most promising theories of nationalism today strive to combine these two historically antithetical approaches.

In my estimation, considerations like the analogy of "teammates in life" go a long way toward vindicating the nationalist line on personal identity. Perhaps more work remains to be done, but I think nationalists are right to defend our identification with conationals as neither irrational nor immoral. Thus, as will become clear shortly, I take this to be the most defensible of the three nationalist theses.

Nations and Associative Obligations

As already indicated, identifying with one's nation involves, among other things, having a sense that one enjoys a special standing among one's conationals, a standing that carries with it additional moral responsibilities. According to nationalists, these perceived special duties are real; the obligations among fellow nationals are more extensive and demanding than the mere samaritan duties thought to exist among strangers. Like the nationalist claim about personal identification, however, this assertion is hotly debated. The problem is that these special obligations seem to conflict with commonsense morality insofar as they are at odds with a proper regard for the ideals of equality and liberty.

---

[8] David Miller, *On Nationality*, pp. 35–36.
[9] Ibid., and Yael Tamir, *Liberal Nationalism*.

According to what Samuel Scheffler has dubbed the "distributive objection," special obligations among conationals are incompatible with an appropriate regard for the equality of all because they extend a morally arbitrary advantage to the nation's members. As Scheffler puts it,

The distributive objection sees associative duties as providing additional advantages to people who have already benefited from participation in rewarding groups and relationships, and it views this as unjustifiable whenever the provision of these additional advantages works to the detriment of people who are needier, whether they are needier because they are not themselves participants in rewarding groups and relationships or because they have significantly fewer resources of other kinds.[10]

In short, why should someone enjoy a privileged status merely because she belongs to my nation? An even more popular concern is the "voluntarist objection," the worry that these special obligations are inconsistent with each individual's normal sphere of autonomy. Scheffler writes: "The voluntarist objection asserts that mere membership in a group or participation in a relationship cannot by itself give rise to any duties at all. Although it is true that we sometimes have special responsibilities to our associates, we have such responsibilities, according to this objection, only insofar as we have voluntarily incurred them."[11] The idea here is that each of us occupies a position of moral dominion over her own self-regarding affairs that keeps her free from all but autonomously chosen commitments. Because nations are nonvoluntary communities, any duties that stem merely from national membership would arise without our consent. Thus, to the extent that voluntarism is a feature of commonsense morality, the special obligations among conationals appear incompatible with our ordinary moral thinking.

Nationalists attempt to defang the distributive objection by emphasizing that the extra rights correlative to the special obligations of nationalism are a supplement to, rather than a substitute for, the basic human rights possessed by all. As David Miller stresses, "The duties we owe to our fellow-nationals are different from, and more extensive than, the duties we owe to human beings as such. This is not to say that we owe *no* duties to humans as such...."[12] Moreover, these national rights are "reiterative," which is to say that each nation has its own set of special claims and

---

[10] Samuel Scheffler, "Families, Nations, and Strangers," p. 7.
[11] Ibid., p. 11.
[12] Miller, *On Nationality*, p. 11 (emphasis in original).

responsibilities.[13] Thus – combining these two points – while Albanians may privilege each other over any particular Czech, for instance, the Albanians must respect all of the Czechs' basic rights, and the Czechs may in turn privilege one another over Albanians. Understood as such, the special obligations posited among conationals do not seem so antithetical to equality.

In response to the voluntarist objection, nationalists contend that our commonsense morality is not as clear-cut as this objection presupposes, because, while most of us do indeed value liberty, we also place a premium on communal ideals like fraternity. Just as ordinary moral thinking affirms the special obligations among siblings and colleagues, for instance, it also leaves ample room for morally significant ties among conationals. Moreover, once one sufficiently appreciates the normative force of the bonds uniting fellow nationals, one sees that these special obligations do not stem from a morally arbitrary source. In short, nationalists maintain that there is room both to conceive of individuals as largely free and equal and to view them as morally encumbered by their communal ties. If so, then the special obligations that accompany national membership need not conflict with commonsense morality.

While much is still being done to develop this line of argument, I remain unconvinced. My chief worry is that, to my knowledge, no one has generated an adequate explanation as to how or why national bonds generate duties. As I have argued elsewhere, no one has built a bridge from the plausible descriptive premise that conationals *do* identify with one another to the more ambitious and controversial normative conclusion that nationals *ought* to do more for one another.[14] That is, there is a huge difference between claiming that Xs are typically inclined to assist one another and asserting that Xs are specially obligated to do so. Until someone offers a compelling explanation as to why the former gives rise to the latter, I think we should question the existence of these extra duties.

Against this type of complaint, nationalists counter that no explanation is necessary because personal identification is a morally basic property.

---

[13] Kai Nielsen is among those who use the term "reiterated." He writes: "It is not only necessary that a liberal nationalism not be an ethnic nationalism: it must be a reiterated generalizable nationalism and not a nationalism of the manifest destiny of a chosen people who can run roughshod over other peoples in terms of its allegedly privileged place in history as being the wisest and the best." ("Liberal Nationalism and Secession," p. 108)

[14] Christopher Heath Wellman, "Associative Allegiances and Political Obligations."

The idea here is that, just as one need say no more than "Jane promised X" to explain Jane's having a special duty to X, one need cite only Jennifer's personal identification with Y to explain her special obligation to Y. As David Miller explains, "The particularist defence of nationality begins with the assumption that memberships and attachments in general have ethical significance. Because I identify with my family, my college, or my local community, I properly acknowledge obligations to members of these groups that are distinct from the obligations I owe to people generally."[15] On this view, we need not give various complicated justifications for why a Jewish American philosopher has special obligations to other Jews, Americans, and philosophers, because it follows straightforwardly from the fact that she identifies with Jews, Americans, and philosophers.

While this tack of conceiving of personal identification as a basic source of moral reasons appears promising as a solution to the present problem, it leads to other conclusions that are less palatable.[16] Consider just two examples. Many sports fans fervently identify with a given team, but it seems wrong to conclude that they therefore have special obligations to support that team. (We might call a person who turns her back on "her" team as soon as they loose a "fair weather fan," but – as I will suggest later – this is an indictment of her *character* rather than an allegation that she has disrespected a *duty* to continue to root for the team.) A second, less benign example is the racist or sexist who identifies with other whites or men. Given that we would be loath to say that a white supremacist has extra duties to other whites or that a misogynist has special obligations to other men, we ought not to embrace the view that all personal identifications create duties.[17] Of course, a nationalist might object that a racist's identification with other whites is irrational or inappropriate, but this move raises problems of its own. First, as we saw earlier, many

---

[15] Miller, *On Nationality*, p. 65.
[16] Here I rely on arguments I make in greater detail in "Relational Facts in Liberal Political Theory: Is There Magic in the Pronoun 'My'?"
[17] Discussing a related point, Simon Caney writes:

> In particular, it is unclear why one should respect features of a person's character by which he or she defines themselves. What if a person's anti-Semitism or chauvinism is an integral part of who they are? To claim here that this feature of their personality should be respected is, of course, utterly unacceptable. So to establish that one should respect someone's nationality one must show that nationality is not obnoxious in the same way that racism and sexism are. One must establish that nations are worthy of respect. ("National Self-Determination and National Secession: Individualist and Communitarian Approaches," p. 162)

theorists question the rationality of national sentiments, and second, the most promising argument for the special duties among conationals relies on the contention that identification creates obligations, not on the view that we are obligated just in case we *ought to* feel connected.[18]

In light of these problems, I remain skeptical of the claim that each nation creates special obligations among its conationals. Although ethicists seem to be focusing on our noncontractual duties with unprecedented vigor, my own view is that this heightened attention will ultimately show that, if there is something ineliminably moral about the bonds connecting conationals, it is better captured by virtue theory than by the language of duties. As the example of the "fair weather fan" illustrates, our real qualm about someone who claims an allegiance during the good times but disassociates during the bad is that she reveals herself to be objectionably self-centered. We think she would be a better, more loyal person – a person with a more laudable character – if her allegiance remained constant through good times and bad. Similarly, a person who takes pride in all of the accomplishments of her conationals and yet distances herself whenever her nation needs support reveals herself to be objectionably selfish. Thus, while I can see that there is something morally suspect about a person who exclaims "*we* won" whenever her team wins and "*they* lost" whenever her team loses, I am reluctant to explain this moral defect in terms of disrespected duties. In sum, much interesting work is currently being done on this topic, but I have yet to be convinced that conationals have special obligations to one another.

The Nationalist Principle

In considering the nationalist principle, it is essential at the outset to distinguish between two versions of the principle. According to the first, political states and cultural nations should be made coextensive, so that every nation has its own state and no state houses more than one nation. According to the second, every nation is *entitled* to its own state.[19] The difference between these two may seem slight, but it is significant because whereas the latter *allows* a nation to form its own state, the former *requires*

---

[18] Note also that authors like David Miller who stress that national sentiment is to be judged principally on the way it inspires us to act rather than on the truth of its presuppositions cannot object to the false assumptions required for racism.

[19] In their seminal article "National Self-Determination," Avishai Margalit and Joseph Raz emphasize that they mean to defend an encompassing group's dominion to choose whether or not to exercise self-determination.

each distinct nation to do so. Because I assume without argument that it is implausible to suppose that two nations may not permissibly stay (or join) together in one multinational state (does one really want to insist that the former Czechoslovakia was morally required to disband, for instance?), I will consider only the latter interpretation of the nationalist principle here. That is, I will explore whether nations have a moral right (as opposed to a duty) to secede from multinational host states.

Another thing to bear in mind is that, although I will focus exclusively upon the nationalist principle's implications for state breaking, there are in fact a variety of ways for a nation to exercise self-determination without controlling its own sovereign political unit. Groups routinely exercise various degrees of cultural self-determination and any number of collective rights within the larger, multinational states. Yael Tamir, for instance, is chief among those who argue that even when cultural self-determination requires some degree of political autonomy (which need not always be the case), there is no reason to assume that this political self-determination must come in the form of complete sovereignty.[20] Moreover, even those theorists who apply the nationalist principle to secession do not always apply it only to state breaking. Rather, authors like David Miller, Margaret Moore, Kai Nielsen, and Daniel Philpott argue that the importance of national self-determination can ground a number of special political rights, including (in some cases) the right to withdraw unilaterally from a multinational host state.[21] Thus, I do not mean to imply that defenders of national self-determination are concerned primarily, let alone exclusively, with state breaking.

Similarly, it is important to acknowledge that the most sophisticated advocates of nationalism stop short of alleging that *all* nations have a right to form their own sovereign states in *any* circumstances. Daniel Philpott, for instance, is representative in his specification that "the right to self-determination is also qualified. . . . Self-determining groups are required to be at least as liberal and democratic as the state from which they are separating, to demonstrate a majority preference for self-determination, to protect minority rights, and to meet distributive justice requirements."[22] The specific conditions on the right vary from author to author, of course,

---

[20] Yael Tamir, *Liberal Nationalism*.

[21] David Miller, *On Nationality* and "Secession and the Principle of Nationality"; Margaret Moore, *The Ethics of Nationalism*; Kai Nielsen, "Liberal Nationalism and Secession"; and Daniel Philpott, "In Defense of Self-Determination" and "Self-Determination in Practice."

[22] Philpott, "Self-Determination in Practice," p. 80.

but it is not uncommon for a theorist to limit the types of nations that qualify for statehood, the types of states they are entitled to create, and the conditions under which they may break from their remainder states. As a consequence, it is important to bear in mind that my description of the nationalist principle as the view that each nation has a right to form its own state is merely a convenient shorthand place marker for the various more nuanced claims for which (the most plausible academic) nationalists argue. In light of these points of clarification, let us examine the reasons to embrace a nationalistic account of political self-determination.

The basic argument for the nationalist principle consists principally of two straightforward and plausible premises: (1) A nation's health directly affects its members' welfare, and (2) political self-determination allows nations to bolster their health. It does not take much effort to motivate either of these claims; consider each in turn.

Given that people often identify so closely with their nations, it is not difficult to connect a nation's health to its members' welfare. As Will Kymlicka and others have argued, nations supply the foundations necessary for us to live rewarding and meaningful lives by making salient the values that guide our choices regarding which types of lives to pursue.[23] Only a healthy nation could suggest a rich and diverse array of meaningful lives, because the strength of a culture determines its ability to support a context of choice within which members set goals and form relationships. A foundering culture will be less able to assist its members in their attempts to construct rewarding lives, since these members will have greater difficulty building relationships and pursuing meaningful goals. Because of this, one's prospects for self-esteem and self-respect depend largely on the health of one's culture. As a result, the first premise, that a nation's health affects the welfare of its members, seems unobjectionable.

The importance of healthy nations to individuals signals the potential value of national self-determination. While there may be no logical connection between a nation's enjoying self-governance and its flourishing, it is clear that self-government is generally conducive to a nation's prosperity and dignity. The most obvious advantage of political sovereignty is as a shield against persecution, but it can also help minority groups who suffer from a majority's neglect, ignorance, or indifference. The core idea here requires little elaboration: A nation stands to prosper when its members can freely debate among themselves what rules should prevail; when its own members draft, promulgate, and adjudicate these rules; and when

---

[23] Will Kymlicka, *Liberalism, Community, and Culture.*

its own members actually take to the streets and enforce these rules. In brief, just as one typically feels most comfortable in one's own home, a nation has a better chance of flourishing when it lives on its own terms.[24]

Given the plausibility of both of these claims, it is not surprising that so many embrace the nationalist principle. Indeed, in many ways the foregoing argument is merely a nationalist transposition of J. S. Mill's influential defense of granting individuals sovereignty over their own lives. Just as Mill favored letting individuals decide how to lead their lives, this argument explains why it is important for nations to have dominion over their own affairs. It is essential to recall, however, that Mill did not propose that individuals should be free to behave however they please; he suggested only that they should enjoy free rein over their *self-regarding* behavior. Thus, even if we are sympathetic to this defense of the nationalist principle, we should be clear that it applies only to a nation's self-regarding matters. (To take an obvious example, just as Mill never meant to suggest that individuals should be free to murder others, we would not want to allege that nations are permitted to "ethnically cleanse" non-nationals in their midst.)

This caveat raises red flags for anyone interested in applying the nationalist principle to state breaking, however, because insofar as secession necessarily involves taking sovereign control over territory currently governed along with the constituents of the remainder state, it does not appear to be self-regarding.[25] Given that secession involves reducing the parent state's territory, there is no question that all of the state's citizens would be affected if their political union were disbanded. As I explained in Chapter 3, though, the operative question is whether the unionist compatriots have not only interests, but *legitimate* interests in the state's remaining intact.[26] Therefore, before we judge whether the nationalist's

---

[24] David Miller puts this point plainly: "Simply put, if you care about preserving your national culture, the surest way is to place the means of safeguarding it in the hands of those who share it – your fellow-nationals." (*On Nationality*, p. 88)

[25] To see that secessionist conflicts are essentially contests over territory, recall the difference between emigration and secession. States would rarely contest a minority group's emigration, but they would likely fight tenaciously if the same group sought to secede. Indeed, although the Serbs fought ferociously to keep the Croats from seceding, they would likely have created a national holiday to commemorate the day that the Croats decided en masse to emigrate to Germany, say.

[26] To appreciate why the distinction between interests and *legitimate* interests is paramount, assume that I am madly in love with Madonna. If so, I would have an interest in her not marrying anyone else, but presumably that interest would not be legitimate. That is, my interests would not generate any moral reasons for Madonna to refrain from marrying someone else.

claim for self-governance over a piece of territory is decisive, we must weigh it against the competing claim of those who would be excluded in the rump state. And because the existing state's claim to its territory is explained in terms of political legitimacy, we cannot adequately assess the nationalist principle without considering it in light of political legitimacy.[27]

To review: The case for the nationalist principle presents a strong prima facie case for national self-determination, but we cannot adequately assess its implications for secession without weighing this presumptive case against a state's claim to the potentially contested territory. Using the samaritan theory of political legitimacy developed in Chapter 2, we can now better assess the nationalist principle, because we can weigh a nation's claim to territory (based on the importance of national self-determination) against the state's claim to its territory (grounded in the importance of ensuring peace and security).

As a nationalist is apt to point out, my account of political legitimacy leaves ample room for nationalist state breaking, because wherever the separatist nation is capable of performing the political functions of ensuring peace and security, the existing state has no justification for its nonconsensual coercion. In other words, when a nation is sufficiently large, wealthy, well-organized politically, and territorially contiguous, it can secede and thereby enhance its national self-determination without jeopardizing the benefits of political stability.

I am sympathetic to this defense of some nations' right to secede, but it is important to notice that this reasoning actually reveals how the nationalist principle misses the mark. This is because, while politically viable nations might have a right to secede, those nations that lack the requisite political capabilities will not have a legitimate claim to be free of the parent state's sovereignty. Furthermore, even in those cases in which a nation has a right to secede, *it will not be the importance of the nation's cultural self-determination that grounds its claim;* rather, it will be its political capacities. That being the case, there is a sense in which a group's cultural status is beside the point; the crucial variable will be the separatists' ability to govern the contested territory in a safe and just manner. To emphasize: It is not true that all and only nations have a right to secede, because non-national groups with the requisite political

---

[27] Again, this is why I went to such lengths in Chapter 2 to develop and defend an account of political legitimacy. Because secessionist conflicts cannot be adjudicated without knowing what it is that grounds the state's claim to its territory, an account of political legitimacy is necessary to generate a principled and systematic theory of secession.

abilities will have a right to secede and politically unviable nations will not. It may well be that most separatist groups are in fact motivated by nationalist aspirations, but those nations whose claims are legitimate will be justified by their *political capabilities*, not by their *cultural attributes*. Thus, once one combines the observation that some non-national groups will have a right to secede with the commonly recognized fact that not all nations have this right, it becomes apparent that we would be wrong to fasten upon a group's nationhood as the key feature that qualifies it for political self-determination.

But even if there is no perfect correlation between a group's being a nation and its deserving political autonomy, there is some truth underlying the principle of national self-determination. As we have seen, this truth is threefold: (1) Nations tend to be more cohesive than other groups of their size; (2) the welfare of a nation is often especially important to the members of the group; and (3) a nation's welfare can be improved by increased political autonomy. The significance of these facts can be captured in the following two ways. First, although the fact that a group constitutes a nation is not directly relevant to its claim to secede (since what is essential is a group's ability to govern itself), it is indirectly significant because a nation's increased cohesion enhances its capacity to perform the requisite political functions and consequently makes it a better candidate for the right to secede. The idea here is that its national allegiance enables a nation to motivate its members to make sacrifices on behalf of the political union. And second, since nationals are (understandably) prone to value political self-determination more highly than nonnationals, this can give the former's claims to political self-determination an urgency missing from the similar claims of nonnationals. This is important, since there may be circumstances in which political stability would be jeopardized if all interested groups of a certain size were allowed to secede, but where the political climate could easily withstand a limited number of these groups forming their own states. Or, as with the disintegration of a large country like the Soviet Union, perhaps a number of secessions will need to be incrementally phased in over time. Under these circumstances, we could utilize additional criteria to distinguish among the eligible secessionist movements, and the nation/non-nation distinction would be an important consideration when prioritizing the competing claims to independence.[28] In the case of Canada, for instance,

---

[28] On page 293 of his article "What's So Special about Nations?," Allen Buchanan argues that "to single out nations as such for rights of self-government that are denied to other groups is morally arbitrary, and this arbitrariness violates the principle that persons are to

Quebec's French-Canadian culture could give its secessionist appeal priority over similar claims advanced by English-Canadian provinces. Thus I suggest that, while the nationalist principle is not perfectly on target, it does capture an important kernel of truth about the (secondary) significance of national allegiances in matters of state breaking.

The Nationalist Rejoinder

Some nationalists are likely to bristle at my suggestion that there is only a kernel of truth in the nationalist principle. In this section, I consider potential difficulties for my approach to secession in light of recent contributions to the debate by Margaret Moore, David Miller, and Alan Patten.

The first thing one might notice about my account is that it seems utterly out of touch with the real world. After explaining my views on secession, Margaret Moore protests:

What is clear in this discussion is the complete ignorance of the dynamic of most secessionist movements. In almost every case of secession, and every secessionist movement, the people who seek to secede are culturally and/or linguistically distinct from the majority population, with a somewhat different history and different relationship to the majority group and the state, and who are situated on their ancestral territory – not recent immigrants. Secession is not simply an issue of political legitimacy or fulfilling the functions of a state but is closely tied up with sub-state nationalism, and the interplay between the state and the community's culture, symbols, and identity.[29]

Were I in the business of describing secessionist movements, Moore's objection would be right on the mark. However, my project is *normative*, not *descriptive*: I aim to answer the moral question of what type of party

be accorded equal respect." The core of Buchanan's objection is that, given that nations are not the only groups with which we identify, proponents of the nationalist principle owe us a more plausible explanation of why we should single out nations as uniquely entitled to secede. Because the functional theory does not require a group to be a nation in order to qualify for a right to secede, it might appear invulnerable to Buchanan's criticism. Insofar as I allege that nations should sometimes be given priority over non-national separatists, however, I should acknowledge that a version of Buchanan's concern would apply to my view as well.

It is tempting to respond that Buchanan's worry is, as a practical matter, insignificant. (After all, it is difficult to imagine a viable secessionist party, composed of people who identify with one another, that is not a nation.) As a conceptual matter, though, I must concede that a non-national, viable separatist party might share a group identification and, if so, that there would be no reason it should be given any less consideration than an analogous national counterpart.

[29] Moore, *The Ethics of Nationalism*, p. 174.

has a right to secede, not the descriptive question of what types of parties typically exhibit an interest in state breaking.

To appreciate the difference between these two very different kinds of projects, consider again my analogy regarding the issuance of driver's licenses. In particular, imagine how we might reason about who should be licensed to drive large trucks. Because it would potentially be harmful to others if all those licensed to drive cars were also allowed to drive trucks, it would make sense to have special exams so that those interested in driving trucks could demonstrate their competence in this capacity. If we restricted truck licenses to only those who could satisfactorily demonstrate that their truck driving would not pose unreasonable risks to others, this would allow us to permit some truck driving without creating too great a risk of harm to the general public.

Against this, one might object in Moorean fashion that such reasoning demonstrates complete ignorance of most truck license applicants: After all, the overwhelming majority of those who seek such licenses are men, so certainly something is wrong with any analysis that makes no mention of the applicant's sex. Here I suspect that most would respond that, while a description of current applicants would indeed be remiss if it said nothing about the preponderance of applicants being male, this in no way shows that being male is (even part of) what should qualify an applicant for such a license. Because one's truck driving competence does not depend upon one's being male, there is nothing objectionable about a normative account specifying who *ought* to be licensed saying nothing about an applicant's sex. Similarly, if a group's nationality is distinct from its capacity to perform the requisite political functions, then being a nation is logically distinct from what qualifies a party for a right to secede. That being the case, there is nothing curious about a normative account of secession like mine making no mention of a group's national status. Of course, if a group's nationhood is likely to affect either its capacity or its willingness to perform the necessary functions (for good or for ill), then nationality might well play an indirect, secondary role in (dis)qualifying a group's candidacy for a right to secede, but there is nothing in my analysis that denies this. On the contrary, I explicitly acknowledge that a group's national status can have a derivative significance.

If the foregoing discussion is on target, then defenders of nationalism would have to do more to deny that a group's nationality is beside the most important moral point. Specifically, they must explain why a group's status as a nation is directly relevant either to its capacity to perform the necessary political functions or its entitlement to a specific piece of territory. Because David Miller has developed promising and influential arguments on both of these counts, let us turn now to his work.

Miller emphasizes that, because they identify so strongly with one another, conationals are more inclined to sacrifice for one another than multinational compatriots. This is key, Miller points out, because liberal democratic states require considerable sacrifices in order to perform their political functions. In particular, constituents must be willing to put aside their individualist pursuits and become the active, engaged citizens necessary to sustain a healthy democracy, and they must be willing to give up a portion of their income so that the state can make welfare transfers to less fortunate compatriots. Drawing upon the tendency of conationals to identify with one another that we discussed earlier, Miller suggests that citizens would be more willing to make such sacrifices for conationals, and thus that one way to help states perform their political functions is to make states and nations coextensive. Using the term "compatriots" to designate fellow nationals, Miller writes:

Where the citizens of a state are also compatriots, the mutual trust that this engenders makes it more likely that they will be able to solve collective action problems, to support redistributive principles of justice, and to practise deliberative forms of democracy. Together, these make a powerful case for holding that the boundaries of nations and states should as far as possible coincide.[30]

Miller may be right that conationals are more apt to sacrifice for one another, but I am skeptical that any more follows from this than that there is a secondary, indirect relevance of nationalism insofar as shared nationality can help a group's capacity to perform the requisite political functions. Admittedly, much more would follow if Miller endorsed the more ambitious claim that *only* national groups could adequately perform the requisite political functions, but he rightly shies away from this more radical thesis, both because it requires the implausible descriptive premise that nations are uniquely capable of securing legitimate political order and because it has the awkward normative implication that all existing multinational states (including Canada, Switzerland, and the United Kingdom, for instance) lack political legitimacy.

Thus, anyone who wants to invoke these types of considerations to defeat the functional theory of secession faces a dilemma. If one begins with only the plausible premise that conational citizens are more inclined to sacrifice for one another than multinational compatriots, then this

---

[30] Miller, *On Nationality*, p. 98.

modest point of departure will not yield the desired conclusion that a party's nationhood is essential to grounding its right to secede. If one begins with the more ambitious premise that only nation-states are capable of performing the requisite political functions, on the other hand, then one has to defend this apparently counterfactual descriptive claim and to allege implausibly that virtually all existing states are in fact illegitimate.

Given that the link Miller highlights between being a nation and having the capacity to perform political functions is not enough to establish more than a derivative role for nationalism in secession, it is worth turning to his second thesis that, through continued occupancy, nations can establish a claim to political authority over land. Miller writes:

The people who inhabit a certain territory form a political community. Through custom and practice as well as by explicit political decision they create laws, establish individual or collective property rights, engage in public works, shape the physical appearance of the territory. Over time this takes on symbolic significance as they bury their dead in certain places, establish shrines or secular monuments and so forth. All of these activities give them an attachment to the land that cannot be matched by any rival claimants. This in turn justifies their claim to exercise continuing political authority over that territory.[31]

There is no question that Miller writes with great sensitivity about how people can and do become attached to particular plots of land. What is less clear, however, is what implications Miller's insights have for linking secession exclusively to nations. To begin, one might wonder why only nations can become attached in this way. Could not a multinational group of people become attached to land in just the way Miller describes? Here Miller might respond that nations are uniquely able to generate these types of claims because such claims require that a group mix its culture with the land, and nations are distinctive in being culturally based groups. Thus, Miller might explain his views as analogous to Locke's: Just as Locke suggested that one could come to have property rights over land by mixing one's labor with it, a group generates a different type of claim over land by mixing its culture with it.[32]

Invoking Locke in this way might motivate Miller's claim that mixing culture with land helps to establish a group's claim to territory, but it raises the question of what type of claim it is. Presumably one would not want to say that mixing culture with a piece of land gives one a *property*

---

[31] Miller, "Secession and the Principle of Nationality," p. 68.
[32] Margaret Moore recognizes this analogy with Locke in *The Ethics of Nationalism*, p. 191.

right to that territory, but neither is it clear that it could give one *political authority* over it. Imagine that a nation were clearly attached to a piece of land but equally clearly lacked the capacity to secure political stability over that territory; would Miller still say that this nation enjoyed a right to exercise political authority over the territory? I presume not. This suggests that the types of considerations that Miller stresses establish a separate type of claim, perhaps to access to the land in question. As Margaret Moore comments: "Historical monuments and national sites can, at best, legitimize a *prima facie* case in favor of rights of *access* but not to control over the territory. . . ."[33] If so, then, whatever we think about Locke's views on property rights, we might say that a group can qualify for the right to political sovereignty only if it is politically viable, and that a group can have a valid claim to some type of access to land if it is appropriately attached to it. Thus, if a group is attached to land that it currently occupies, then it has a claim not to be displaced, and if the group does not currently occupy the territory, then it might have at least a claim to some type of visitation. In sum, although there are important truths in each of Miller's observations, neither gives us reason to abandon the functional account of secession for one that features nationalism more centrally.

Finally, let us consider the argument in Alan Patten's recent article "Democratic Secession from a Multinational State." Patten values national self-determination, but he nonetheless dislikes plebiscitary theories like mine because they permit national minorities to secede from states that "introduce and respect constitutional arrangements that provide space for self-government for members of a national minority."[34] Because it is so important to secure the equal recognition of the different identities, Patten argues that we must dismiss any theory that would allow the division of states that achieve this equal recognition.

The pivotal move in Patten's argument is that states should recognize minority national groups because recognition of one's group is a fundamental good. As Patten explains, "the recognition of national identity is 'good' for individuals in two different ways. Recognition allows individuals to fulfill their aspiration to participate in collective self-government alongside members of the group with which they identify, and it promotes

---

[33] Ibid., p. 190 (emphasis in original).

[34] Alan Patten, "Democratic Secession from a Multinational State," p. 566. Views like mine are sometimes labeled "plebiscitary" because, insofar as they require that a separatist group neither suffer injustice nor constitutes a nation, they appear to grant a right to secede to any group that can garner a majority of pro-separatist votes in a plebiscite. (My view is also sometimes called a "choice" theory.)

the value of communal integrity."[35] Once one appreciates the importance of equal recognition, it is not difficult to see Patten's dissatisfaction with plebiscitary theories: They would allow a group to dismantle a state that effectively secures equal recognition in order to create a new state that does not. Patten's alternative is to permit plebiscitary secessions from states that deny equal recognition but to prohibit unilateral withdrawal from states that realize this fundamental good. He writes:

> My proposal suggests that the decision whether to grant a secessionist claim made by a substate national minority should take into account the degree of recognition enjoyed by the group within the existing state. Where a national minority does enjoy significant recognition, it should not normally be regarded as possessing a plebiscitary right to secede. Where multinational constitutional arrangements providing for recognition are not in place, a national minority should be regarded as having a plebiscitary right to secede, so long, at least, as the various conditions required by moderate and qualified versions of the democratic account are satisfied.[36]

As should be clear from my discussion of the indirect importance of nationalism, I am not unsympathetic to Patten's claims about the importance of equal recognition. It is not clear to me, however, why he draws from this the conclusions he does regarding secession. If equal recognition is as important as Patten suggests, then it seems reasonable to conclude that only states that constitutionally secure it live up to the dictates of justice. But from this it follows that the liberal conception of a just state should be amended to include provisions for equal recognition, not that secession should be permitted from only those states that do not secure equal recognition. To see this, notice what types of conclusions we would draw regarding another issue of justice, slavery.

It would not be difficult to construct an argument concerning slavery analogous to that which Patten develops for equal consideration. Just as Patten claims that equal recognition is a fundamental good, we could argue that being subjected to slavery is a fundamental bad. Thus, just as we might want states to constitutionally secure equal recognition, we would like states to constitutionally prohibit slavery. Would we therefore conclude that secession should not be allowed from any state that prohibits slavery? Presumably not. Rather, we would require that no one has the right to secede in order to create a new state that allows slavery. Given this, why conclude that the importance of equal recognition implies that

[35] Ibid., p. 569.
[36] Ibid., p. 583.

secession from states that secure such recognition must be prohibited? The more natural conclusion would seem to be that a separatist group could have a right to secede only on the condition that the state it subsequently created itself secured equal recognition. What is more, the conclusion Patten draws from the value of recognition is all the more curious given his explicit awareness that plebiscitary theorists routinely specify that secession is permitted only where "the creation of the new state is unlikely to generate serious violations of standard liberal rights, or to conflict with the realization of other standard elements of liberal justice."[37] Thus, it seems as though the correct thing for Patten to suggest is not that plebiscitary theories must be rejected, but that the standard roster of liberal rights should be expanded to include the constitutional protection of equal recognition.

Here Patten might counter that my analogy to slavery is inapt because equal recognition is not something that the seceding territory can simply reestablish internally in the way that it could prohibit slavery.[38] In response, I concede that securing equal recognition may not always be easy, but I do not understand why a newly sovereign state cannot constitutionally recognize the national identities of its minorities just as its parent state did. (If Great Britain can accommodate those in Northern Ireland who identify with Ireland, for instance, then what precludes a newly sovereign Northern Ireland from doing the same for those citizens who identify with Great Britain?) Even if we assume that a particular secessionist territory would for some reason be unable to secure equal recognition on its own, however, why could it not simply form a confederation with the parent state? If we suppose that Northern Ireland could not form its own state without violating the equality of those citizens who continue to identify with Great Britain, for instance, then why may Northern Ireland not secede on the condition that it retain the necessary confederal arrangement with Britain?

What is more, notice that the possibility of confederal arrangements raises other issues for Patten's argument. If Patten genuinely believes both (1) that states do not treat equally those citizens whose identities they fail to constitutionally recognize and (2) that equal recognition is not always something that can be established internally, then he seems committed to the view that all states (not just secessionist territories) are required to enter into confederations when this is necessary to constitutionally

---

[37] Ibid., p. 563.
[38] I am grateful to Patten for pressing me on this point.

secure the identities of their citizens. Patten would apparently require Great Britain to form a confederal agreement with Ireland, for instance, if this were necessary to secure the identities of those in Northern Ireland who identify with Ireland.

Patten explicitly considers this apparent implication and argues that both because constructing institutions that recognize the different national identities is extremely difficult and because attempts to do so may weaken existing democratic institutions, "there is no duty to enter into equality-enhancing multinational confederal arrangements."[39] Patten's position here seems plausible when considered on its own, but it fits awkwardly with his requirement that separatists be prohibited from seceding from states that have effectively secured equal recognition. In particular, if equal recognition is not important enough to ground an obligation for existing states even to *attempt* to form confederal arrangements with other countries, then why is it sufficiently compelling to block the self-determination of separatist groups, even those perfectly willing to constitutionally secure the equal recognition of the identities of all of their citizens? Put another way, if the political self-determination realized in a well-ordered democracy is important enough to explain why a state has no duty even to explore forming a confederal arrangement, then it seems curious that the political self-determination that could be realized by a separatist movement is *necessarily* outweighed by the value of the equal recognition that an existing state may have secured for its citizens. In short, Patten appears to face the following dilemma: If he believes that justice requires states to secure equal recognition, then he should not shy away from the implication that states unable to do so internally must make arrangements with other countries. If he does not believe that equal recognition is required by justice, on the other hand, then it is unclear why he thinks that it is important enough to trump claims to political self-determination.

In sum, even if Patten is right that equal recognition is desirable (as I believe he is), this gives us no reason to abandon plebiscitary theories of secession. Only if equal recognition were a requirement of justice (a claim Patten appears to deny) would it have any implications for secession, and even then it would imply only that secession would be permissible just in case the separatists constitutionally secured equal recognition in their newly sovereign state. And because the work of Moore and Miller similarly gives us no reason to jettison the functional theory of secession, we need

---

[39] Patten, "Democratic Secession from a Multinational State," p. 582.

not shrink from our suggestion that a group's nationality can play at most a supporting role in its bid for sovereign statehood.

National Self-Determination in the Shadow of Past Abuses

In light of the foregoing analysis, I remain convinced that an exclusively nationalistic account of secession misses the mark. But while I deny that the nationalist principle is the whole story, I admit that it can sometimes be part of the story. As I have argued, there are times when national groups should be given priority. In staunch opposition to this, some argue against even this limited and secondary role of nationalism in determining rights to political self-determination. The claim here is that, because nations have so often abused their political power, a group's nationalism *defeats* rather than *buttresses* its case for political legitimacy. Even a quick glance at the nationally fueled horrors committed in Africa, the former Yugoslavia, and the former Soviet Union, for example, should be enough to alert one to the special dangers that can result from nations' wielding political control. In this final section, I consider the objection that the functional theory of secession is wrong even to leave the door open to nationally motivated secession.

In *Political Philosophy*, Jean Hampton argues strenuously against the construction of nation-states. Unlike many who condemn cultural affiliation as mere atavism, Hampton acknowledges the importance of cultural community. Despite her appreciation for what Margalit and Raz call "encompassing groups," Hampton emphasizes the dangers of designing political units to coincide with cultural communities. She cautions:

The key to peaceful coexistence may come not from separation and exclusivity but from interdependence and tolerance of diversity in a multicultural society. Those advocates of the nation-state or unicultural state who believe my argument is wrong must develop a consequentialist defense of these states in the face of the history of violence generated by nationalism and uniculturalism in the twentieth century.[40]

Hampton's view is noteworthy in that it attacks the putative strength of those who champion national self-determination. That is, after noting that the best defense of the nationalist principle invokes the good consequences of building nation-states, Hampton cites a number of examples that undermine this descriptive claim. Her quick survey leads her to conclude that "recent history would seem to show that even if a

---

[40] Hampton, *Political Philosophy*, p. 242.

unicultural state sometimes protects cultural units in some parts of the world, it is one of the worst vehicles for the preservation of cultures in situations where substantial numbers of people who belong to other groups also reside in the same territory – and that includes most areas of our world today."[41]

To begin, two quick points are in order. First, there is room to question the lesson that Hampton draws from the historical evidence. For instance, Hampton comments that the new states spawned by the former Yugoslavia have been unable to coexist, peaceably, but this example is misleading, because the warring began within the multinational Yugoslavia rather than between the subsequent nation-states. (Here it is helpful to recall David Owen's balanced reflection upon the break-up of Yugoslavia: "Of course the world has to be aware of the dangers of drawing state borders along ethnic lines; but the world also has to recognize the dangers of ignoring ethnic and national voices.")[42] The example of Yugoslavia raises a second, related concern about Hampton's case against nation-states. Although Hampton is surely correct that peace would come from "interdependence and tolerance of diversity in a multicultural society," the undeniable fact is that many multicultural states find themselves with a lamentably short supply of anything like tolerance and mutual respect. Given what this means to oppressed minorities, it seems recklessly unfair to tell the Kurds, for instance, that they may not create a sovereign Kurdistan because in the best-case scenario we would all just learn to tolerate one another. As Jacob Levy emphasizes:

... it strains credulity to think that there would be more political cruelty and violence in the world were Tibet an independent state, and it seems very likely that there would be much less. The violence that accompanied East Timor's separation from Indonesia was terrible, but so was the violence that was a constant condition of its presence inside the state; and the violence of separation was comparatively brief.[43]

Despite these two concerns, I think there is something importantly right about Hampton's worries. We must be careful, however, about how this concern shapes our understanding of political self-determination. To see this, recall once more my analogy of a state's procedure for allocating driver's licenses. In my view, the most important point of Hampton's argument is that we must concern ourselves not only with a group's *ability*

---

[41] Hampton, *Political Philosophy*, p. 241.
[42] David Owen, *The Balkan Odyssey*, p. 343.
[43] Levy, *The Multiculturalism of Fear*, p. 43.

to perform the functions of a government, but also with its *willingness* to do so in a reasonably just manner. This is analogous to a state's interest in issuing licences only to those able *and willing* to drive in a sufficiently safe fashion, an interest that justifies the authorities in revoking the license of one who drives drunk, for instance. Furthermore, imagine that an inordinately high percentage of hazel-eyed people drive drunk. Given this statistical correlation and our concern to avoid harmful automotive circumstances, we should be especially cautious about extending driving privileges to hazel-eyed applicants.

All of this appears correct. What seems incorrect, however, is that this statistical correlation justifies denying driver's licenses to all hazel-eyed applicants.[44] Perhaps it would be permissible to scrutinize hazel-eyed applicants with greater care or to construct other institutional safeguards, but these measures must stop well short of summarily rejecting all hazel-eyed applicants merely because of the statistical correlation.[45] This latter option is unacceptable for its statistical prejudice; each individual deserves a chance to demonstrate her ability and willingness to drive in a safe manner. The analogous conclusions for nationalist appeals to self-determination are clear. If there is a statistical correlation between national groups and those who abuse political autonomy, then certainly we must be careful about extending political powers to nations, but it does not follow that we should deny all national appeals to political self-determination. Instead, we might review more closely nationalist claims and/or grant nations only provisional or restricted powers.

At this point, a critic might object that there is no reliable method to determine in advance which national groups are (or will become) inclined to abuse their political power. A hazel-eyed person would be on her best behavior when applying for a driver's license, and a national group would likely promise angelic conduct when petitioning for independence. We can minimize this problem, however, with institutional safeguards. Just as the Division of Motor Vehicles issues restricted driver's licenses that permit offenders to drive only to and from work or during

---

44 Patricia Williams offers a compelling account of the injustice of this type of statistical prejudice in her book *The Alchemy of Race and Rights*, pp. 51–55. Here Williams recounts her experience of being denied entrance to a Benneton clothing store because she is African-American.

45 I appreciate that "profiling" in any guise is controversial, and I am not committed to defending it here. Rather, I mean to insist only that, *even if certain types of profiling are permissible*, it would not follow that all hazel-eyed candidates may be summarily denied the right to drive, for instance.

certain hours of the day, we might extend political privileges to national groups on a conditional and/or incremental basis. Under such an arrangement, a nation would keep its existing autonomy and gain additional dominion only so long as it exercised this sovereignty in a fashion that was sufficiently respectful of basic human rights. Alternatively, a national group might be extended political self-determination on the condition that it make decisions democratically, that it make key policies under United Nations supervision, or that it create a board to review and redress individual and group rights violations. Some combination of these types of safeguards (coupled with closer examination of nationalist appeals) seems permissible and might go a long way toward preventing nations from abusing their newfound political power. But all of this is quite different from (and more acceptable than) simply denying all national appeals to political self-determination. The crucial point is that just as the poor record of hazel-eyed drivers does not entail that a particular hazel-eyed person will drive drunk, an individual nation's inability or unwillingness to govern justly cannot and should not be inferred automatically from the dismal performance of other nations.

A second point that should not be forgotten, however, is that national groups have no monopoly on political abuse. The history of national political power may be a textbook for cynics, but the history of non-national political sovereignty is no light read either. As Michael Walzer observes: "The crimes of the twentieth century have been committed alternatively, as it were, by perverted patriots and perverted cosmopolitans. If fascism represents the first of these perversions, communism, in its Leninist and Maoist versions, represents the second."[46] Given that no regime is immune from abusing its political autonomy, factors other than nationalism may lead political groups to misuse their power. Kai Nielsen and Will Kymlicka have each proposed that nationalism may be a red herring; both suggest that having been politically oppressed is the operative factor leading groups to become politically abusive.[47] Kymlicka writes: "I suspect that the extent to which a nationalist movement is liberal will depend largely on whether or not it arises within a country with long-established liberal institutions. . . . Any nationalist movement that seeks to impose illiberal practices on a population accustomed to the benefits of

---

[46] Michael Walzer, "Spheres of Affection," pp. 126–127.

[47] Will Kymlicka proposes this in his article "The Sources of Nationalism: Commentary on Taylor," and Kai Nielsen makes this point both in "Secession, the Case of Quebec" and in "Liberal Nationalism and Secession."

liberal governance will not acquire any popular support."[48] Thus, just as
parents who were abused as children are more likely to beat their children, groups that were oppressed as a minority may be prone to mistreat
minorities in their own sovereign state. If so, we should expect minorities
to be mistreated in the new national states resulting from the break-up of
the former Yugoslavia, but we should not anticipate similar rights abuses
in an independent Scotland or Quebec.

If Nielsen and Kymlicka are correct, then Hampton might want to
revise her recommendations. Rather than caution against extending
political power to any nation, she might warn us against empowering
mistreated national groups. Even this less sweeping advice is problematic,
however, because it unfairly saddles current victims with additional abuse.
Clinging to the status quo in these circumstances is especially worrisome
both because it sacrifices actual victims for the sake of potential future
casualties and (at least ordinarily) because it results in a greater number
of people being treated unjustly. To appreciate the importance of these
points, imagine denying the Kosovars a right to secede from the former Yugoslavia because they have been treated unjustly by the Serbs and
thus are statistically likely to mistreat any Serbs who remain in an independent Kosovo. First, the victimized Kosovars in the former Yugoslavia
would be denied independence (and thereby left vulnerable to further
abuse) merely because there is a *substantial probability* that Serbs in Kosovo
would subsequently be mistreated. Second, the potential Serb victims in
a sovereign Kosovo would be less numerous than the Kosovars in the former Yugoslavia (and Serbs would have an independent Serbia as a haven).
And third, there is every reason to expect that the international community could more effectively monitor an emerging state of Kosovo than it
could an established Yugoslavia. In sum, if it is true that past abuse rather
than national allegiance fosters the inclination to mistreat others politically, then authors like Hampton are stuck on the horns of a dilemma.
If the nation lobbying for secession is not being victimized, then there
is no statistical rationale for denying its independence; if the nation is
being treated unfairly, on the other hand, then we cannot merely cite the
potential for injustice as a justification for resisting the political division,
as *actual* injustice already exists.

No one can be sure that Nielsen and Kymlicka are correct, but certainly their proposal is worth investigating. At the very least, we must not
dogmatically oppose all national separatists or cling blindly to some other

[48] Kymlicka, "The Sources of Nationalism: Comments on Taylor," p. 64.

policy that forces us to turn our backs on this or any other suggestion that might reduce political tyranny. Thus, even if Hampton is right to warn us against recklessly extending political powers to nations (as I believe she is), the reasonableness of this apprehension in no way undermines the *importance* of national self-determination; it only highlights the necessity to carefully supervise those nations and their additional political powers.

Conclusion

My principal concern in this chapter has been to further explain and defend the functional theory of secession by critically examining its more established competitor, the nationalist principle. If my arguments have been sound, then there is some truth in nationalism, but this truth plays only a supporting role in the drama of political self-determination and thus does nothing to undermine my claim that any group able and willing to perform the requisite political functions has a right to secede as long as its withdrawal would not politically incapacitate the remainder state. Nationalists have been correct to insist that many nations have a right to secede, but they have been wrong to think that nations qualify for this right principally because of their cultural characteristics. In light of this, I would encourage politicians, political theorists, and international lawyers who evaluate candidates for secession to shift their focus from cultural attributes to political abilities and, even more importantly, I implore secessionist movements to cease dealing exclusively in nationalistic rhetoric and to spend more of their precious energy bolstering their capacity to govern in a secure, efficient, and just manner.

6

Political Coercion and Exploitation

The most sophisticated critics of primary right theories of secession raise institutional concerns: They contend that, no matter how compelling the moral case for political self-determination, the right to secede should not be institutionally protected. In the next chapter, I will survey concerns about designing international laws that permit unilateral political divorce; in this chapter, I consider arguments against creating domestic constitutions that honor a primary right to secede. In particular, I examine Cass Sunstein's arguments that institutionally recognizing the right to secede will corrupt democratic decision making by allowing minority groups to hold their compatriots hostage.[1] The worry is that, by threatening to secede, groups will be able to coerce and/or exploit their fellow citizens out of more than their fair share of the benefits of political cooperation. In response, I acknowledge that respecting secessionist rights might well change the dynamics of political decision making, but I regard this largely as providing reasons *in favor* of constitutionally recognizing the right to secede. In my view, democracies are currently corrupt and stand to be *improved* by extending to groups the political leverage that would likely accompany having the right to exit.

This chapter is divided into four sections. First, I recapitulate Cass Sunstein's objection and suggest that one of his chief concerns is about secessionist groups potentially coercing and/or exploiting their compatriots. I then argue that, because coercion and exploitation are sometimes permissible, we must restrict our inquiry to *impermissible*

[1] Cass Sunstein, "Constitutionalism and Secession."

128

coercion and exploitation. I propose that impermissible coercion and exploitation are united by the common manner in which they violate the coercee's/exploitee's rights. In the third section, I explain why the functional theory of secession bars separatist groups from undermining the political process. Finally, I turn Sunstein's objection on its head, arguing that only by allowing secessionist rights can we effectively protect all parties from impermissible coercion and exploitation. In other words, respecting political self-determination is the only way to correct the perversion of the democratic processes endemic to the status quo.

The Objection

In "Constitutionalism and Secession," Cass Sunstein suggests that, "whether or not secession might be justified as a matter of politics or morality, constitutions ought not to include a right to secede."[2] Sunstein's worry is that a constitutional right to secede would give subunits excessive strategic bargaining power. In essence, the concern is that constitutionally protecting the right to secede is tantamount to equipping minority groups with a dangerous weapon with which to hold their compatriots hostage. As he puts it:

To place such a right in a founding document would increase the risks of ethnic and factional struggle; reduce the prospects for compromise and deliberation in government; raise dramatically the stakes of day-to-day political decisions; introduce irrelevant and illegitimate considerations into those decisions; create dangers of blackmail, strategic behavior, and exploitation; and, most generally, endanger the prospects for long-term self-governance.[3]

Each of these concerns deserves attention, but for the purposes of this chapter let us focus specifically upon the worry that constitutionally recognizing secession opens the door for "blackmail, strategic behavior, and exploitation."[4]

Sunstein cautions that an ability to secede might lead disaffected groups to threaten their fellow citizens. He worries not only that minorities will play this trump card when majorities outvote them, but also that all groups will engage in strategic behavior in order to gain "benefits or

---

[2] Ibid., p. 634.

[3] Ibid.

[4] Part of the reason I focus on this portion of Sunstein's argument is that others have raised concerns with different portions of his analysis. See, for example, Daniel Weinstock's article "Constitutionalizing the Right to Secede," Wayne Norman's paper "Domesticating Secession," and Chapter 4 of Allen Buchanan's book *Secession*.

diminish burdens by making threats that are strategically useful and based on power over matters technically unrelated to the particular question at issue."[5] In fact, Sunstein is especially worried about citizens with a disproportionate share of the vital resources utilizing their power to make political arrangements even more self-serving. Such exploitation would be possible because "any subunit whose resources are at the moment indispensable, and that might be able to exist on its own, is in an extraordinary position to obtain benefits or to diminish burdens on matters formally unrelated to its comparative advantage."[6] In short, respecting the right to secede would have a profoundly negative effect upon each subunit's incentive structure. Rather than work together to secure a fair arrangement among all subunits, distinct groups would be likely to coerce their compatriots with threats of secession. Each group could exploit the others by playing upon their fellow citizens' fear of political division. The cumulative effect of all this strategic bargaining is that the political environment would shift from a cooperative enterprise in which arrangements are decided on relevant grounds to a self-interested competition in which each subunit gains political advantages based solely on its relative value to the state.

The best way to steer clear of this adversarial political environment, according to Sunstein, is to constitutionally rule out the right to secede. He recommends that "a waiver of the right to secede is a sensible precommitment strategy, one that is likely to remove a serious threat to democratic processes."[7] Sunstein notes that this waiver solves a collective action problem, because, while each subunit would prefer individually to have and utilize the strategic power of a right to secede, the cumulative effect of everyone's capitalizing upon this power is dramatically worse than the situation in which no subunit has this power. In order to avoid the horrible effects of everyone's selfishly invoking their right to separate, the best strategy is collectively to restrict all. In this fashion, Sunstein portrays the prohibition on secession as the only way to avoid a nasty Prisoner's Dilemma and the destructive threats that would inevitably accompany it. Ultimately, Sunstein worries that constitutionally recognizing a right to secede would allow a minority group to coerce and exploit the majority out of much more than its fair share of the benefits of political cooperation.

---

[5] Sunstein, "Constitutionalism and Secession," p. 648.
[6] Ibid., p. 650.
[7] Ibid., p. 652.

In the remainder of this chapter, I will (1) distinguish between permissible and impermissible coercion and exploitation, (2) show why my permissive stance on state breaking precludes impermissible political coercion and exploitation, and (3) explain why allowing the right to secede is actually apt to improve political dialogue and negotiation. Before doing so, however, it is worth noting that, even if Sunstein is right to warn us about the bad consequences of constitutionally protecting the right to secede, his argument as it stands is incomplete. The problem is that we cannot assess his conclusion that "whether or not secession might be justified as a matter of politics or morality, constitutions ought not to include a right to secede" unless we antecedently presume that the moral right to secede is insufficiently important to outweigh the bad consequences that Sunstein predicts.[8] We are in no position to assume this, however, because many rights ought to be respected even if their exercise might lead to suboptimal circumstances. (As it is now standard to say, many rights "trump" consequential considerations.) Consider, for instance, the analogous right of marital divorce. Even if we can reliably predict that allowing couples to divorce will give wives and husbands less incentive to work through their marital problems in constructive ways, no one would deny that the right to divorce should be legally protected. On the contrary, we value freedom of association enough to insist that divorce be legally available even if allowing exit from marriages will lead some to have less happy unions.

To put the same point in constitutional terms, think of the right to free speech. Protecting free speech clearly impedes many important social goals. It allows hate groups to flourish; it makes it much more difficult to secure the equality of oppressed groups (by protecting pornography, for instance); and it even impedes measures to improve democratic decision making (as we recently saw with the U.S. Supreme Court's judgment that the Feinstein/McCain campaign finance law was unconstitutional). I acknowledge with some sympathy the complaints of critics who insist that liberal democracies like the United States exaggerate the relative importance of the right to free speech, but even if these criticisms are entirely on target, they do not undermine my main point: The presence of negative consequences does not necessarily entail that a right should not be constitutionally protected – it depends upon how important the right is. We would never curtail the right to vote or the right not to be enslaved merely because constitutionally respecting these rights would

[8] Ibid., p. 634.

usher in the unpleasant political environment that Sunstein predicts, for instance, so we cannot embrace Sunstein's conclusion unless we tacitly assume that secessionist rights are not as important as other rights that we constitutionally protect. I do not here insist that the right to political self-determination is as important as the right not to be enslaved; I merely seek to call attention to the fact that Sunstein's argument presumes that it is not. Thus, even if Sunstein is right to warn of negative consequences, his argument remains incomplete. In short, without an argument that the right to secede is a relatively unimportant right that should not be given the weight of other, more standard rights, we should not assume that arguments like Sunstein's (even if correct) are decisive.

Coercion and Exploitation

In response to Sunstein's concerns about political coercion and exploitation, I suggest that any instance of coercion or exploitation may or may not be impermissible, and we should reject a theory of secession only if it opens the door to impermissible coercion or exploitation. Ultimately, I will show that the functional theory is innocent on this score, but first let me explain both how I understand coercion and exploitation and how I distinguish between permissible and impermissible instances of each. Consider the following four scenarios:

Death Threat: Albert holds a knife to Barbara's throat and explains that he will kill Barbara unless she has sex with him.

Disappointment Threat: Albert stares longingly at Barbara and explains that he will be bitterly disappointed if she does not have sex with him.

Drowning Offer: Albert comes across Barbara in the middle of a vast and otherwise unpopulated lake. Barbara is exhausted from struggling to stay afloat since her boat capsized. Albert explains that Barbara may board his boat only if she will have sex with him.

Fancy Boat Offer: From the shore of the lake, Barbara stares longingly at Albert's fancy new boat. Albert recognizes Barbara's desire for a ride and explains that Barbara may board his boat only if she will have sex with him.

I presume that Albert's behavior is impermissible in Death Threat and Drowning Offer and permissible in Disappointment Threat and Fancy Boat Offer. (I do not deny that Albert's behavior in Disappointment

Threat and Fancy Boat Offer may be woefully *suberogatory*, but this does not mean that he has a *duty* to act differently.)[9]

Let us say that A threatens B when A attempts to motivate B to do X by placing additional costs on B's doing not-X. In Death Threat, for example, Albert's threat increases Barbara's motivation to have sex with Albert by adding the loss of Barbara's life to the option of not having sex with him. The key feature of a credible threat (I will hereafter write as if all threats are credible) is that it closes a conjunctive option that would otherwise be open. In Death Threat, for instance, Albert's threat closes Barbara's option of not having sex with Albert and continuing to live.

An offer is the opposite of a threat. A makes B an offer when A opens an option (perhaps at a price) that is currently closed to B. In Drowning Offer and Fancy Boat Offer, for instance, Albert *opens* Barbara's previously closed option of boarding Albert's boat (at the cost of having sex with Albert). Because the (im)permissibility of these four cases cuts across the distinction between threats and offers, we cannot account for the latter with the former. Given that some threats are permissible and some offers are impermissible, we might explain the impermissibility of Death Threat and Drowning Offer by singling out Death Threat as a *coercive* threat and Drowning Offer as an *exploitative* offer. Although this move seems promising, it too is ultimately inadequate, because not all coercive or exploitative acts are impermissible.

First, consider coercion. Coercion motivates an individual to act by applying pressure to her will. A coerces B when A pressures B to act in a manner X by attaching an additional cost to B's doing not-X. Unlike compulsion, coercion does not destroy an otherwise available alternative so much as it diminishes its relative appeal by increasing its cost. The paradigm of coercion is a threat. Coercion closes some options completely, but these are only conjunctive options. In Death Threat, for example, Albert closes Barbara's conjunctive option of continuing to live and not having sex with Albert. Finally, note that coercive impositions can fail to compel if the coercee judges the threatened alternative to be less costly than the coercer's demand (in Disappointment Threat, for instance, no one would be surprised if Barbara would rather disappoint Albert than have sex with him).

Many theorists add that coercion is prima facie wrong. This claim may be reasonable because, given a presumption in favor of individual

---

[9] An action is suberogatory when it is morally permissible but nonetheless reflects badly upon an agent's moral character.

liberty, any act that closes another's options requires special justification. It seems wrong to insist that every act of coercion is all-things-considered impermissible, however, because this would exclude paradigm cases of coercion. Consider three examples: A parent tells her child, "Clean your room, or you will be grounded!"; a teacher tells her student, "Stop misbehaving, or I will send you to the principal's office!"; and a police officer tells a criminal, "Stop, or I will shoot!" Each is a familiar threat, and all three strike me as clear instances of coercion. One might be tempted to list only the last of these three as coercive, since the first two threats are relatively mild, but there is no reason why coercion must satisfy a threshold of intensity. Coercing is a type of pressuring, and so, just as pressure exists at all levels, coercion can be applied and experienced to varying degrees. If the added cost of a threat is small (as it might be for Barbara in Disappointment Threat), then we should conclude not that coercion is absent, only that it is relatively insignificant. Most of all, it is important to recognize that even very severe acts of coercion (like the police officer's threat) can sometimes be warranted. Thus, although threatening to punish or shoot a person may be prima facie wrong, such actions need not be all-things-considered impermissible. We may safely conclude, then, that the mere fact that an act is coercive is not enough to show that it is impermissible. This skeletal account of coercion leaves a number of important issues unaddressed, but it should be sufficient for our purposes here.[10]

Now consider exploitation. A exploits X when A utilizes X for A's advantage. Like coercion, exploitation need not always be a pejorative; we do not criticize an artist for exploiting her talents, an entrepreneur for exploiting a market, or an athletic team for exploiting an opposing team's weakness. Exploitation can be wrong, however, when one exploits another person. In Drowning Offer, for instance, we are right to blame Albert for capitalizing upon Barbara's peril. But even exploiting a person's characteristics need not always be impermissible. For example, there is nothing wrong with the fast food industry capitalizing upon our desire for quick and inexpensive food. (And, although Albert in Fancy Boat Offer may fall well short of many moral ideals, presumably it is not *impermissible* for Albert to capitalize upon Barbara's desire to ride in a speedboat.) Thus, it appears that not only is exploitation (like coercion) sometimes

---

[10] One important moral issue left unaddressed by this analysis of coercion and exploitation is the moral accountability of the coercee/exploitee. On this issue, see Joel Feinberg, *Harm to Self*.

permissible, it is (perhaps unlike coercion) not even necessarily prima facie wrong.

We now stand at a crossroads in the discussion. On the one hand, we can defer to the common understanding of coercion and exploitation and define the two terms as I have done here. On the other hand, we might insist that the traditional notion of each is confused for its failure to recognize that both concepts have an ineliminable moral element. The first option is attractive because it allows us to capture all of the apparent cases of coercion/exploitation, but this inclusiveness comes at a price. If we define both concepts amorally, we cannot appeal merely to the coercion of Death Threat or the exploitation of Drowning Offer in order to explain either's impermissibility. Adopting a normative definition of coercion/exploitation has the opposite advantages and drawbacks. It helps us to explain the wrongness of Death Threat and Drowning Offer, but it forces us to deny the existence of obvious instances of coercion/exploitation wherever it is permissible. Although some authors opt for the second route, I prefer the first.[11] Were I unable to generate a plausible account of when coercion or exploitation is impermissible, I could not recommend the first path as superior. If I can provide such an explanation, on the other hand, then I can advocate my approach for its ability to capture all of the benefits and none of the costs of the second option. That is, I can explain the impermissibility of cases like Death Threat and Drowning Offer without flouting our common understanding of coercion and exploitation. With this in mind, consider my account of why Death Threat and Drowning Offer, but not Disappointment Threat or Fancy Boat Offer, are impermissible.

Coercion is impermissible when one *wrongly* coerces another person, and exploitation is impermissible when one *wrongly* exploits another person. This much is obviously true but equally unhelpful, since it merely transfers the question to deciding when coercion/exploitation is *wrong*. From our earlier analysis, we know that A impermissibly coerces B when A wrongly closes one of B's conjunctive options, and we understand that A wrongly closes one of B's conjunctive options when A wrongly attaches a cost to an option. Likewise, we know that A impermissibly exploits B when A wrongly opens an option at a price for B. Because merely opening a benign option could not be forbidden, the element that makes an

---

[11] For instance, Alan Wertheimer defends a moralized conception of coercion in his book, *Coercion*. The seminal discussion of the relative merits of moralized and nonmoralized conceptions of coercion is Robert Nozick's "Coercion."

offer impermissibly exploitative must be the price attached to opening this option. But notice: Unless A has a duty to open an option for B, A is at liberty to affix any cost whatsoever to opening that option. And notice further that, in the absence of some morally relevant transaction or association between A and B, A could have no duty to open an option for B unless B were imperiled and A could help B to avert this peril by opening an option for B at no unreasonable cost to A. If this is correct, then we are now in a better position to specify when exploitation is forbidden. A wrongly exploits B when A attaches an excessive cost to opening an option for B, where this cost is excessive because B needs this option to avoid extreme peril *and* A could open this option at a lower price without incurring an unreasonable loss. (As I explained in Chapter 2, A would have no such samaritan duty to B if B were not sufficiently imperiled or if A's assistance would be unreasonably costly.)

In each case, A's coercion or exploitation is impermissible just in case A wrongly attaches a price to one of B's options. But what is it about affixing this cost to an option that is impermissible? I believe this question is best answered in terms of rights. Coercion or exploitation is impermissible where one attaches a cost to an option when the coercee/exploitee has a right to this option at either no cost or less cost. In coercion, the coercer attaches a cost to an option the coercee already had, and in exploitation, the exploiter attaches a cost to an option the exploitee did not have. Furthermore, A wrongly coerces B just in case B has a right to the option A closes, and A wrongly exploits B when B has a right to the option A opens only at a price. Given this, coercion is impermissible when the coercer *wrongly harms* the coercee, and exploitation is impermissible when the exploiter *wrongly fails to benefit* the exploitee. If this is so, then the existence of either coercion or exploitation is beside the moral point. What is (morally) crucial is whether one wrongly either harms or fails to benefit another. At the end of the day, I suggest that the harm and benefit principles are the keys to explaining whether or not any given instance of coercion or exploitation is permissible. To evaluate this proposal, let us consider it in light of the four scenarios introduced earlier.

Death Threat and Disappointment Threat are threats; Drowning Offer and Fancy Boat Offer are offers; and I have alleged that Death Threat and Drowning Offer are impermissible, while Disappointment Threat and Fancy Boat Offer are permissible. In my view, Albert's threat in Death Threat is forbidden because Barbara has a right not to be killed by Albert. Albert's threat in Disappointment Threat is permissible, on the other hand, because Barbara has no right that Albert not be disappointed. Albert's offer in Drowning Offer is impermissible because Barbara has a right to board Albert's boat at no (or minimal) cost.[12] Barbara has this positive right against Albert because the combination of Barbara's extreme peril and Albert's ability to rescue her at no unreasonable cost renders Albert duty-bound to help Barbara. Albert's offer in Fancy Boat Offer is permissible, however, because, under these circumstances, Barbara has no antecedent right to ride in Albert's speedboat. If Barbara agreed to have sex with Albert in Fancy Boat Offer, we might say that Albert has exploited Barbara's interest in boats, but we would be wrong to label this exploitation impermissible. (Though, again, Albert may fall short of a moral ideal.)

The common element uniting the impermissibility of the coercion in Death Threat and the exploitation in Drowning Offer is Barbara's right to an option. The two are distinct because Death Threat is a coercive threat and Drowning Offer is an exploitative offer. Given this difference, the two rights derive from separate sources. Barbara's right in Death Threat is subsumed under the harm principle, because Albert wrongly harms Barbara (that is, Albert wrongly makes Barbara worse off than she would otherwise be) by impermissibly attaching a cost to an option that Barbara already had. Barbara's right in Drowning Offer, on the other hand, derives from a benefit-to-others principle, because Albert wrongly fails to benefit Barbara (that is, Albert wrongly fails to make Barbara better off than Barbara would otherwise be) by impermissibly affixing a cost to an option that Albert opens for Barbara. Death Threat and Drowning Offer are united in being forbidden because, regardless of whether Albert opens or closes one of Barbara's options (and thus independent of whether it is a threat or an offer), Barbara has a right to that option at either no cost or less cost.

Before applying this analysis to secession and political self-determination, let us quickly check my distinction between permissible and impermissible coercion/exploitation in light of some standard "real-life" cases. Consider kidnapping, political coercion, graduate assistant stipends, and people who sell their body parts (e.g., "spare" kidneys) on the black market. Let us begin with the two instances of coercion. A kidnapper and a political state both coerce their subjects, but a kidnappee is impermissibly coerced, whereas a citizen of a just state is permissibly coerced. My distinction specifies that kidnapping is impermissible because the victim's right to liberty is violated by the kidnapper,

---

[12] Perhaps Barbara would fall short of some moral ideal if she did not express gratitude after Albert helped her, but this is distinct from Barbara's having a duty to Albert and completely different from Barbara's having a duty to have sex with Albert.

and that political coercion is permissible because the citizens have no rightful claim to be free of the state's imposition. (Moreover, note that this explanation is confirmed by the fact that anarchists typically claim that political coercion is impermissible precisely because states have no right to limit their constituents' liberty.) Next, consider the exploitation of graduate students and those whose economic hardship forces them to sell their organs to buy food or medical treatment.[13] Research universities often exploit the zealous interest of graduate students by offering them relatively small salaries in return for substantial loads of work. If this exploitation is permissible, it is because no one has a right to obtain extra-market subsidies in to pursue her chosen profession. If buying a starving person's kidney for a thousand dollars is impermissibly exploitative, on the other hand, it is because we all have positive rights to samaritan assistance at no charge. In this case, our samaritan right consists of a claim both to eat and to retain our kidneys. My rights-centered account of the permissibility of coercion and exploitation is confirmed by these analyses. In each case, it focuses on precisely that issue which either determines the deontic status of the act or excites the relevant controversy.

At the beginning of this section, I noted that the core of Sunstein's objection is that constitutionally protecting the right to secede would enable subunits to coerce and exploit their compatriots. Because some coercion and exploitation is permissible, however, the mere fact that a threat is coercive or that an offer is exploitative cannot explain the impermissibility of the threat/offer. I have argued that coercion or exploitation is forbidden just in case it violates a right either by closing access to an existing option to which the coercee has a right or by failing to open an option to which the exploitee has a right. In the end, the existence of either coercion or exploitation is not morally telling. What is of central moral importance is whether one wrongfully harms or fails to benefit another.

Coercion, Exploitation, and Secession

Having analyzed coercion and exploitation, we are now in a better position to assess Sunstein's worry about recognizing the right to secede. If I am right to distinguish between permissible and impermissible coercion and exploitation, then presumably we need concern ourselves only with the latter. Thus the operative question is whether constitutionally

[13] See Michael Kinsley's article "Take My Kidney, Please," about a man who sold his kidney in order to finance an operation for his daughter.

protecting rights to political self-determination would enable parties *impermissibly* to coerce or exploit their compatriots. As I have argued, this question is tantamount to asking whether recognizing the right to secede allows political subunits to coerce or exploit their compatriots in a way that violates their rights. I will show that we need not worry about the functional theory on this front, because while the functional theory of secession undeniably empowers minority groups, it does not allow them to wrongly take advantage of their fellow citizens.

The functional account is dramatically revisionist insofar as it extends political self-determination to any group that can perform the requisite political functions. As I suggested at the end of Chapter 4, this implies that the American British colonies, the antebellum South, Lithuania, Slovenia, Croatia, Chechnya, and Quebec are among those who had (have) a duly qualified moral right to secede. Take Quebec as a test case for Sunstein's objection; consider to what extent my account would allow Quebec to coerce the rest of Canada. For now, assume that a majority of the *Québecois* want to secede and that a majority of their compatriots would prefer that Canada remain intact. The *Québecois* (both those for and against independence) could capitalize upon their compatriots' interest in unity, threatening to secede unless they are given X, Y, and Z. At this point, the rest of Canada must consider the marginal costs and benefits and decide whether to give in to the demands or to allow the secession. Either way, the remaining citizens of Canada (hereafter simply Canada) may not complain. If Canada decides to give Quebec X, Y, and Z, then it does so voluntarily because of its preference for a continued union. If Quebec secedes, on the other hand, then Canada knows that its new political arrangement is better than its other options. It is true that Quebec would either gain additional benefits or secede after issuing a coercive threat, but this is not an instance of impermissible coercion, because Quebec has a right to secede and Canada has no right to a continued union at no additional cost. Because of this, Canadians should feel righteously aggrieved neither if Quebec secedes nor if Canada must sacrifice in order to preserve the union. As such, the relationship between Canada and Quebec is akin to that between a customer (me) and a sports store.[14] I am repeatedly shocked by the

[14] One might protest that political deliberation cannot be analogous to a market transaction; when one walks away from a discussant in the forum it is entirely different from not accepting an offer in the market. I appreciate this distinction between the market and the forum (to borrow Elster's language), but one must remember that secessionist conflict is not so much a deliberation within an existing forum as a decision to create a new forum.

escalating price of running shoes. When I shop in a sports store, I must choose whether to pay roughly a hundred dollars or settle for a "second-rate" pair of shoes. But, while I lament the fact that they are so expensive, I am in no position to complain. Whether I pay an exorbitant amount or go without my preferred shoes, I should not feel righteously aggrieved, because I have no right to acquire the shoes without paying the additional cost.

At this point, one might object that not all secessionist threats can be received in the calm manner in which Canada might respond to Quebec. Sometimes a political division would destroy the rump state, and a separatist movement that understands this might exact a princely sum. When the stakes are this high, the potential remainder state cannot be cavalier about doing the cost/benefit analysis. Sunstein appeals to these circumstances when he warns that "any subunit whose resources are at the moment indispensable, and that might be able to exist on its own, is in an extraordinary position to obtain benefits or to diminish burdens on matters formally unrelated to its comparative advantage."[15] When a secessionist party is "indispensable" to its state, the situation is much different from the sports store case where I am shopping for exorbitantly priced shoes. The demands of an indispensable separatist party can put the remaining citizens between a rock and a hard place; they must either sacrifice an enormous amount for their political stability or live precariously in a vulnerable state. In short, some secessionist threats appear obviously impermissible in that they confront a potential remainder state with a choice closer to Barbara's options of either drowning or being raped than to my options of having either fancy shoes or a hundred dollars.

I recognize that not all secessionist threats could be accommodated as easily as Quebec's, and I do not mean to suggest that no secession would leave a parent state vulnerable. Indeed, when the separatist party is indispensable (as opposed to merely desirable), the threat can be impermissibly coercive. This, therefore, is precisely the point upon which we should push the functional theory of secession, since it would be a significant failure of any theory if it sanctioned impermissible coercion. As I will explain, however, my account is immune to attack on this front. To illustrate the functional theory's strength on this count, we must consider its recommendations for the political self-determination of indispensable subunits. Before doing so, however, it is important to notice that a political subunit

---

[15] Sunstein, "Constitutionalism and Secession," p. 650.

might be indispensable for a variety of reasons; it might contain essential natural resources, human capital, military bases, and so on. Although there are various ways in which a subunit might be indispensable, we can place each into one of two groups depending upon whether or not the essential attribute can be transferred between countries. In other words, we can distinguish between those resources (like financial assistance and military protection) that can be transferred from the new country to its parent state, and other features (like territorial contiguity and population) that cannot be replaced after political division. In either case, the functional account precludes impermissible coercion because it prohibits a secessionist party from removing a commodity essential to the remainder state. Consider each type of good separately.

If the separatist territory contains an indispensable resource that can be transferred (say, it contains a dam upon which the entire country depends for electrical power), then the functional theory would allow the secession only on the condition that it continue to share the power generated by the dam.[16] This restriction upon the right to secede is critical, because it prohibits the secessionist party from impermissibly coercing its compatriots. The former may permissibly threaten to secede, but it may not threaten to secede with all of the electrical power. The secessionist party has a right to political self-determination but (we are supposing) has no right to the exclusive use of the dam's power supply. If the country as a whole has a right to the power, then the secessionist party has no right to deny them this, and threatening to do so would be impermissibly coercive. This, of course, is analogous to a spouse who may be at liberty to divorce her husband but has no right to neglect her share of the financial and childrearing responsibilities. Above all, it is important to recognize that there is nothing about the functional approach that forces its advocates to permit this latter type of coercion. Secondly, the functional theory's treatment of secessionist movements whose resources are indispensable and nontransferable is even more straightforward. If political divorce would strip the rump state of a crucial good that could not be replaced after the division (as when political stability is jeopardized because of diminished population or incongruous territory, for instance), then the secession is impermissible. It is true that a secessionist group that threatened to leave under these circumstances would be impermissibly coercing its compatriots, but this is no criticism of the functional theory,

---

[16] This entire discussion presumes that the country as a whole has not only an interest in but also a right to this electricity.

because it authorizes such a group neither to secede nor to threaten to secede.

Upon closer examination, then, we see that proponents of the functional account need not apologize for the room this theory leaves for coercion. It is true that this view allows political subunits to threaten to politically divorce their compatriots, but it never allows them to impermissibly do so. And as we established in the previous section, we need shy away only from those accounts that allow impermissible coercion. Having shown the functional theory to have a clean record with respect to coercion, let us consider its implications for exploitation.

Recall that threats are coercive; offers can be exploitative; and among the latter, some offers can be impermissibly exploitative. In order to establish the functional approach's innocence on this score, we need only to show that it does not allow political units to make impermissibly exploitative offers. To see this, consider two possible annexation proposals offered by Richland. Imagine Richland to be an affluent country bordered by two less wealthy states, Poorland and Chaosland. Poorland is a bucolic country that has few problems managing its political affairs despite a weak economy and a low standard of living. Chaosland is in much worse shape than Poorland. Its political structure is ineffective, and the country is actually being "run" by competing gangs. The quality of life is miserable, because the Chaosians have neither the resources (because they are so poor) nor the incentive (since the fruits of all labor would be stolen) for substantial industry or agriculture.

Imagine that Richland offered to annex Chaosland on the condition that the Chaosians and their descendants would forever be slaves, to be cared for by and assigned tasks by the state of Richland. This offer would be exploitative if the Chaosians, in a desperate attempt to escape their perilous circumstances, accepted Richland's offer. What is more, this offer would be *impermissibly* exploitative because Richland is wrong to put this price upon rescuing the Chaosians from the perils of anarchy. The Chaosians have a right to political assistance from Richland. This right may not include an offer to join Richland as equal partners, but it involves at least a claim to political assistance from the wealthier country until the gangs are suppressed and political order is restored. Because of this, Richland's offer to Chaosland is impermissible, and any theory of political legitimacy that condones the offer is suspect.

This conclusion need not alarm proponents of the functional account, however, because the latter prohibits this offer. As I explained in Chapter 2, samaritanism implies that duties to supply political stability can be owed to all humans rather than merely to compatriots. Thus, in the same fashion in which it insists upon Antonio's duty to help Bathsheba, my view recognizes Richland's responsibility to assist Chaosland and thereby prohibits Richland from placing the unconscionable price of slavery upon their offer to establish political stability. In other words, samaritanism condemns this hypothetical offer because it acknowledges Chaosland's right to assistance at no (or at least at significantly less) cost.[17] The problem with Richland's offer, then, is that it impermissibly fails to open an option to which the Chaosians have a right – namely, the option of costless assistance.

Now suppose that Richland offered to annex Poorland on the condition that the Poorlanders and their descendants would forever be second-class citizens with no political rights to vote, run for elected office, and so on. This offer is certainly not noble; if it effectively capitalized upon the Poorlanders' interest in joining Richland, it could correctly be characterized as an exploitative offer (insofar as the Richlanders exploited the Poorlanders' interest in joining them). But it is not an *impermissibly* exploitative offer. Recall that an offer opens an option, sometimes at a price. An offer is exploitative when the offerer gains something by capitalizing upon a characteristic of the offeree, and an offer is impermissibly exploitative, on my view, when the offerer gains something by wrongly placing a price upon opening an option to which the offeree has a right. Richland's offer would be exploitative if the Poorlanders accepted it, but it would not be impermissibly exploitative, because the latter (we are supposing) have no antecedent right to assistance from Richland. The Poorlanders should rationally decide whether they are better off as equal citizens of Poorland or as second-class citizens of Richland; but whatever they decide, they may not be righteously aggrieved at being limited to those choices, because they have no right to the preferred option of being full citizens of Richland.

This case presents a much greater challenge to the functional theory, because Richland's offer to Poorland seems clearly objectionable, and yet, according to my account, it is not impermissibly exploitative. (To appreciate the full force of this objection, imagine a secessionist analogue. That is, suppose that Richland and Poorland were distinct subunits of a single

---

[17] The Chaosians do not necessarily have a right to merge politically with Richland, of course, but they do have a right to some sort of assistance – perhaps to humanitarian intervention, assuming that this assistance would not be unreasonably costly to Richlanders.

state rather than separate countries. In this case, the objection continues, surely it would be impermissible for the Richlanders to threaten to secede from the Poorlanders unless the latter agree to surrender their rights to vote, run for public office, etc.) The crux of the problem is that, because the Poorlander's are not so badly off as to be imperiled, they do not qualify for any samaritan rights. As a consequence, the functional approach does not require the Richlanders to assist the Poorlanders, and it thus seems unable to prohibit the former from making any type of offer to the latter.

Although Richland's second hypothetical offer to Poorland cannot be handled as easily, it does not force us to dismiss the functional theory of political legitimacy and the correlative account of secession. As I see it, there are two plausible lines of defense. The first involves simply "biting the bullet." According to this response, adequate reflection upon our political responsibilities confirms that, despite our initial reaction, Richland's offer to Poorland is indeed acceptable. A second response capitalizes upon the fact that an offer might be unacceptable even when it is not objectionably exploitative. In other words, for reasons unrelated to exploitation, one can explain the impermissibility of Richland's offer to Poorland. Consider both of these responses.

It admittedly seems awkward to suppose that the Richlanders may rightfully make such an offer, but this implication is not as radical as it might first appear. If it turns out that the Richlanders have a duty to share their resources with the Poorlanders, then of course it would be impermissible for them to place political restrictions upon their offer to assist Poorland. But notice that we cannot assert that the Richlanders must support the Poorlanders without presupposing redistributive duties that extend well beyond samaritanism. What is more, a thoroughgoing application of this more ambitious redistribution would call for substantially greater (and more awkward) revisions of current state practice than the functional theory with its mere samaritanism. Most obviously, affluent countries would be obligated to dedicate the vast majority of their wealth to foreign aid.

Although I think there is something to this response, it is not the only route open to a defender of the functional account. A second, and I think preferable, approach is to suggest that although Richland's offer is not impermissibly exploitative, it is objectionable on other grounds. In particular, it seems plausible to insist that, while the Richlanders are not required to open their political association to the Poorlanders, they nonetheless must welcome the Poorlanders as political equals if they do decide to merge with them. In other words, even though the Poorlanders have no antecedent right to join Richland, they do have a right to political-equality-if-admitted.

This solution is promising, because the functional theory specifies that only a just state can legitimately coerce its citizens, and equal citizenship is a bedrock moral value necessary for a state to be just. As Jean Hampton explains:

> If a country persisted in denying rights of citizenship to . . . nonnationals, it would be allowing a system of different classes of residents in that society, with nonnationals forced to accept unequal treatment and second-class status. The ideals of liberalism would certainly rule out such a policy. . . . [L]iberalism . . . recognizes the right of any long-standing, productive, and law-abiding resident of a country to gain eventual citizenship if he so chooses, even if he cannot meet all of the genetic and cultural requirements that would mark him as a member of the nationality of the dominant group in that country. And this latter right is grounded in the liberal and democratic requirement that all people in a political society should be treated fairly, no matter how much any of them might differ from the majority.[18]

As Hampton makes plain, liberal principles have ample resources to explain the Poorlander's conditional right to political-equality-if-admitted. Indeed, Michael Walzer argues for just such a right in his seminal discussion of "membership."[19] Walzer explores issues analogous to those operative here when he addresses the thorny question of guest workers. In the end, Walzer concludes that foreign workers have a conditional right similar to the one I attribute to the Poorlanders: They have no general claim to enter a host country, but they do have a right to political-equality-if-admitted. He writes:

> . . . the principle of political justice is this: that the processes of self-determination through which a democratic state shapes its internal life, must be open, and equally open, to all those men and women who live within its territory, work in the local economy, and are subject to local law. . . . Democratic citizens, then, have a choice: if they want to bring in new workers, they must be prepared to enlarge their own membership; if they are unwilling to accept new members, they must find ways within the domestic labor market to get socially necessary work done.[20]

This conditional right to political-equality-if-admitted allows me to prohibit Richland's offer to Poorland without labeling it impermissibly

---

[18] Jean Hampton, *Political Philosophy*, pp. 235–236.
[19] Michael Walzer, *Spheres of Justice*, Chapter 2, pp. 31–63.
[20] Ibid., pp. 60–61.

exploitative. In this way, it allows me to avoid a potential counterexample without abandoning my commitment to samaritanism and the corresponding distinction between permissible and impermissible exploitation. This move may not satisfy all critics, however, because one might worry that the conditional right incorporates an ad hoc and indefensible asymmetry. Such an objection questions how I can insist upon political equality among compatriots if I do not require it between foreigners. Consistency seems to require either a global acceptance or a global rejection of this egalitarianism: If I endorse political equality, then why do the Poorlanders not have a general (unconditional) right to join the Richlanders as political equals? And if I reject political equality, then why do the Poorlanders have even the conditional right, if invited to join Richland, to do so on equal footing? This challenge seems especially poignant for me, because in championing samaritanism as I have, my account of legitimacy explicitly relies upon the political responsibilities that we have toward one another as fellow humans capable of suffering in a stateless environment. As a consequence, the critic continues, it is particularly awkward that I should suddenly invoke an asymmetric, conditional right to political equality when faced with a potential counterexample.

In response, I acknowledge that I cannot introduce such an asymmetry without an explanation, but the right to political-equality-if-admitted is neither ad hoc nor indefensible; there are good reasons to suppose that political inequality among fellow citizens is more worrisome than financial disparity between states. Walzer's thoughts provide a good place to start on this matter. He opines:

These guests experience the state as a pervasive and frightening power that shapes their lives and regulates their every move – and never asks for their opinion. Departure is only a formal option; deportation, a continuous practical threat. As a group, they constitute a disenfranchised class. They are typically an exploited or oppressed class as well, and they are exploited or oppressed at least in part because they are disenfranchised, incapable of organizing effectively for self-defense. . . . They are locked into an inferior position that is also an anomalous position; they are outcasts in a society that has no caste norms, metics in a society where metics have no comprehensible, protected, and dignified place. That is why the government of guest workers looks very much like tyranny: it is the exercise of power outside its sphere, over men and women who resemble citizens in every respect that counts in the host country, but are nevertheless barred from citizenship.[21]

[21] Ibid., p. 59.

Here Walzer captures the problem with political inequality: second-class citizens are denied crucial means to self-respect, dignity, and autonomy. An individual without political rights must endure a subordination that is more than unappealing; it is oppressive enough to stifle self-esteem as well as personal and moral development. Without developing this point further, it should be clear that political subordination raises more numerous and pressing concerns than mere economic inequality among states. And since considerably more is at stake when a subject is held politically captive by her compatriots than when a citizen has fewer resources than a foreigner with whom she does not regularly interact, we are right to be especially worried about the former situation. This also justifies the asymmetry between the two types of concerns that, in turn, give rise to the conditional right to political-equality-if-admitted.

Finally, and perhaps most importantly, notice that recent analyses of equality in general confirm that the conditional right to political-equality-if-admitted is not merely an ad hoc move to avoid a potential counterexample. Think, for instance, of Elizabeth Anderson's landmark essay "What Is the Point of Equality?" Here Anderson argues that a proper regard for equality need not lead us to ensure that each has all (but no more) than she deserves; rather, it should move us to eliminate those inequalities that create socially oppressive relationships. In other words, equality is an essentially *relational* concept: The extent to which we should worry about an inequality between the haves and the have-nots depends upon the relationship between the two; any given inequality would be much less problematic if experienced by two groups who live separately and in ignorance of one another than if the haves and have-nots coexist in the same society.

In developing what she calls "democratic equality," Anderson proposes: "Negatively, people are entitled to whatever capabilities are necessary to enable them to avoid or escape entanglement in oppressive relationships. Positively, they are entitled to the capabilities necessary for functioning as an equal citizen in a democratic state."[22] Anderson is particularly concerned to offer an account of political equality, but her more general insight is that our principal reason to root out inequality is that it can be harmful to those in the subordinate relationship, and once one grasps this insight, it becomes clear that one cannot properly evaluate any given inequality without knowing the relationship between those with unequal shares. As Anderson puts it, "democratic egalitarians

---

[22] Elizabeth Anderson, "What Is the Point of Equality?," p. 316.

are fundamentally concerned with the relationships within which goods are distributed, not only with the distribution of goods themselves."[23] It is not hard to see how this conception of equality vindicates the conditional right to political-equality-if-admitted. Given that the relationship between the haves and have-nots is relevant, and that the relationship between compatriots is significant, there is nothing ad hoc or otherwise suspicious about being more concerned about an inequality between compatriots than one would be about the same inequality between parties who were not fellow citizens.

At this point, a critic might counter that, even if political subordination is both personally and morally destructive, my commitment to self-determination stands in the way of my prohibiting Richland's offer to Poorland on these grounds. The basic idea here is that, because I value autonomy, I cannot deny people the right to choose dangerous ways of life. I would never prohibit mountain climbing because of the inherent dangers, for instance, so neither should I prevent the Poorlanders from accepting political subordination if they decide it is worth the sacrifice to share in Richland's wealth. Just as each individual has the right to take great risks for the thrills of mountain climbing or an investor may risk her savings in a business venture, each Poorlander may endure the hardships of political subordination in exchange for the material comforts of wealth. It would be a different matter if Richland *forced* the Poorlanders into this subordination, but we are inquiring whether Richland may permissibly *offer* the Poorlanders such a position. What is more, the objection continues, I cannot protest that the Poorlanders cannot autonomously make this decision because I have explicitly supposed that (unlike the Chaosians) they face no peril that would undermine their deliberation. In short, the premium I place upon individual liberty seems incompatible with my prohibition of Richland's offer on the grounds that it would leave the Poorlanders in a politically subordinate position.

This objection raises a fundamental question in liberal theory: Does the best understanding of liberal rights include the right to alienate one's autonomy? For instance, is one at liberty to sell oneself into slavery? Following John Stuart Mill, many have argued that it is either impossible (one *cannot* waive certain rights) or impermissible (one *may not* waive these rights) to sell oneself into slavery.[24] If these authors are right, then perhaps their arguments would also explain why there is no right to accept

---

[23] Ibid., p. 314.

[24] John Stuart Mill, *On Liberty*, Chapter 5, paragraph 11. For an excellent discussion of the issues surrounding this question, see Feinberg, *Harm to Self*, pp. 71–79.

a position of political subordination. (Indeed, by insisting that democratic principles preclude consenting to political inequality, Michael Walzer utilizes this type of argument to explain why guest workers cannot be said to consent to their position.)[25] Such a move is controversial, however, as authors like Joel Feinberg argue that there is nothing conceptually confused or morally impermissible about autonomously consenting to a position that restricts one's autonomy.[26] (Consider Feinberg's example of someone who sells herself into slavery for ten million dollars because she believes that she could not have a more meaningful life than one in which she donates such a vast sum to charity.)

Fortunately, we can avoid this controversy, because the case against Richland's offer to Poorland need not rely exclusively on the impossibility or impermissibility of waiving one's rights to autonomy. Richland's merger with Poorland is distinct from the question of guest workers because the former involves both a minority and children. This is significant because, in the case of guest workers, each person who endures the position of political subordination consents. In the case of Richland and Poorland, on the other hand, all those Poorlanders who vote against the merger are placed in a position of political subordination against their will; they are involuntarily moved from an autonomous position of equality to a station of inferiority. What is more, even if the Poorlanders unanimously voted to join Richland, they would be choosing to bring their children up in an environment of political subordination. In a very real sense, they would be selling their children into a subordinate political status. I take it for granted that this is impermissible; it is wrong for the same reasons that one may not sell one's children into slavery. Thus, even though Richland's offer to Poorland is not impermissibly exploitative, it is nonetheless impermissible. Ultimately, both of Richland's offers are impermissible. Their invitation to Chaosland is impermissibly exploitative, and their offer to Poorland is forbidden because it would nonconsensually place individuals in a position of political subordination.

In conclusion, we must admit that the functional theory of secession opens the door to political coercion and exploitation, but we can do so without flinching because our account precludes *impermissible* coercion and exploitation. The samaritanism essential to the functional account of political legitimacy ensures that an indispensable subunit may not threaten to secede from its compatriots and that a wealthy country cannot

---

[25] Walzer, *Spheres of Justice*, p. 58.
[26] Feinberg, *Harm to Self*, pp. 71–79.

place an objectionable price tag on assisting an imperiled neighbor.[27] But, while I am pleased because my theory leaves no room for impermissible coercion and exploitation, some might object to a view that allows minority groups to coerce or exploit their compatriots in any fashion. Let us address this worry now.

Is Any Coercion or Exploitation Appropriate?

It is tempting to protest that, whereas I applaud the functional account for prohibiting some but not all political coercion and exploitation, it would

---

[27] It is worth noting that my solution is not the only one in the literature. On pages 98–100 of his book *Secession*, Allen Buchanan shares Sunstein's worry about a group using its right to secede for strategic bargaining power. Unlike Sunstein, though, Buchanan does not recommend a constitutional ban on secession; instead, he advocates institutional devices designed to deter groups from threatening secession. In particular, he recommends requiring secessionist parties to pay an exit cost and/or to demonstrate that more than a simple majority (perhaps a super-majority of two-thirds or three-quarters) of those in the contested territory prefer secession. Buchanan contends that these additional hurdles would dissuade disingenuous parties from feigning an interest in seceding by placing additional costs upon political divorce. That is, since the institutional obstacles would make exiting more difficult, all but those who genuinely and passionately desired independence would abandon their separatist movements. The end result, Buchanan hopes, is that many groups who might otherwise simulate an interest in secession for strategic bargaining power would instead direct their energy and resources toward making their union a more productive and harmonious whole.

Although Buchanan's proposals might inhibit some groups from bluffing to secede, I have several reservations about placing these types of obstacles in the way of political division. First, there is reason to doubt that these measures would be as effective as Buchanan hopes. For instance, placing a tax on exit might not dissuade all from threatening to secede, since a group would know that it must pay the fee only if it actually secedes – not for merely threatening to do so. Similarly, requiring more than a simple majority would not *eliminate* political coercion; it would only *limit* the potential for coercion to those groups who satisfied the threshold requirements. In response to my counterpoints, Buchanan might suggest raising the institutional hurdles so that even fewer groups would be initially eligible to leave and so that those who were eligible would face even greater exit fees. This response only exacerbates my second worry, however, that placing additional institutional hurdles on political divorce can make secession impossible and/or too costly for groups who have a right to political independence. This is so because any measure that limits the room for political coercion by blocking secession would potentially strip deserving groups of their effective right to secede. This is no small concern, since (as Buchanan and Sunstein both acknowledge) groups can have compelling interests in independence. Furthermore, impoverished and mistreated groups who most need autonomy are likely to be those least able to overcome additional obstacles blocking their path to independence. Buchanan's solution is not ideal, then, since it allows some of the coercion he seeks to avoid and impedes some of the movements he wants to allow. My proposal, on the other hand, distinguishes between permissible and impermissible coercion/exploitation and allows all of the former and none of the latter.

be preferable if *all* coercion and exploitation were eliminated. While my distinction between permissible and impermissible coercion might be helpful in some realms, the objection continues, it is inapplicable to this context because political deliberation should be completely free of coercion and exploitation. A country's policies ought to be shaped by whatever is best for the whole, not by whichever subunit is able to exert the most pressure in favor of its self-interested aims. Indeed, this is the central motivation for Sunstein's project: We must do all that we can to make our political negotiation approximate the ideals of deliberative democracy, and one key piece of this puzzle is constitutionally prohibiting secession in order to eliminate strategic threats of state breaking. Sunstein supports this point by citing the analogous benefits of restricting divorce: "A decision to stigmatize divorce or to make it available only under certain conditions ... may lead to happier as well as more stable marriages, by providing an incentive for spouses to adapt their behavior and even their desires to promote long-term harmony."[28]

I prefer to turn this objection on its head and use it against those who would eliminate all political coercion. Whereas Sunstein cites the incentive to improve a relationship from which one cannot exit, I would emphasize the potential for tyranny in any union from which there is no escape. Consider Sunstein's analogy with divorce. The author rightly notes that many spouses work to improve their marriages only because institutional and social costs make divorce an unattractive option. Other theorists, on the other hand, complain of the gross injustice endured by spouses only because they feel chained to their partners. For instance, feminists have long protested that women experience considerable pressure to endure horrible marital conditions.[29] The economic, legal, and social costs of divorce for women are so high that many are effectively forced to remain in miserable marriages. Furthermore, men often capitalize upon these asymmetrical exit costs by demanding that the marriage be tailored to suit their preferences. Lamentably, women all too often submit to these lopsided unions for lack of a better alternative. In short, I suspect that discouraging divorce actually chains women to their tormentors more often than it facilitates healthy partnerships. If this is accurate, it suggests that prohibiting secession would have more than just the healthy effects that

---

[28] Sunstein, "Constitutionalism and Secession," p. 649.

[29] For an explanation of the tyranny of marriage in the past, see John Stuart Mill's *The Subjection of Women*, and for a study of the injustice of contemporary marital relations, see Susan Moller Okin's text, *Justice, Gender, and the Family*.

Sunstein supposes. Ironically, if Sunstein's comparison between secession and divorce is apt, it gives us all the more reason to permit secession and its attendant political coercion.[30]

Throughout this chapter, we have worried about minority groups using their secessionist rights as weapons with which to coerce compatriots. Our overriding concern has been that political deliberation could deteriorate into nothing more than a thinly veiled power struggle in which minority groups gain an effective veto power over the majority. As my inversion of Sunstein's divorce example intimates, however, our narrow focus may have led us to overlook another side of the story. The truth is that political deliberation is seldom an open and selfless quest for the best solutions to the community's most pressing problems. More often, policy is the product of the majority's short-sighted, self-interested aims. Over the long haul, minority groups are repeatedly ignored by majorities who are willing to appease them only to the extent necessary to avoid civil unrest. Not only do minorities inevitably lose out in the long run, they often have insufficient leverage with which to protect even their most pressing interests. Donald Horowitz describes this state of affairs in blunt terms: "International actors generally took a hard line against secession except in the rarest case (Bangladesh), and then only when it became a *fait accompli*. To put the point sharply, the former view was that international boundaries were fixed and regimes could do what they wished within them. This was the international framework for a good deal of tyranny."[31] Given this more realistic account of contemporary political decision making, we can see that there are actually advantages to allowing minority groups to secede. As I will now explain, the threat of secession

[30] Indeed, in a footnote, Sunstein acknowledges that restricting exit is a double-edged sword. See Sunstein, "Constitutionalism and Secession," pp. 649ff.

[31] Donald Horowitz, "Self-Determination: Politics, Philosophy, and Law," p. 190. Margaret Moore makes a similar point when discussing minority national groups:

In *Democracy and America*, Tocqueville argued that, in a well-functioning democracy, the outvoted minority will respect the majority decision in the expectation that, at some later time, they will be part of a winning coalition and will require minority compliance. The reverse would also seem to hold true – though Tocqueville did not spell this out – that a majority will tend to refrain from upsetting the minority because they anticipate THEY will be in need of majority self-restraint when they are converted into a minority status. This dynamic does not occur in a state in which different national communities consistently vote for nationally aligned parties – there is no outlet for minority disaffection, there is no moderating influence on minority demands, and no mechanisms, at least internal to the democratic system, to prevent the majority from oppressing the minority. (*The Ethics of Nationalism*, p. 89)

enables minority groups to protect themselves from the tyranny of the majority and, as a result, secures the mutually beneficial political arrangements that the social contract proudly advertises but seldom delivers.

Given that minorities are routinely left vulnerable to discriminatory policies designed to benefit the majority, prohibiting secession only heightens the problem. If subunits are unable to exit, then (like a spouse who has no option of divorce) they are held captive in unions with partners who have insufficient reason to treat them as equals. If a minority can secede, on the other hand, then not only can it escape existing tyranny, it can threaten to secede before the mistreatment becomes too severe. Thus the minority's option of threatening to secede often functions more as a shield against impermissible coercion than as a weapon with which to impermissibly coerce compatriots. As Daniel Philpott puts it, "If the moral criteria of the moral right to secede are correct, then this is just the sort of group whom we desire for the law to empower. Their advantaged negotiating position with the central government seems entirely appropriate: their leverage, we more accurately think of as 'empowerment' rather than 'blackmail'."[32] I suspect that authors like Sunstein have failed to appreciate this point because they have focused so narrowly upon a secessionist movement's power. But while it is good to be alert to the evils that may accompany recognizing rights to political self-determination, we must not lose sight of the fact that the status quo offers few viable alternatives to the minorities who are all too often treated as second-class citizens. The protective power of secession is corroborated by Albert Hirschman in his seminal book *Exit, Voice, and Loyalty*. Hirschman notes that "[t]he chances for voice to function effectively as a recuperation mechanism are appreciably strengthened if voice is backed up by the *threat of exit*, whether it is made openly or whether the possibility of exit is merely well understood to be an element in the situation by all concerned."[33] In other words, if you cannot exit an association, your associates may have little incentive to respect your voice. Political theorists have often advocated a citizen's right to leave her country, but they have traditionally understood this right wholly in terms of emigration (hence the expression that disgruntled citizens should "vote with their feet"). The problem with this 'solution' is that threatening to emigrate does not make one's voice more authoritative, since countries normally do not worry about losing citizens in the same way that a business minds losing customers. Indeed, while

[32] Daniel Philpott, "Self-Determination in Practice," p. 95.
[33] Albert O. Hirschman, *Exit, Voice, and Loyalty*, p. 82.

some countries worry about losing accomplished artists, athletes, and scientists, many would actually prefer that members of disgruntled national minorities flee.[34] Only secessionist exit makes one's voice more effective, because states are typically more concerned with losing territory than citizens. And because organizations are motivated to improve the conditions only of those who have leverage against the group as a whole, only exiting with territory can amplify a political subunit's voice.

In light of the foregoing, we can see how opening the door to political coercion may actually *improve* decision making, enabling subunits to secure the benefits of political cooperation promised by social contract theorists. Respecting rights to political self-determination accomplishes this by changing states from unchecked monopolies to suppliers in a competitive market. The social contract tradition contains a diverse family of views united by their core understanding that political arrangements should be mutually beneficial. This insight is fundamental to the tradition because the notion of a contract presumes autonomous parties who voluntarily bind themselves in order to advance their interests. I suspect that this tradition has led to at least as much confusion as clarity, however, because, while it is true that states *ought* to be mutually beneficial arrangements that *look as if* they might be voluntarily accepted, they are seldom mutually beneficial and rarely voluntarily adopted. As we have seen, there is more than an accidental relationship between mutual benefit and voluntary agreement: Not only is one unlikely to voluntarily enter a relationship that is not beneficial, coercive relationships are less prone to benefit the coercee. Thus traditional social contract theorists have confused matters by promising benefits that are unlikely in the absence of voluntary unions, while simultaneously denying that exit is permissible. To emphasize: When secessionist exit is ruled out, the union becomes coercive, and the majority has little incentive to accommodate minority groups. In sum, contract theorists have traditionally touted political benefits that can be purchased only with an arrangement that allows secessionist exit; given their distaste for political divorce, then, social contract theorists are left unable to deliver the goods they advertise.

In the end, I do not condemn social contract theorists for advocating mutual advantage, since states can and should be designed to benefit minorities as well as the majority; their mistake lies in failing to recognize

---

[34] Lamentably, one need not imagine cases like the Gypsies or the Kurds to see this; on a smaller scale, consider how many U.S. communities deliberately make their environments inhospitable to homosexuals or blacks.

the type of political arrangements necessary for states to approach contract theory's own ideal. In particular, countries are unlikely to supply the best goods when they enjoy monopolistic control over captive customers. The only way for social contract theorists to ensure that states are responsive to their subunits is to amplify the latter's voices with the threat of political divorce. Without allowing subunits to secede, I know of no way to expose states to the market pressures of competition, and this is why the functional theory's allowance for unilateral state breaking actually has beneficial, rather than deleterious, consequences.

In closing, let me emphasize that these positive results provide the most compelling reasons to respect rights to political self-determination. Many oppressed subunits would flourish in an independent state, but the most precious advantage of honoring political self-determination is not the actual political divorces; it is the reduction of oppressive conditions that lead minorities to long for independence in the first place. As Lenin explains: "To defend this right [to secession] does in no way mean encouraging the formation of small states, but to the contrary, it leads to a freer, ... wider formation of larger states – a phenomenon more advantageous for the masses and more in accord with economic development."[35] Thus, I defend secessionist rights not just because some groups are entitled to independence, but primarily because the threat of secession can be a healthy catalyst that stirs apathetic states from their monopolistic slumber and invigorates countries with competitive incentives. In short, institutionally protecting secessionist rights can provide for both just divisions and healthier unions.

Conclusion

Concerned to create the conditions necessary for deliberative democracy, Sunstein recommends constitutionally prohibiting secession. We are now in a position to see why, *even if Sunstein is right that allowing secession might encourage strategic bargaining among political subunits*, his argument faces two considerable challenges. First, if there are moral rights to secede, then it is not enough merely to show that institutionally protecting these rights will have costs; one must demonstrate that these costs are grave enough to justify constitutionally restricting moral rights. Second, equipping political subunits with the threat of secession is also beneficial insofar as it gives minority groups a degree of political leverage with which to

---

[35] Quoted in Lee C. Buchheit, *Secession: The Legitimacy of Self-Determination*, p. 120.

shield themselves. Thus, one must balance the potential costs against the expected benefits of constitutionally protecting the right to secede. It is open to debate, of course, whether the benefits or the costs will be greater. However, because a moral right hangs in the balance, there is a presumption against those who would restrict political self-determination. Putting these two points together, then, we see that Sunstein has the burden of proof (doubly) on his shoulders: Not only must he demonstrate that (1) the costs of institutionally protecting secessionist rights are clearly greater than the benefits, he must show that (2) the net costs are so substantial as to justify denying moral rights to political self-determination. In sum, while Sunstein is no doubt correct that we must consider the likely effects of institutionally protecting secessionist rights before designing constitutions in accordance with the recommendations of the functional theory of secession, his argument as it stands is not enough to show that we must constitutionally prohibit secession.

7

Secession and International Law

This chapter explores the wisdom of reforming the international legal system's stance on state breaking in light of the moral rights validated by the functional theory of secession. This matter cannot be settled conclusively without empirical information that is currently unavailable, but I argue both (1) that the case in favor of the functional theory places the burden of proof on those who would restrict secessionist rights and (2) that there are good reasons to doubt that Remedial Right Only theorists will be able to withstand this burden.

Ideal Theory and International Law

International law's stance on secession is even less permissive than that of contemporary political theory. In the Introduction I mentioned that, while many theorists now acknowledge that a group can have a remedial right to secede when it has suffered severe and long-standing injustice at the hands of its state, most deny that a group could have a unilateral right to political divorce when it has not been treated unjustly. The existing international legal system is more conservative than political theory; not only does it not protect primary rights to secede, it fails to recognize even most remedial rights. Currently, international law invokes a "saltwater" test (restricting secessionist rights to overseas colonies), so it does not recognize Chechnya's right to secede, let alone Scotland's or Quebec's. Thus, clearly it would require a huge transformation to revise the international legal system in accordance with the recommendations of the functional theory of secession. It is not difficult to imagine, however, how this revision might be achieved.

There are a variety of ways in which international law could institutionally protect primary rights to secede, but David Copp offers what I take to
be a particularly sensible proposal.[1] Copp recommends that the International Court of Justice be called on to adjudicate secessionist conflicts in
essentially the same manner in which it presides over conflicts between
sovereign states. Copp suggests that any separatist group should be permitted to petition the International Court of Justice, and the Court's first
task would be to determine whether this group qualified for the right to
secede. (Copp and I have slightly different accounts of the primary right
to secede, but on my view this would require the Court to determine
whether both the separatists and the remainder state would emerge able
and willing to perform the requisite political functions.)[2] If the Court
judged the group to be the type of party that might qualify for a right to
unilateral exit, the Court would then oversee a plebiscite in the proposed
secessionist territory to ensure that a majority did indeed desire independence.[3] Assuming that a majority in fact favored separation, the Court
would then oversee the political divorce settlement to ensure that, as in
marital divorce, both the separatists and the rump state were given a fair
share of the collective debts and assets. Copp then recommends that the
Court oversee a second plebiscite "to determine whether the group still
wants to secede, given the negotiated terms, and to determine whether it
does in fact have a stable desire to form a state."[4] If the majority's preference for divorce remains constant, then the parent state may make one
last appeal to the court (arguing, perhaps, "that the secessionist group
did not intend in good faith to abide by the settlement").[5] If this final
appeal fails (or is not made), then the Court would oversee the separation, ensuring that the secessionists and the rump state both honor the
separation agreement and generally respect each other's rights. Copp
suggests that at this stage, "[t]he right of a secessionist society not to be
interfered with in forming a state is of a piece with the right any state
has not to be interfered with in governing its territory. So these rights

---

[1] David Copp, "International Law and Morality in the Theory of Secession," pp. 231–236.
My summary here simplifies Copp's proposal a bit, cutting out some of the steps; I do
this for the sake of brevity, not because I think any of Copp's recommendations are
unimportant.

[2] On Copp's view, the Court would also have to judge that the separatists constitute a
"society."

[3] As noted in Chapter 3, Harry Beran has explained how democratic principles can be used
to determine the boundaries of the separatist territory.

[4] Copp, "International Law and Morality in the Theory of Secession," p. 234.

[5] Ibid., p. 235.

of secessionist societies are essentially the same rights that international law now accords to states, and they would have the same legal force as existing rights of existing states."[6]

It is tempting to suppose that my arguments in Chapters 3 and 4 illustrate the necessity for reforming the international legal system in this fashion; after all, if there is a moral right to secede, then international law should protect this right. This inference is too quick, however, because the fact that A has a moral right to X does not necessarily imply that we should *institutionally protect* A's moral right to X. Using an analogy to euthanasia, Allen Buchanan nicely explains this point about institutional reasoning:

It may not be difficult to describe a particular hypothetical case in which a physician would be morally justified in actively terminating the life of a hopelessly ill, incompetent patient whose quality of life is extremely poor. And one may be able to formulate the conditions C, D, and E, that make this case one in which active termination of life is morally justified.

But it is quite a different matter to show that it would be morally justifiable for physicians to apply the rule "Whenever conditions C, D, and E obtain, they may actively terminate life." Whether it would be a moral improvement or a moral disaster for physicians to act on the rule the philosopher abstracts from a particular favored case will depend upon a number of factors that are conspicuously absent from the description of that particular case. For instance, one must take into account the overall character of the institutions within which the physicians work and in particular whether reimbursement schemes or other features of the institutional framework create incentives that generate an unacceptable risk that physicians would exercise this authority wrongly. The more general problem is this: even if it is possible by calm reflection on a hypothetical case to formulate conditions under which a certain action would be morally justified, the real world agents who are supposed to follow a rule that is abstracted from the hypothetical case may not reliably identify those conditions and perform the action only when they obtain.[7]

Transposing Buchanan's insight to my own analysis of secession, we can see that *even if I have argued flawlessly to this point*, it would be premature to derive conclusions regarding international law without first considering the potential consequences of altering the international legal system. In fact, because my analysis to this point has been largely *ideal* and *noninstitutional*, we must evaluate two types of considerations before making any recommendations about existing international law: (1) the transition from

---

6 Ibid.

7 Allen Buchanan, *Justice, Legitimacy, and Self-Determination*, pp. 22–23.

noninstitutional to institutional analysis and (2) the difference between ideal and nonideal theory. Consider each of these distinctions.

In light of Buchanan's discussion of euthansia, the distinction between institutional and noninstitutional analysis should be relatively clear. One's analysis is satisfactorily institutional only if one considers the likely consequences of designing the relevant institutions in certain ways, and one's analysis is noninstitutional if one considers only a single case in isolation. With the exception of the last chapter (in which I considered the merits of constitutionally protecting secessionist rights), my analysis has been largely noninstitutional.

As for the second distinction, let us say that one's theory is ideal just in case one assumes that moral agents will generally be constrained by the dictates of morality. Thus, Allen Buchanan distinguishes ideal and nonideal theory as follows:

Ideal theory sets the ultimate moral targets, articulating the principles that a just society or a just international order would satisfy, on the assumption that there will be full compliance with these principles. Nonideal theory provides principled guidance for how to cope with the problems of noncompliance and how we are to move closer toward full compliance with the principles of ideal theory.[8]

Because I have not yet considered how the various parties should respond if and when international actors fail to respect the value of political self-determination, my analysis to this point has been ideal.

Finally, notice that because I am considering whether *existing* international law ought to be changed (as opposed to what *ideal* international laws would be), I am drawing upon my earlier *ideal, noninstitutional* analysis to shed light on a *nonideal, institutional* question. There is nothing wrong with making these transitions, but, as Buchanan's discussion of euthanasia makes plain, we must be careful not to rush from sound arguments regarding ideal, noninstitutional theory to unwarranted conclusions regarding existing international law. Let me stress, however, that none of this means that my analysis in the preceding chapters is irrelevant to the question of international law. On the contrary, if my defense of the functional theory of secession is compelling, it creates at least a *presumptive* case for reforming international law. This presumptive case might be defeated by considerations of how institutional changes may affect (potentially noncompliant) actors, but there is no reason why my arguments in favor of the moral right to unilateral secession do not supply

[8] Ibid., p. 55.

an ideal that international law should approximate in the absence of compelling reasons to deviate from this ideal. As Kai Nielsen puts it, "the international legal system should be altered so that it comes to be in accordance with that moral right. The moral tail should wag the legal dog. We should not tailor moral or normative political theory and our moral principles to square with the legal system."⁹ To appreciate this point, consider again the analogous debate regarding euthanasia.

If one can establish via sound ideal, noninstitutional reasoning that there is a moral right to physician-assisted euthanasia whenever conditions C, D, and E obtain, then this establishes a presumption in favor of legally allowing euthanasia in those circumstances. Buchanan is right to remind us that we cannot automatically infer that these acts of euthanasia should be legally permitted, because without doing the appropriate nonideal institutional analysis, one cannot be sure that these laws would not have unintended (but nonetheless morally relevant) consequences. But nothing about Buchanan's observation should lead us to deny that our initial analysis of euthanasia supplies an ideal that should be legally approximated to whatever extent is possible without creating negative consequences. After all, there are a variety of considerations relevant to designing the best laws, but surely a chief factor must be the moral rights of those subject to the laws. In short, even if moral rights are not *all* that should be considered when designing governing institutions, certainly they are an important part thereof. And, just as the moral right to physician-assisted euthanasia provides (admittedly defeasible) moral reasons in favor of creating domestic laws that permit euthanasia, the moral right to unilateral secession provides (defeasible) moral reasons in favor of securing international legal rights to political divorce. In sum, while the arguments in support of the functional theory of secession may not create a *conclusive* case in favor of revising international criminal law, they certainly supply a *presumptive* case for doing so. Thus, our principal task in this chapter must be to review the case *against* creating international legal rights to secession to determine whether it can outweigh the arguments already supplied on behalf of these rights.

The most prominent and sophisticated arguments against creating international legal rights to unilateral secession have been advanced by Allen Buchanan. While Buchanan has no doubt been gratified by the remarkable extent to which his groundbreaking work has attracted increased attention to the morality of secession, he may be discouraged

⁹ Kai Nielsen, "Liberal Nationalism and Secession," p. 129.

that so few have paid more than scant attention to the surrounding institutional issues. Whatever might be said in favor of secessionist rights considered in an institutional vacuum, Buchanan insists that international law should *not* protect primary rights to secede in the fashion that I (following Copp) have proposed here. Buchanan is not against all rights to political divorce (indeed, he criticizes the "saltwater" test and seeks to *expand* the list of grievances that can qualify a group for an international legal right to secede), but he is emphatically opposed to creating any international legal right to secede in the absence of injustice. At the heart of Buchanan's argument are concerns about the types of incentives that international laws can create. He argues in favor of remedial rights to secede because of the beneficial incentives that institutionally protecting these rights will have, and he argues against primary rights because of the "perverse" incentives that would be created by international laws designed to protect them.[10] To appreciate Buchanan's argument, let us review the incentives he supposes would be attached to the various possible international laws on secession.

First, notice why Buchanan thinks Remedial Right Only theory "gets the incentives right." He writes:

On the one hand, states that protect basic human rights and honor autonomy agreements are immune to legally sanctioned unilateral secession and entitled to international support for maintaining the full extent of their territorial integrity. On the other hand, if, as the theory prescribes, international law recognizes a unilateral right to secede as a remedy for serious and persisting injustices, states will have an incentive to act more justly.[11]

In other words, if international law recognizes rights to secede *only* in cases of injustice, then political leaders will be motivated to govern justly because they know both that (1) doing so will lead the international community to support the state in any potential secessionist conflict and that (2) sufficient cases of injustice would lead the international community to support the separatists.

[10] Let me explicitly stress that I do not mean to imply that Buchanan's entire argument against primary rights to secede rests on the consideration of incentives. I say that incentives constitute the "heart" of his argument only to indicate that I think that they are his most important consideration. I will review other pieces of his argument later in this chapter when I consider potential methodological objections to my own account, but even so, I will omit various portions of Buchanan's very complex and integrated argument. I strongly encourage the reader not to take my discussion here as a complete summary of Buchanan's views. One would be well advised to read *Justice, Legitimacy, and Self-Determination* in its entirety to appreciate the portions of Buchanan's argument that I omit here.

[11] Buchanan, *Justice, Legitimacy, and Self-Determination*, p. 370.

As Buchanan explains, the incentive structure would be altogether different if the international legal system also respected primary rights to secede:

If state leaders know that unilateral secession will be considered a right under international law for any group that can muster a majority in favor of it in any portion of their state, they will not be receptive to proposals for decentralization. They will view decentralization as a first step toward secession, because creation of internal political units will provide the basis for future secessions by plebiscite.

International recognition of a plebiscitary unilateral right to secede would also create perverse incentives regarding both immigration and economic development. States that did not wish to risk losing part of their territory (which includes virtually all of them) would have a strong reason for limiting immigration (or internal migration) that might result in the formation of a pro-secession majority in a portion of the state's territory. And to deter secession by existing internal political units, the state might even seek to prevent them from becoming sufficiently developed to be economically viable. (The Soviet Union's policy of dispersing major industries among the Republics was very likely motivated at least in part by precisely this consideration.)[12]

Thus, not only would leaders lose some of their incentive to govern justly (because being a just state would no longer insulate one from the threat of secession), institutionally protecting primary rights to secede would discourage decentralization, open immigration, and freedom of migration, because each of these policies potentially nurtures separatism. In brief, there seems every reason to think that institutionally protecting only remedial rights to secede would create positive incentives and that protecting primary rights would both eliminate those helpful incentives and create additional detrimental ones.

Because political leaders are loath to lose territory and have unparalleled power to promote or destroy peace and justice, Buchanan is right to call attention to these relatively neglected considerations. Moreover, I think Buchanan accurately describes some of the incentives that could be attached to laws protecting remedial and primary rights to secede. For several reasons, however, I am not convinced that these considerations are sufficiently weighty to defeat the presumptive case created by the moral right to secede.

To begin, there are at least two reasons to think that the "perverse" incentives about which Buchanan warns us are not that strong. First of all, the negative incentives to which Buchanan refers already exist, so the operative question is to what extent they would be magnified by the international community's support of primary rights to secede. I say this

[12] Ibid., pp. 377–378.

because (as Buchanan's reference to the former Soviet Union illustrates), even in the absence of any international legal right to secede, countries all too often disempower minority groups in an effort to preempt potential independence movements. As Copp explains:

> ... it is a matter of speculation whether implementation of my proposal would create incentives significantly different from those that already exist. States that contain secessionist groups already have to worry about the possibility of secession. There is not now a legal right to secede, but there are secessionist movements all over the world, and the states facing these movements need somehow to deal with the threat to their territorial integrity. This fact creates incentives for states to attempt to block secession or to undermine the motivation for it in various ways. It is not obvious that my proposal would create significant new incentives for them to act in harmful ways.[13]

Thus, if political leaders already have incentives to avoid desirable policies like decentralization, then we have reason to avoid creating international laws that protect primary rights to secede only if we know that such laws would *substantially strengthen* those incentives; but this is an empirical question about which there is less reason to be sure. To emphasize: It is one thing to speculate about the *kind* of incentives a law might create, but it is another thing altogether to guess *how much* an existing incentive might be strengthened by this same law. Secondly, historical evidence indicates that separatist sentiment is typically pacified, rather than enflamed, when minority groups are given additional political powers. As John McGarry explains:

> While states are often reluctant to decentralize, for fear it will promote secession, there is evidence that timely and genuine decentralization achieves exactly the opposite effect. While Francoist centralization coincided with a significant increase in support for Basque separatism, the granting of autonomy to Basques in 1979 resulted in support for independence dropping from 36 percent to 12 percent. The long-time existence of the Canadian and Swiss federations also show that extensive decentralization is consistent with state unity.[14]

---

[13] Copp, "International Law and Morality in the Theory of Secession," p. 243.

[14] John McGarry, "'Orphans of Secession': National Pluralism in Secessionist Regions and Post-Secession States," pp. 225–226. Regarding Canada, McGarry adds:
> Canada's current troubles do not undermine this argument. To a considerable extent, the rise in support for Quebec separatism since the 1970s can be traced to a move away from the concept of bi-national partnership on the part of English-speaking Canadians towards a view of Canada as a nation-state in which all individuals and provinces should be treated equally. Similarly, the breakup of several Communist multinational federations should not cast any doubt on decentralization as a strategy, as these states were in fact highly centralized.

On reflection, this observation is commonsensical: After all, it would be crazy *not* to think that many formerly middle-of-the-road Chechens may have become ardent separatists precisely because of Moscow's brutal campaign to quell the secessionist movement. Thus, leaders with some sense of what actually fuels separatist fires will recognize that they have no incentive to avoid decentralization *no matter what stand the international legal system takes on rights to political divorce.*

Another factor to bear in mind is that, while Buchanan highlights the reasons *against* institutionally protecting primary rights to secede, these must be balanced against the considerations *in favor of* legally securing these rights. As I emphasized in the last chapter, for instance, arming minority groups with an effective right to secede gives these groups political leverage, and this leverage in turn provides the central government with incentives not to mistreat these minority groups. In addition, secessionist movements are likely to emerge whether or not the international legal system condones them, so instituting something like Copp's proposal would be beneficial insofar as it would allow us to bring "secessionist problems to the International Court where the issues could be decided in a peaceful and orderly manner."[15] As Michael Freeman observes, "The restrictive interpretation of the right to self-determination does not inhibit claims to self-determination, but it does inhibit their peaceful and just resolution, since it denies their legitimacy."[16]

In light of the foregoing, it appears that, even if Buchanan is right that international laws protecting primary rights to secede will generate some perverse incentives, it is not at all clear how much weight to give this consideration. Once one recognizes both that some of these incentives will exist whether or not the international legal system protects primary rights and that there would also be some *positive* side-effects of institutionally recognizing these moral rights, it is questionable whether Buchanan's concerns are decisive.[17] However, because moral rights hang in the balance, there are two things about which we can be confident: (1) The burden of proof to establish the empirical fact of the matter lies squarely

---

[15] Copp, "International Law and Morality in the Theory of Secession," p. 243.

[16] Michael Freeman, "The Priority of Function over Structure: A New Approach to Secession," p. 15.

[17] As Daniel Philpott says, "The absence of institutions of self-determination may allow unionist evils, just as the presence of such institutions might admittedly promote the ill effects of self-determination. The difficult question is the magnitude of each effect." ("Self-Determination in Practice," p. 92)

on the shoulders of those who would *restrict* these moral rights, and (2) it would not be sufficient to show that there is merely a slight advantage in favor of restricting these rights. To appreciate each of these points, consider how we might have reasoned in the United States a hundred years ago when deliberating whether to give women the legal right to vote. Against such a proposition, one might have suggested that enacting a law granting all literate women the right to vote would have created perverse incentives for men to keep women illiterate. Such an incentive is certainly relevant, but, given that women have a moral right to vote, women should not be denied this legal right unless we have compelling evidence both (1) that the marginal effect of this increase in incentive would often be decisive and (2) that the resulting harm would be substantial. Similarly, given that qualified groups have primary moral rights to secede, we should legally protect these rights unless those who advocate legal restrictions can offer compelling evidence that sufficient harms would ensue.

My own view is that the case against secessionist rights cannot be sustained, but my stance is admittedly speculative; I am a philosopher, and at the end of the day I must defer to those better equipped to answer these empirical questions.[18] For the sake of argument, however, let us suppose that I am wrong. Before closing I would like to emphasize that even if the empirical evidence comes back against institutionally protecting primary rights to secede, this does not settle the matter once and for all. Instead, because the harmful effects of institutionally recognizing secessionist rights stem from noncompliance, denying political self-determination must be regarded as a *temporary* strategy, one that we should endorse only until we can satisfactorily reform the illiberal actors. To see why this is so, notice how we would address analogous concerns in medicine.

In his article "Physician-Assisted Suicide: A Tragic View," John Arras offers an argument regarding euthanasia analogous to Buchanan's case

---

[18] Again, Philpott strikes me as adopting the appropriate agnostic stance:

> Political philosophers have the most to say about basic moral principles. The principles offer general insights for international law and domestic constitutions, but as the questions become more specific, dealing with the advantages of certain constitutional clauses, the good and ill effects of the UN intervention, the dynamics of secessionist politics, and so on, the less the philosopher will have to say and the more we find ourselves turning to sociologists, political scientists, and constitutional lawyers, who can tell us better what sort of effects are likely to ensue from our proposed institutions. ("Self-Determination in Practice," p. 100)

against internationally legalizing primary rights to secede. Arras writes:

It is highly doubtful that the context of physician-patient conversation within this new dispensation of "turnstile medicine" will be at all conducive to humane decisions untainted by subtle economic coercion.

In addition, given the abysmal and shameful track record of physicians in responding adequately to pain and suffering, we also can confidently predict that in many cases all reasonable alternatives will not have been exhausted. Instead of vigorously addressing the pharmacological and psychosocial needs of such patients, physicians no doubt will continue to ignore, undertreat, or treat many of their patients in an impersonal manner. The result is likely to be more depression, desperation, and requests for physician-assisted death from patients who could have been successfully treated.[19]

Thus, just as Buchanan warns against institutionally instantiating primary right theories out of concern that political leaders in the real world might resort to injustice before relinquishing any of their territory, Arras maintains that it would be unwise to legalize physician assisted-suicide on the grounds that physicians would give patients the type of care necessary to ensure that laws legalizing physician-assisted suicide would always work as designed. For the purposes of argument, let us assume that Arras is absolutely right. Would it then follow that we should once and for all turn our backs on the ideal of legalizing physician-assisted suicide and euthanasia? Presumably not; rather, it would show at most that we should not legalize these acts *until we have adequately addressed the deficiencies in the existing medical system.* Moreover, if there is a moral right to physician-assisted suicide, this right supplies additional, weighty reasons to reform the practice of medicine so that physicians no longer "ignore, undertreat, or treat many of their patients in an impersonal manner."

I recommend that we reason in similar fashion about rights to political self-determination. That is, even if it turns out that the potential injustices committed by political leaders currently make it reckless for us to legally enforce primary rights to secede, this should not lead us permanently to abandon the goal of institutionally realizing moral rights to political self-determination. Instead, it should inspire us to do all that we can to foster international respect for justice in general, and for rights to political self-determination in particular. Finally, while it is undeniable that many leaders would go to horrible extremes before ceding control over any of their territory, the rapidly changing landscape of international law gives

---

[19] John D. Arras, "Physician-Assisted Suicide: A Tragic View," p. 228.

us ample reason to suppose that substantial progress will soon be made on this front. As Buchanan notes:

Little more than fifty years ago few informed persons would have predicted that international law would place substantial limitations on the state's right to treat its own citizens as it sees fit. Given the short time span of these developments, as well as their radical departure from the statist paradigm of traditional international law that has dominated since the mid-seventeenth century and reached its apogee in the nineteenth, it is not unreasonable to work within the system for further improvements.[20]

Buchanan's evaluation of history and his optimism about the future both strike me as right on target; I would add only that political self-determination is beginning to enjoy the ascendance that human rights have already experienced. Fifty years ago it would have been unthinkable for a country to respond to a separatist movement in the way in which Czechoslovakia responded to Slovakia. And while there remain too many countries that would treat independence movements in the manner in which Russia has treated Chechnya, Canada's principled deliberation regarding Quebec is a harbinger of good things to come. Assuming that liberal democratic values continue to blossom on the international landscape, we will decreasingly have to worry about renegade political leaders mistreating potential separatist movements. And, if that is the case, whatever worries we currently have about noncompliant leaders being motivated by the perverse incentives of international laws will continue to diminish.

To review: While the arguments from the previous chapters in defense of the functional theory of secession do not by themselves conclusively demonstrate that we should design international laws protecting primary rights to secede, they do create a presumption in favor of doing so. This presumptive case is vulnerable to being defeated by competing considerations, but the burden of proof is upon those who would restrict political self-determination, and the evidence suggests that this burden cannot be sustained. Even if one could provide a compelling case that substantial harms would result from revising the international legal system, though, this would not show that we should permanently abandon the ideal of institutionally protecting primary secessionist rights. At most, such a case could show only that we should not institutionally instantiate primary rights to political divorce until the democratic value of political self-determination has taken firmer root in the geopolitical terrain.

[20] Buchanan, *Justice, Legitimacy, and Self-Determination*, p. 58.

Methodological Objections

One might object to the preceding analysis on methodological grounds. In particular, Allen Buchanan argues that it is inappropriate to move from ideal to institutional theory in the way in which I do. For issues such as euthanasia, there is nothing methodologically suspect about first analyzing individual cases and then going on to ask the institutional question of whether the best system of laws would accommodate whatever conclusions one has arrived at in ideal theory. Buchanan insists that it is wrong to proceed in this fashion when analyzing state breaking, however, because the right to secede is "inherently institutional." As Buchanan explains, "I am not denying the distinction between ideal and nonideal theory. My point, rather, is that both ideal and nonideal theory must be institutional because the right to secede is inherently institutional. . . ."[21]

Thus, the real problem with my approach, according to Buchanan, is that I mistakenly take my earlier, noninstitutional analysis of secession to be relevant to my analysis of the institutional questions. On my view, the moral rights to secede validated by the functional model serve as an ideal that, other things being equal, we should strive to realize. In other words, international law should be amended in accordance with this ideal unless there are sufficiently weighty considerations against doing so. The problem with this approach, according to Buchanan, is that my initial, noninstitutional analysis of secession is not only beside the point, it is fundamentally flawed in its own right. Indeed, noninstitutional analyses are apt to mislead one's exploration of institutional matters in this arena because the former are derived with no regard to how they might fit into a larger institutional framework. Buchanan puts it plainly:

To summarize the key methodological point: Whether a particular account of the right to secede is defensible will depend upon whether embodying its principles in the international legal order would, all things considered, promote the proper goals of the system. That is why an account of the right to secede, if it is to provide guidance for reforming international law, must be embedded in a more comprehensive moral theory of international legal institutions.[22]

Given that Buchanan's concerns stem not from the general distinction between ideal and nonideal theory, but from his more specific insistence that the right to secede is inherently institutional, we should begin by reviewing his argument for this latter claim. In explaining secession's

---

[21] Ibid., pp. 346–347.
[22] Ibid., p. 348.

institutional nature, Buchanan calls attention to the connection most separatists make between secession and statehood. He writes:

> ...secessionists typically assert that they have the right to their own legitimate state, and a legitimate state is an institutionally defined entity, an entity defined as having certain rights, powers, and immunity under international law.
>
> So, if we understand their assertion as they do, to say that the Chechens have a right to secede – in the claim-right sense of 'right' – is at the very least to say that (1) they are morally justified in attempting to establish Chechnya as a legitimate *state* and that (2) others are morally prohibited from interfering with this attempt to create this new legitimate *state*. Both (1) and (2) are institutional statements, because they both employ the concept of a state, which is an institutional concept – not just in the sense that states are institutions – but because to be a legitimate state is to be an institutionally defined entity, an entity that has a certain status according to the institutions of international law.[23]

For several reasons, I am unconvinced by this argument. First and most obviously, even if Buchanan is correct that secessionists typically understand the right to secede as including the right to their own legitimate state (indeed, even if secessionists *invariably* conceive of political divorce in this way), this does not entail that secession is in fact conceptually linked to legitimate statehood, because there is no reason why these "typical" secessionists could not be wrong. Furthermore, if secessionists have this conception, they *are* in fact wrong, because as a conceptual matter there is no necessary connection between secession and legitimate statehood. One can see this by considering the possibility of a group of anarchists who want to secede in order to live in a state of nature, or a group that does not seek independence but instead would like to separate from its current state merely in order to merge with another (as Northern Ireland might, for instance, if it sought to sever its political association with the United Kingdom in order to unite with Ireland). In addition, if secession were inherently institutional because it was inextricably linked to international law, then it would not be possible even to sensibly speak of secession in the absence of international law. But this must be wrong, because international law has arrived on the scene relatively recently, and surely secession was conceivable (and perhaps even permissible) before there were any international laws on the subject.

Moreover, it is mysterious to me why Buchanan should emphasize the particular understanding of secession that he ascribes to most

[23] Ibid., p. 24.

secessionists, since he himself rejects it. When clarifying his own conception of the right to secede, Buchanan carefully distinguishes between two positions. He writes:

According to the first option, a morally defensible international law of secession would only recognize a right to secede understood as the right of a group to throw off the state's authority and attempt to constitute an entity that will be recognized as a legitimate state; according to the second, the right to secede is the right of a group to have its own legitimate state. On the second option, the right to break away and the right to recognition go together; on the first they do not.

The proposal for international legal reform I am advancing is the first option.[24]

As Buchanan later explains: "The rationale for separating the right to repudiate state control over a portion of the state's territory and to attempt to establish an independent state, on the one hand, and the right to legitimate statehood, on the other, is straightforward: The grounds of the two rights differ."[25] I have no quarrel with Buchanan's explicitly distinguishing between the right to secede and the right to legitimate statehood as he does, but it is then curious that he should claim that the right to secede is inherently institutional merely because secessionists tend not to distinguish between the two.

Finally, notice that even if there were a conceptual link between the right to secede and the right to legitimate statehood, this would give us no reason to question the functional theory of secession, because insofar as the latter restricts secessionist rights only to those cases in which the separatists and the rump state are able and willing to perform the requisite political functions, it authorizes secession only for those groups that should qualify as legitimate states.

If I am correct that the right to secede is not inherently institutional merely because secessionists typically consider the right to political divorce to include the right to a legitimate state, then there is nothing methodologically suspect about invoking the conclusions that I derive from my noninstitutional analysis as an ideal to be institutionally approximated. In other words, if there is no reason to suppose that secession is necessarily an institutional concept in a way that euthanasia is not, then we should morally analyze the two in roughly the same fashion. Just as a noninstitutional conclusion that euthanasia can be permissible gives us (defeasible) moral reasons to legally permit euthanasia in certain duly restricted circumstances, the noninstitutional conclusion that some

[24] Ibid., p. 335.
[25] Ibid., p. 336.

parties have the moral right to secede provides (defeasible) reasons to design international laws that recognize and enforce primary rights to political divorce.

At this point, Buchanan might protest that, even if secession is not inherently institutional, international law still should not recognize primary rights to secede because protecting these rights will impair international law's capacity to secure those goods that the international legal system is designed to promote. Specifically, Buchanan suggests that international law is justified as an institutional system because it promotes peace and justice, and that protecting primary rights to secede will diminish international law's capacity to make the world a more peaceful and just place. If this is correct, it is of course a weighty consideration against creating laws that protect secessionist rights. However, it is important to recognize two things about this latter argument. First, unlike the previous argument that secession is inherently institutional, this line of argumentation relies on a *value judgment* rather than a conceptual claim. Thus, whatever the merits of this latter argument, it is not an objection to the *methodology* I have adopted in exploring whether to revise international law. Second, as I shall go on to argue, there are reasons to question the limited values that Buchanan espouses.

The Aims of International Law

Central to Buchanan's argument that international law's aims preclude it from respecting primary rights to secede is his contention that the chief goal of the international legal system is the promotion of peace and justice. This means both that (1) the international legal system would not be justified unless it made the world more peaceful and just, and that (2) the international laws we recommend for such a system should be those that, taken as a whole, maximally secure peace and justice in the world. So far, so good. But this very general description raises a more specific question concerning political self-determination: Does justice include group claims to self-determination, or is justice understood in purely individualistic terms, so that only the self-determination of individual human beings qualifies as a matter of justice? Buchanan's position on this crucial issue is laid out most clearly when he acknowledges the lone case of permissible group self-determination, the rights of (some) indigenous groups to limited legal intrastate autonomy. Here he explicitly endorses what he calls "justificatory individualism" (the view "that only the interests of individuals can serve as the ultimate ground of moral justification, that only individuals are moral subjects")[26] and emphasizes that he recommends intrastate autonomy for indigenous peoples only as an effective remedy for violations of individual human rights.[27]

Some might criticize Buchanan for cashing out justice in such individualistic terms. Why think that neither a legitimate state's complaint about being forcibly annexed nor a colony's grievance against its colonial oppressor qualifies as a claim of justice, for instance? Indeed, if my arguments in Chapter 3 are correct, then one can wrongly disrespect individuals when one interferes with their group's self-determination. But we need not press Buchanan on this point in order to question his reluctance to institutionally respect primary rights to secede. Instead, we can merely suggest that, *if* Buchanan excludes claims of group self-determination from the realm of justice, then the goals of international law cannot properly be restricted to promoting only peace and justice; the international legal system should be designed to promote peace, justice, *and political self-determination.* Moreover, absent an argument to the contrary, there is no reason to suppose that any one of these three goods should be regarded as lexically prior to the other two. Any reasonable pluralism recognizes that competing values must be weighed against one another and that even our most prized values are vulnerable to being outweighed in sufficiently extraordinary circumstances. Thus as important as peace is, there may be circumstances in which one should prefer a slightly less peaceful world if the decrease in peace resulted in considerably greater justice or political self-determination. To give a pair of historical instances in which people rightly sacrificed peace to promote justice, think of the efforts in the United States to abolish slavery and, later, to promote civil rights. In each case, the more peaceful route would have been to maintain the status quo, but I believe activists in both cases correctly judged that substantial gains in justice justified the disruption of peace.

By the same token, peace and justice (even taken together) should not be regarded as lexically prior to the value of political self-determination. To see this, consider the U.S.-led occupation of Iraq. To begin, I should say that (putting aside a host of important reservations about the timing, unilateralism, and "marketing" of the current war) I believe that there are circumstances in which a war to topple Hussein's horribly oppressive regime could be justified despite the inevitable disruption of peace

---

[26] Ibid., p. 414.
[27] Ibid.

because this war promised to make Iraq such a dramatically more just state. However, as I pen this chapter, there is considerable pressure upon the U.S.-led occupying force to cede its political power to the Iraqi people. The first thing to recognize is that one cannot explain the deonto-logical (as opposed to merely instrumental) moral reasons to transfer this power without assuming the nonderivative importance of group self-determination. Put contrapositively, if political self-determination were not a basic value, then the only moral reason for the United States to cede its political power over Iraq would be the contingent, instru-mental argument that Iraqi self-government would be more peaceful and just (where justice is cashed out, à la Buchanan, solely in terms of respect for individual rights). Most importantly, though, I take it that settling upon the correct decision in this case would involve finding the right balance between peace, justice, and political self-determination. Thus, every reasonable person agrees both that (1) the United States should not transfer the power if it would result in a complete and ongoing absence of peace and justice, and that (2) the United States most definitely should cede power when it can do so with a negligible diminution of peace and justice. Between these two poles, reasonable and fully informed people may disagree as to how valuable politi-cal self-determination is relative to peace and justice. Some will sug-gest that once a relatively low threshold of peace and justice can be assured, the United States must respect the Iraqis' claim to political self-determination, while others will maintain that the minimal level of guar-anteed peace and security must be set much higher because the impor-tance of group political self-determination pales in comparison to that of peace and justice. We need not pinpoint the precise level at which the importance of political self-determination becomes paramount; for our purposes, it is enough merely to note that (even if group politi-cal self-determination should not be subsumed under the banner of justice) political self-determination is a competing value, important enough to justify trade-offs between it and the other goods of peace and justice.

The lesson we should take from this discussion of Iraq is that, even if Buchanan is right to emphasize that peace and justice are important goods to be secured by international law (as I believe he is), there is no reason to suppose that these must be the *only* goods. If the international legal system should also seek to promote political self-determination, then there may be circumstances in which the goods of peace and justice should be sacrificed in the interest of substantial gains in group autonomy.

In short, international laws should be designed so that, taken as a whole, they maximally secure peace, justice, *and* political self-determination. Moreover, even if Buchanan could somehow establish that peace and justice enjoy lexical priority over political self-determination, at the very least political self-determination should be promoted whenever doing so would in no way be injurious to either peace or justice. Put in terms of state breaking, this means that international laws should at least be designed to protect primary rights to secede wherever institutionally protecting these rights requires us to sacrifice the promotion of neither peace nor justice. On Buchanan's view, however, we need not protect secessionist rights even in this minimalist case, because not only does Buchanan give lexical priority to peace and justice, he places no nonderivative value whatsoever on group self-determination.

In the end, then, the prevailing reason that Buchanan has to reject my views concerns neither the "inherently institutional" nature of the right to secede nor the distinction between ideal and nonideal or institutional and noninstitutional theory. The most basic and decisive reason why Buchanan has no sympathy for my permissive stance on secessionist rights is that he does not value political self-determination. As a consequence, we may be at something of an impasse, because as I specified in this book's introduction, my goal is to furnish a *conditional* argument: I do not argue for self-determination; rather, I merely argue that *if* one values self-determination, *then* one should endorse primary rights to secede. Buchanan and I ultimately come to divergent conclusions regarding international legal rights to political divorce, then, only because he does not share my confidence in the nonderivative importance of political self-determination.

At this point, Buchanan might object that this characterization of our differences is misleading. After all, he is an ardent defender of *individual* self-determination; Buchanan merely denies the deontological value of *group* self-determination, and he does so only because he believes it is incompatible with value-individualism (what he calls "justificatory individualism"). Here I think Buchanan is mistaken. As I outlined in Chapter 3, one can explain the deontological reasons to respect group self-determination without endorsing value-collectivism. It is true that rights to political self-determination are *exercised* by groups, but it is the individuals, qua members of these groups, who are *wronged* when these rights are violated. Specifically, one wrongly disrespects the individual members of a group when one denies the self-determination of a group that is capable of performing the requisite political functions.

For the sake of argument, however, let us suppose that my account of group autonomy is problematic. Even granting this assumption, I contend that Buchanan should value collective self-determination, because as explained earlier, the implications of denying the deontological reasons to respect group autonomy are less plausible than value-collectivism. In particular, one cannot fully capture what is wrong with either colonization or the forcible annexation of legitimate states unless one acknowledges the importance of group self-determination. To appreciate the significance of these implications, notice the divergent views Buchanan and I take on these two issues.

Buchanan and I agree that international law's current stance on colonization wrongly utilizes a "saltwater" test, but we disagree about what makes it impermissible to colonize a group of people. On this issue, Buchanan writes:

> The most obvious deficiency of existing international law regarding unilateral secession is the apparent arbitrariness of the restriction to classic decolonization. Presumably what justifies secession by overseas colonies of a metropolitan power is that the colonized are subject to exploitation and unjust domination, not the fact that a body of saltwater separates them and their oppressors. But if this is so, then the narrow scope of the existing legal right of self-determination is inappropriate. The existing right to secession as decolonization appears to be justice-based, yet the idea that serious injustices can justify secession points to a more expansive right.[28]

Unlike Buchanan, I do not presume that colonies are justified in seceding only if they are subject to exploitation and unjust domination. As Margaret Moore writes: "Justice may be a good criterion for assessing government; but it does not seen [sic] to be the primary factor in understanding the quest to secede, or even making sense of the massive movement to decolonize in the 1960's; or the importance that the international community is currently placing on democratic legitimacy."[29] I believe that a colony could have a right to independence even if it were being neither exploited nor unjustly dominated by the metropolitan state. (As I suggested in Chapter 4, the American colonies would have had a right to secede from Britain even if the British had offered to reduce their taxes and give the colonists political representation.) Of course, Buchanan would have no trouble explaining why, as an institutional matter, he would design international laws that forbid colonization of all kinds

[28] Ibid., p. 339.
[29] Margaret Moore, "Introduction," p. 6.

(i.e., whether or not the colonies were exploited or treated unjustly), because in the real world, peace and justice would be best promoted by a blanket prohibition on colonization. But, unless one accepts the deontological value of group self-determination, one cannot explain how a group of people are wronged by an individual case of nonexploitative, non-unjust colonization. One could not explain, for instance, why the Americans could have been wronged by Britain's nonexploitative colonization. I take this to be a weighty reason to accept that there are deontological reasons to respect group self-determination.

Buchanan and I are similarly divided over the issue of forcible annexation. On this topic, he writes:

But why should unjust annexation in itself be regarded as a ground for acknowledging a unilateral right to secede in international law?

The most obvious answer is that international legal recognition of a right to secede in order to reclaim unjustly annexed territory would serve as a deterrent to unjust annexations and would to that extent reinforce the existing international legal restrictions on the aggressive use of force by states. And there are a number of considerations that speak in favor of limiting the aggressive use of force. . . . In addition, at least in a system in which the existence of states is taken as a provisional given, the citizens of legitimate states ought to be regarded, at least with a very strong presumption, as being entitled to govern themselves. Hence international law should protect them against violations of their right to self-government.[30]

It is striking that Buchanan speaks of the "right to self-government" and that he would characterize an annexation as "unjust." (Given his justificatory individualism, it would seem that he could at most object to an annexation as being "illegal" or "contrary to the rules that would be set forth in an ideal international legal system.") In fairness to Buchanan, I do not think he is being inconsistent by invoking self-government here; on my reading, Buchanan recommends a blanket prohibition on forcible annexations in part because the existing international legal system values self-determination, but principally because he believes that this is the best way to secure peace and promote justice. But, as with his account of colonization, I find this explanation wanting. To see why, imagine that Canada could forcibly annex the United States and, without any disruption of peace or justice (understood in individualist terms), manage the annexed territory in a more peaceful and just fashion. Suppose, for instance, that Canadians abolished the death penalty, dramatically reduced the homicide rate, increased support for public education, and

---

30 Buchanan, *Justice, Legitimacy, and Self-Determination*, p. 356.

supplied a decent minimum level of universal health care to all those who occupied the territory formerly known as the United States. Even in this imaginary case, it seems awkward to suppose that the Americans would not be wronged by the annexation. Again, I understand that Buchanan could readily explain why, as an institutional matter, it would be best to have a prohibition on all annexations of reasonably just governments. But this alone is not enough, because it fails to capture the conviction that people can be wronged by *a single instance of annexation*, even when this political acquisition disrupts neither the security of peace nor the promotion of individual rights.

Finally, let us consider whether democracy can be adequately defended without assuming the deontological value of group self-determination. This is a crucial issue in exploring the divergence between our two views, because whereas I know of no way to supply an adequate non-instrumental defense of democracy without invoking the basic value of group self-determination, Buchanan purports to do just that. In his criticism of authors like Daniel Philpott who believe that individual autonomy grounds both democracy and (by extension) secessionist rights, Buchanan denies any link between democratic governance and individual autonomy. However, by appealing to individual equality, he believes that a right to democracy can nonetheless be defended without abandoning justificatory individualism. On Buchanan's view, democracy is unquestionably *instrumentally* valuable because it tends more than any other type of government to maximize peace and respect for human rights, and there are *noninstrumental* reasons to promote democracy because it alone is consistent with the fundamental equality of individual persons. On its face, this view seems right, but on reflection it becomes clear that one can raise concerns about grounding democracy in individual equality, concerns analogous to those Buchanan raises against basing democracy on the value of individual autonomy.

To begin, notice that there is nothing to preclude a monarchy from passing only laws that treat everyone equally (indeed, one could imagine a constitutional monarchy in which the monarch is prohibited from creating any inegalitarian laws). To this proposal an egalitarian might object that even a monarchy that treats all subjects equally would not respect the fundamental equality of all citizens, because the monarch has more political power than her subjects. This response is problematic, however, because representatives in a representative democracy also have a disproportionate amount of political influence, and few would suggest that only direct participatory democracies are consistent with equality.

At this point, a defender of representative democracy might stress that, although the representatives undeniably have greater political power, this is not inconsistent with treating all subjects equally as long as the political offices are equally open to all citizens. This response will not vindicate all and only democracies, however, because one can imagine a constitutional monarchy in which the monarch is chosen by lottery. As long as the constitution effectively prohibits inegalitarian laws and the lottery gives each subject an equal chance to be monarch, it is unclear how one could object that this political order fails to respect the fundamental equality of all of its citizens. Thus, those who defend democracy in terms of individual equality face a dilemma: If each person must actually possess equal political power, then only (certain forms of) direct participatory democracies will be legitimate. And if representative democracies do not violate egalitarianism, then neither do certain types of monarchies.

I share Buchanan's twofold conviction that representative democracies are legitimate and that there are deontological reasons to avoid even egalitarian monarchies, but the preceding discussion illustrates that democracy must be grounded in something other than equality. I suggest that what makes a democracy preferable to an egalitarian monarchy is that only the former allows people to choose the laws to which they will be subject and/or the representatives who will make those laws. (Indeed, when a person is given political power via a lottery system, it is not clear that she is in any meaningful sense a "representative.") In other words, if people have a right to democratic governance, it must be because they have a right to determine who politically represents them. And since the leaders are determined by the group as a whole rather than by each individual, what ultimately grounds democracy is *group* self-determination. Thus, if one wants to argue that there are both instrumental and deontological reasons to support democracy (as Buchanan and I both do), it appears that one must admit that there are deontological reasons to respect group self-determination.

In the end, then, it appears that remaining true to ordinary moral thinking on the issues of colonization, forcible annexation, and democracy requires granting that there are noninstrumental moral reasons to respect group self-determination. Thus, even if there were irremediable problems with my value-individualist account of group autonomy, I would be reluctant to deny the deontological importance of group self-determination. Given this judgment, we can now better evaluate Buchanan's concerns about approaches like mine. As Buchanan acknowledges, his objection does not depend upon the distinction between ideal and nonideal theory; it focuses instead on the inherently institutional nature of the right to secede. Because Buchanan's argument that secession is inherently institutional is flawed, however, his distaste for primary rights to secede ultimately boils down to a question of values. Whereas he thinks there are no noninstrumental reasons to make room for group self-determination, I believe that the international legal system should be designed to maximize peace, justice, *and political self-determination*. My support for the deontological value of group self-determination is twofold. In addition to my value-individualist account of group autonomy, I cite the deontological reasons to respect group self-determination as the only way to explain the wrongness of colonization, forcible annexations, and restrictions on democratic governance. Thus, not only do I insist that my account of secessionist rights within international law cannot be rejected on methodological grounds, I suggest that the values I invoke are thoroughly defensible.

Conclusion

We can distinguish between two questions regarding international law, one *predictive* and the other *prescriptive*. *Is it likely* that the current political leaders will legally protect primary rights to secede? And *should* these leaders now bring the international legal system in line with the functional theory of secession? The answer to the predictive question is clearly no. International actors remain far too concerned with losing territory and insufficiently impressed with liberal democratic values to design laws that could threaten their territorial integrity. Answering the prescriptive question is much more difficult. On the one hand, the moral rights to political self-determination give us compelling reasons to reform existing international law immediately. On the other hand, the potential perverse incentives of these new laws provide reasons to refrain from institutionally protecting rights to political self-determination until democratic principles enjoy a greater international following. The relative weight of these two competing concerns is open to debate, and the question cannot be decided conclusively until more empirical evidence is amassed. In the meantime, we can at least affirm one, more modest conclusion: Once liberal democratic values have ascended to such an extent that the world's leaders might in fact legalize primary rights to secede, there will be a decisive moral case in favor of doing so.

8

The Velvet Transformation

If there is any truth to Kant's bold prediction that democracies will not go to war with one another, it merely puts the icing on the cake of democracy. People already appreciate that the importance of self-determination gives constituents a right to democratic governance, so Kant's predicted consequences merely buttress the already decisive case in favor of democracy. In stark contrast, secession appears to lack not only the icing but also the cake on which to put it. People generally deny that self-determination gives constituents the right to determine the contours of their political boundaries, and the horrific consequences one could imagine resulting from licensing unilateral state breaking appear to defeat any case that might be made on behalf of secessionist rights. This book is first and foremost about making the case for the moral right to secede, but, in the spirit of Kant, I would like to close with my own hopeful prediction: *We are not far from the day when political theorists and international actors respect the importance of political self-determination, and when that day arrives, groups will not vote in favor of secession.*

The international community is in the midst of a breathtaking "velvet transformation," a transformation that features the dramatic ascendance of regional and global integration, international law, democracy, human rights, group rights, and self-determination. Even the keenest observers of international relations are surely surprised to see how quickly and extensively these emerging phenomena are taking root, spreading, and profoundly changing the geopolitical terrain. Of course, it is no accident that these particular elements are flourishing in concert with one another; each plays a part in providing an environment hospitable to the others.

Part of the impetus toward democracy and human rights has come
from the newfound willingness of the international community to impose
international law via humanitarian intervention in cases of genocide and
other gross rights abuses, but more often the motivation stems from
the carrot rather than the stick. Increasingly, countries find that it is
enormously advantageous to enter into military, legal, and economic
pacts with each other. Whether in relatively established alliances (like
the European Union) or the newly emerging associations (such as the
African Union), the tendency toward regional and even global cooperation has been a striking catalyst for the promotion of democratic values and human rights. Moreover, the various unions and treaties constitute a burgeoning international law that increasingly has the will and
muscle to enforce its judgments. Finally, as the international appreciation for democratic principles continues to grow, political theorists
and international actors are beginning to acknowledge that condemning overseas colonies is just a start; the value of self-determination has
broad and far-reaching implications for individuals as well as for nonstate
groups.

The most obvious effect of these developments, of course, has been
the erosion of state sovereignty. Whereas governments in the Westphalian
order long enjoyed virtually unrestricted dominion over all affairs that
did not spill beyond their territorial borders, they now find themselves
ever more bound to conduct their internal affairs in a fashion that accords
with international law. There may be some reasons to lament the loss of
sovereignty, but few can deny that it has brought about a marked and
growing decrease in injustice and a corresponding increase in respect
for democracy, human rights, and self-determination.

None of these observations is novel, of course, but I am not sure that
people have sufficiently appreciated the implications for the future of
secessionist conflicts. First of all, we should expect a sharp reduction
in separatist passion. Recent history has proven that it is never wise to
underestimate nationalism's potential to fan the flames of political division (especially since it remains unclear how immigration and terrorism –
to name just two potentially explosive developments – will play out), but
it seems reasonable to suppose that the reduction in cases of injustice
in general and group grievances in particular should lead to a similar diminution in disgruntled minority groups. Moreover, both because
national sovereignty is becoming ever less important and because states
are becoming more receptive to extending special political rights to
various collectives, disaffected groups will be less inclined to press for

independent statehood. Of course, existing states will in turn put up less resistance to secessionist demands, in part because minority groups are less inclined to grasp for independence and, more importantly, because of the diminishing significance of national sovereignty. Thus, these developments have put in motion a virtuous circle, in which separatist passion and statist resistance will mutually wane. The consequences of the velvet transformation are *circular* because the continued reduction in each phenomenon causes additional, corresponding reductions in the other (separatist passion is often fueled by the host state's reluctance to acknowledge the minority group's rights, and countries are often reluctant to respect group rights for fear it will inspire and empower separatists). And these consequences are *virtuous* because they reduce the emotionally charged and politically divisive tension that too often impairs reasonable negotiations between politically distinct groups.

To concretize this discussion, consider the Scottish separatist movement. Whereas twenty years ago it would have been unthinkable for the United Kingdom to allow Scotland to secede without a fight, it is not so clear how vigorously they would resist such a movement today. And projecting into the future, as the European Union continues to assume a more prominent role, it is reasonable to suppose that in another two decades the United Kingdom would do almost nothing to stand in the way of Scotland's separation. Just as importantly, these same developments will make it less likely that many Scots would be so motivated to secede in twenty years time. Indeed, in some ways this dynamic is echoic of the changes we have already witnessed with respect to the British monarchy. Several hundred years ago, many British citizens would have killed or died in defense of the crown. Now that the political power has shifted elsewhere, however, the stakes are much lower. The British may remain divided over the legitimacy and usefulness of retaining the monarchy, but this issue is no longer such an explosive one.

Here a critic might cite the break-up of the former Czechoslovakia as a telling counterexample to my prediction. After all, the Slovaks chose to secede even though the Czechs put up no real resistance. In some ways, this case is illustrative of the dynamics I predict (in particular, it is striking that Havel realized that the very principles of self-determination that justified his velvet revolution also justified the velvet secession), but this political divorce is not really a counterexample, both because the former Czechoslovakia had not fully embraced the value of self-determination (the Slovaks did not yet have all of the individual and group rights it would be reasonable to suppose they would have eventually been granted in a more mature, democratic Czechoslovakia, for instance) and, more importantly, because *a majority of the Slovaks never actually voted in favor of secession.* It is important to remember that this political division was precipitated not by a majority voting in favor of separation in a clear and free plebiscite but merely by the election in Slovakia of Vladimir Meciar, who received a minority of votes on a platform that included, among other things, a stated interest in Slovakia's independence.

A more revealing counterexample would occur if the majority of those in Quebec voted to secede from Canada. I say this because Canada has to an exemplary extent already embraced the values of democracy, human rights, group rights, and political self-determination to which the international community as a whole is currently gravitating. Not only does Canada's federalism afford a great deal of autonomy to each of the provinces, its highest court has impressively acknowledged that the country has a responsibility to enter into open-ended negotiations with Quebec if a clear majority of those in the province should vote in favor of secession. Thus, if such a majority were to vote for separation, it would bode ill for my prediction. It is important to note, however, that none of the various plebiscites in Quebec has produced a majority vote in favor of secession, and there is every reason to expect that the number of those who favor an independent Quebec will actually decrease in the coming years as Canada continues to respect Quebec's right to political self-determination and its own national sovereignty becomes less important.

This changing landscape of international relations is important because, even if the majority of political theorists were to be won over by the moral arguments in the preceding chapters, we should not expect this to make a substantial difference in the real world until the incentive structures of existing governments change. In this regard, secessionist rights are reminiscent of the right not to be enslaved: No matter how compelling the theoretical claims of abolitionists, the practice of slavery was unlikely to end as long as slave holders had a sizable economic stake in its continuation. Similarly, irrespective of the strength of arguments that people should have a say in the redrawing of territorial borders, it would be Pollyannaish to expect these arguments to find any purchase in the real world as long as leaders have such a stake in denying political self-determination. Just as the practice of slavery ended only when its abolition ceased to be prohibitively expensive to slave owners, rights to political self-determination will be respected only as their costs to rulers become less substantial. If this is the case, then my prediction is doubly significant. Not only does it show that respecting secessionist rights will soon cease to have the feared consequences, it indicates that we are not far from the day when theoretical arguments like those I offer in this book can play a more substantial role in shaping the way rulers in the real world actually govern.

Bibliography

Abbott, Philip (1998). "The Lincoln Propositions and the Spirit of Secession." In Percy B. Lehning (ed.), *Theories of Secession*, pp. 182–207. London: Routledge.

Alexander, Larry (ed.) (1998). *Constitutionalism: Philosophical Foundations.* Cambridge: Cambridge University Press.

Anderson, Benedict (1993). *Imagined Communities: Reflections on the Origin and Spread of Nationalism.* London: Verso.

Anderson, Elizabeth (1999). "What Is the Point of Equality?" *Ethics* 109: 287–337.

Arras, John D. (2003). "Physician-Assisted Suicide: A Tragic View." In Tom L. Beauchamp and LeRoy Walters (eds.), *Contemporary Issues in Bioethics*, 6th ed., pp. 225–234. Belmont, CA: Thomson Press.

Baker, David (1990). *Political Quotations.* Detroit: Gale Research.

Barnett, Randy (1977). "Restitution: A New Paradigm for Criminal Justice." *Ethics* 87: 279–301.

Baron, Marcia (1995). *Kantian Ethics Almost without Apology.* Ithaca, NY: Cornell University Press.

Barry, Brian (1991). "Self-Government Revisited." In *Democracy and Power: Essays in Political Theory I.* Oxford: Clarendon Press.

Beauchamp, Tom L., and Walters, LeRoy (eds.) (2003). *Contemporary Issues in Bioethics*, 6th ed., Belmont, CA: Thomson Press.

Beiner, Ronald S. (1998). "National Self-Determination: Some Cautionary Remarks Concerning the Rhetoric of Rights." In Margaret Moore (ed.), *National Self-Determination and Secession*, pp. 158–180. Oxford: Oxford University Press.

Beitz, Charles (1979). *Political Theory and International Relations.* Princeton, NJ: Princeton University Press.

Benson, Bruce (1990). *The Enterprise of Law.* San Francisco: Pacific Research Institute.

Bentham, Jeremy (1843). "Anarchical Fallacies." In John Bowring (ed.), *The Works of Jeremy Bentham*, vol. 2. Edinburgh: William Tait.

Beran, Harry (1984). "A Liberal Theory of Secession." *Political Studies* 32: 21–31.

(1987). *The Consent Theory of Political Obligation.* New York: Croom Helm.

(1988). "More Theory of Secession: A Response to Birch," *Political Studies* 36: 316–323.

(1998). "A Democratic Theory of Political Self-Determination for a New World Order." in Percy Lehning (ed.), *Theories of Secession*, pp. 32–59. London: Routledge.

Birch, A. H. (1984). "Another Liberal Theory of Secession." *Political Studies* 32: 596–602.

Bishai, Linda (1998). "Altered States: Secession and the Problems of Liberal Theory." in Percy Lehning (ed.), *Theories of Secession*, pp. 92–110. London: Routledge.

Brandon, Mark E. (2003). "Secession, Constitutionalism, and American Experience." In Stephen Macedo and Allen Buchanan (eds.), *Secession and Self-Determination*, pp. 272–314. New York: New York University Press.

Brilmayer, Lea (1989). "Consent, Contract, and Territory." *Minnesota Law Review* 74: 6–10.

(1991). "Secession and Self-Determination: A Territorialist Reinterpretation." *Yale Journal of International Law* 16: 177–202.

Brubaker, Roger (1998). "Myths and Misconceptions in the Study of Nationalism." In Margaret Moore (ed.), *National Self-Determination and Secession*, pp. 233–265. Oxford: Oxford University Press.

Buchanan, Allen (1975). "Revisability and Rational Choice." *Canadian Journal of Philosophy* 5: 396–408.

(1985). *Ethics, Efficiency, and the Market.* Totowa, NJ: Rowman and Allanheld.

(1989). "Assessing the Communitarian Critique of Liberalism." *Ethics* 99: 852–882.

(1991). *Secession: The Morality of Political Divorce from Fort Sumter to Lithuania and Quebec.* Boulder, CO: Westview.

(1993). "The Morality of Inclusion." *Social Philosophy and Policy* 10(2): 233–257.

(1996). "What's So Special about Nations?" In J. Couture, K. Nielsen, and M. Seymour (eds.), *Rethinking Nationalism. Canadian Journal of Philosophy*, supplementary volume 22.

(1997a). "Secession, Self-Determination, and the Rule of International Law." In Robert McKim and Jeff McMahan (eds.), *The Morality of Nationalism.* Oxford: Oxford University Press.

(1997b). "Theories of Secession." *Philosophy and Public Affairs* 26: 30–61.

(1998a). "Democracy and Secession." In Margaret Moore (ed.), *National Self-Determination and Secession*, pp. 14–33. Oxford: Oxford University Press.

(1998b). "The International Institutional Dimension of Secession." In Percy Lehning (ed.), *Theories of Secession*, pp. 227–256. London: Routledge.

(2003a). "Introduction." In Stephen Macedo and Allen Buchanan (eds.), *Secession and Self-Determination*, pp. 1–15. New York: New York University Press.

(2003b). "The Quebec Secession Issue: Democracy, Minority Rights, and the Rule of Law." In Stephen Macedo and Allen Buchanan (eds.), *Secession and Self-Determination*, pp. 238–271. New York: New York University Press.

(2004). *Justice, Legitimacy and Self-Determination: Moral Foundations for International Law.* Oxford: Oxford University Press.

Buchheit, Lee C. (1978). *Secession: The Legitimacy of Self-Determination.* New Haven, CT: Yale University Press.

Caney, Simon (1998). "National Self-Determination and National Secession: Individualist and Communitarian Approaches." In Percy Lehning (ed.), *Theories of Secession*, pp. 151–181. London: Routledge.

Cassese, Antonio (1995). *Self-Determination of Peoples: A Legal Reappraisal.* Cambridge: Cambridge University Press.

Christiano, Thomas (2003). "The Authority of Democracy." *The Journal of Political Philosophy* 12: 266–290.

Cohen, Joshua (ed.) (1996). *For Love of Country: Debating the Limits of Patriotism.* Boston: Beacon Press.

Copp, David (1997). "Democracy and Communal Self-Determination." In Robert McKim and Jeff McMahan (eds.), *The Morality of Nationalism*, pp. 277–300. Oxford: Oxford University Press.

(1998). "International Law and Morality in the Theory of Secession." *The Journal of Ethics* 2: 219–245.

Dahl, Robert (1989). *Democracy and Its Critics.* New Haven, CT: Yale University Press.

Denitch, Bogdan (1994). *Ethnic Nationalism: The Tragic Death of Yugoslavia.* Minneapolis: University of Minnesota Press.

Dowding, Keith (1998). "Secession and Isolation." In Percy Lehning (ed.), *Theories of Secession*, pp. 71–91. London: Routledge.

Dworkin, Ronald (1975). "The Original Position." In Norman Daniels (ed.), *Reading Rawls*, pp. 16–53. New York: Basic Books.

(1977). "Hard Cases." In *Taking Rights Seriously*, pp. 81–130. Cambridge, MA: Harvard University Press.

(1986). *Law's Empire.* Cambridge, MA: Harvard University Press.

Edmundson, William (1998a). "Legitimate Authority without Political Obligation." *Law and Philosophy* 17: 43–60.

(1998b). *Three Anarchical Fallacies.* Cambridge: Cambridge University Press.

Feinberg, Joel (1970). "The Nature and Value of Rights." *Journal of Value Inquiry* 4: 243–257.

(1979). "Civil Disobedience in the Modern World." *Humanities in Society* 2: 37–60.

(1980). "The Child's Right to an Open Future." In William Aiken and Hugh LaFollette (eds.), *Whose Child? Children's Rights, Parental Authority, and State Power.* Totowa, NJ: Rowman and Littlefield.

(1984). *Harm to Others*, vol. 1: *The Moral Limits of the Criminal Law.* Oxford: Oxford University Press.

(1986). *Harm to Self.* Oxford: Oxford University Press.

Franck, Thomas (1992). "The Emerging Right to Democratic Governance." *American Journal of International Law* 86: 46–91.

Freeman, Michael (1998). "The Priority of Function over Structure: A New Approach to Secession." In Percy Lehning (ed.), *Theories of Secession*, pp. 12–31. London: Routledge.

Frey, R. G., and Wellman, Christopher H. (eds.) (2003). *A Companion to Applied Ethics.* Malden, MA: Blackwell.

Friedman, David (1996). "Anarchy and Efficient Law." In John T. Sanders and Jan Narveson (eds.), *For and Against the State*, pp. 255–288. Lanham, MD: Rowman and Littlefield.

Gauthier, David (1994). "Breaking Up: An Essay on Secession." *Canadian Journal of Philosophy* 24: 357–372.

Gellner, Ernest (1983). *Nations and Nationalism.* Ithaca, NY: Cornell University Press.

Gilbert, Margaret (1993). "Group Membership and Political Obligation." *Monist* 76: 119–131.

Gilbert, Paul (1998a). "Communities Real and Imagined: Good and Bad Cases for National Secession." In Percy Lehning (ed.), *Theories of Secession*, pp. 208–226. London: Routledge.

(1998b). *The Philosophy of Nationalism.* Boulder, CO: Westview.

Godwin, William (1798 [1946]). *Enquiry Concerning Political Justice*, 3rd ed., ed. F. E. L. Priestley. Toronto: University of Toronto Press.

Goodin, Robert (1988). "What Is So Special about Our Fellow Countrymen?" *Ethics* 98: 663–686.

Green, Leslie (1990). *Authority of the State.* Oxford: Clarendon Press.

Hampton, Jean (1997). *Political Philosophy.* Boulder, CO: Westview.

Hardimon, Michael (1994). "Role Obligations." *Journal of Philosophy* 91: 333–363.

Hardin, Russell (1995). *One for All: The Logic of Group Conflict.* Princeton, NJ: Princeton University Press.

Hart, H. L. A. (1955). "Are There Any Natural Rights?" *Philosophical Review* 64: 175–191.

(1973). "Bentham on Legal Rights." In A. W. B. Simpson (ed.), *Oxford Essays in Jurisprudence*, 2nd series, pp. 171–201. Oxford: Clarendon Press.

Hartney, Michael (1991). "Some Confusions Concerning Collective Rights." *Canadian Journal of Law and Jurisprudence* 4: 293–314.

Hirsch, Fred (1976). *Social Limits to Growth.* Cambridge, MA: Harvard University Press.

Hirschman, Albert O. (1970). *Exit, Voice, and Loyalty.* Cambridge, MA: Harvard University Press.

Hobbes, Thomas (1990 [1651]). *Leviathan*, ed. Richard Tuck. Cambridge: Cambridge University Press.

Hohfeld, Wesley (1919). *Fundamental Legal Conceptions.* New Haven, CT: Yale University Press.

Horowitz, Donald L. (1985). *Ethnic Groups in Conflict.* Berkeley: University of California Press.

(1998). "Self-Determination: Politics, Philosophy, and Law." In Margaret Moore (ed.), *National Determination and Secession*, pp. 181–214. Oxford: Oxford University Press.

(2003). "A Right to Secede?" In Stephen Macedo and Allen Buchanan (eds.), *Secession and Self-Determination*, pp. 50–76. New York: New York University Press.

Hume, David (1739 [1978]). *A Treatise of Human Nature*, 2nd ed., ed. L. A. Selby-Bigge. Oxford: Oxford University Press.

(1987 [1748]). "Of the Original Contract." In *Essays: Moral, Political, and Literary*, ed. Eugene F. Miller, pp. 465–487. Indianapolis: Liberty Classics.

Hurka, Thomas (1997). "The Justification of National Partiality." In Robert McKim and Jeff McMahan (eds.), *The Morality of Nationalism*, pp. 139–157. Oxford: Oxford University Press.

Jennings, Ivor W. (1956). *The Approach to Self-Government*. Cambridge: Cambridge University Press.

Jeske, Diane (1996). "Associative Obligations, Voluntarism, and Equality." *Pacific Philosophical Quarterly* 77: 289–309.

Kant, Immanuel (1965). *The Metaphysical Elements of Justice*, trans. John Ladd. New York: Macmillan.

Kedourie, Elie (1985). *Nationalism*. London: Hutchinson.

Kinsley, Michael (1989). "Take My Kidney, Please." *Time*, March 13, p. 88.

Klosko, George (1992). *The Principle of Fairness and Political Obligation*. Lanham, MD: Rowman and Littlefield.

Kukathas, Chandran (1995). "Are There Any Cultural Rights?" In Will Kymlicka (ed.), *The Rights of Minority Cultures*, pp. 228–256. Oxford: Oxford University Press.

Kymlicka, Will (1989a). *Liberalism, Community and Culture*. Oxford: Clarendon Press.

(1989b). "Liberal Individualism and Liberal Neutrality." *Ethics* 99(4): 883–905.

(1990). *Contemporary Political Philosophy*. Oxford: Clarendon Press.

(1994). "Individual and Community Rights." In Judith Baker (ed.), *Group Rights*, pp. 17–33. Toronto: University of Toronto Press.

(1995a). *Multicultural Citizenship: A Liberal Theory of Minority Rights*. Oxford: Clarendon Press.

(1995b). *The Rights of Minority Cultures*. Oxford: Oxford University Press.

(1996). "The Sources of Nationalism: Commentary on Taylor." In Robert McKim and Jeff McMahan (eds.), *The Morality of Nationalism*, pp. 56–65. Oxford: Oxford University Press.

(1998). "Is Federalism a Viable Alternative to Secession?" In Percy Lehning (ed.), *Theories of Secession*, pp. 111–150. London: Routledge.

Lehning, Percy (ed.) (1998a). *Theories of Secession*. London: Routledge.

(1998b). "Theories of Secession: An Introduction." In Percy Lehning (ed.), *Theories of Secession*, pp. 1–11. London: Routledge.

Levinson, Sanford (1995). "Is Liberal Nationalism an Oxymoron?" *Ethics* 105: 626–645.

Levy, Jacob (2000). *The Multiculturalism of Fear*. Oxford: Oxford University Press.

(2003). "Indigenous Self-Government." In Stephen Macedo and Allen Buchanan (eds.), *Secession and Self-Determination*, pp. 119–135. New York: New York University Press.

Lincoln, Abraham (1955). *The Collected Works*, ed. Roy P. Basky. New Brunswick, NJ: Rutgers University Press.

Livingston, Donald W. (1998). "The Very Idea of Secession." *Society* (July/August): pp. 38–48.

Locke, John (1988 [1689]). *Second Treatise of Government*, ed. Peter Laslett. Cambridge: Cambridge University Press.

Lomasky, Loren (1987). *Persons, Rights, and the Moral Community.* Oxford: Oxford University Press.

MacCormick, Neil (1982). "Nation and Nationalism." In *Legal Right and Social Democracy.* Oxford: Clarendon Press.

Macedo, Stephen (1990). *Liberal Virtues: Citizenship, Virtue, and Community in Liberal Constitutionalism.* Oxford: Oxford University Press.

    (2003). and Buchanan, Allen (eds.). *Secession and Self-Determination.* New York: New York University Press.

MacIntyre, Alasdair (1983). "The Magic in the Pronoun 'My.'" *Ethics* 94: 113–125.

    (1984a). *After Virtue,* 2nd ed. Notre Dame: University of Notre Dame Press.

    (1984b). "Is Patriotism a Virtue?" (The Lindley Lecture). Lawrence: University of Kansas Press.

Margalit, Avishai, and Raz, Joseph (1990). "National Self-Determination." *Journal of Philosophy* 87: 439–461.

Mason, Andrew (1997). "Special Obligations to Compatriots." *Ethics* 107: 427–447.

McDonald, Michael (1991). "Should Communities Have Rights? Reflections on Liberal Individualism." *Canadian Journal of Law and Jurisprudence* 4: 217–237.

McGarry, John (1998). "'Orphans of Secession': National Pluralism in Secessionist Regions and Post-Secession States." In Margaret Moore (ed.), *National Self-Determination and Secession,* pp. 215–232. Oxford: Oxford University Press.

McKim, Robert, and McMahan, Jeff (eds.) (1997). *The Morality of Nationalism.* Oxford: Oxford University Press.

McMahan, Jeff (1997). "The Limits of National Partiality." In Robert McKim and Jeff McMahan (eds.), *The Morality of Nationalism,* pp. 107–138. Oxford: Oxford University Press.

Mill, John Stuart (1978 [1859]). *On Liberty,* ed. Elizabeth Rappaport. Indianapolis: Hackett.

    (1988 [1869]). *The Subjection of Women,* ed. Susan M. Okin. Indianapolis: Hackett.

    (1993[1861]). "On Representative Government." in *Utilitarianism, On Liberty, Considerations on Representative Government,* ed. Geraint Williams. London: Everyman.

Miller, David (1988). "The Ethical Significance of Nationality." *Ethics* 98: 647–662.

    (1993). "In Defense of Nationality." *Journal of Applied Philosophy* 10: 3–16.

    (1995). *On Nationality.* Oxford: Oxford University Press.

    (1998). "Secession and the Principle of Nationality." In Margaret Moore (ed.), *National Self-Determination and Secession,* pp. 62–78. Oxford: Oxford University Press.

Miller, Richard W. (1998). "Cosmopolitan Respect and Patriotic Concern." *Philosophy & Public Affairs* 27: 202–224.

Monroe, D. H. (1953). *Godwin's Political Philosophy.* Oxford: Oxford University Press.

Moore, Margaret (1998a). "Introduction: The Self-Determination Principle and the Ethics of Secession." In Margaret Moore (ed.), *National Determination and Secession,* pp. 1–13. Oxford: Oxford University Press.

(ed.) (1998b). *National Self-Determination and Secession.* Oxford: Oxford University Press.

(1998c). "The Territorial Dimension of Self-Determination." In Margaret Moore (ed.), *National Self-Determination and Secession,* pp. 134–157. Oxford: Oxford University Press.

(2001). *The Ethics of Nationalism.* Oxford: Oxford University Press.

(2003). "An Historical Argument for Indigenous Self-Determination." In Stephen Macedo and Allen Buchanan (eds.), *Secession and Self-Determination,* pp. 89–118. New York: New York University Press.

Murphy, Jeffrie G. (1980). "Blackmail: A Preliminary Inquiry." *Monist* 63(2): 156–171.

Murphy, Mark C. (1999). "Moral Legitimacy and Political Obligation." *APA Newsletter on Philosophy and Law* 99: 77–80.

Nielsen, Kai (1993). "Secession: The Case of Quebec." *Journal of Applied Philosophy* 10: 29–43.

(1998). "Liberal Nationalism and Secession" in Margaret Moore (ed.), *National Self-Determination and Secession,* pp. 103–133. Oxford: Oxford University Press.

Norman, Wayne (1998). "The Ethics of Secession as the Regulation of Secessionist Politics." in Margaret Moore (ed.), *National Self-Determination and Secession,* pp. 34–61. Oxford: Oxford University Press.

(2003). "Domesticating Secession." In Stephen Macedo and Allen Buchanan (eds.), *Secession and Self-Determination,* pp. 193–237. New York: New York University Press.

Nozick, Robert (1969). "Coercion." In Sydney Morgenbesser et al. (eds.), *Philosophy, Science and Method,* pp. 440–472. New York: St. Martin's Press.

(1974). *Anarchy, State, and Utopia.* New York: Basic Books.

Nussbaum, Martha (1996). "Patriotism and Cosmopolitanism." in Joshua Cohen (ed.), *For Love of Country: Debating the Limits of Patriotism.* Boston: Beacon Press.

Okin, Susan Moller (1989). *Justice, Gender, and the Family.* New York: Basic Books.

Oldenquist, Andrew (1982). "Loyalties." *Journal of Philosophy* 79: 173–193.

Orentlicher, Diane F. (2003a). "Democratic Principles and Separatist Claims: A Response and Further Inquiry." In Stephen Macedo and Allen Buchanan (eds.), *Secession and Self-Determination,* pp. 77–86. New York: New York University Press.

(2003b). "International Responses to Separatist Claims: Are Democratic Principles Relevant?" In Stephen Macedo and Allen Buchanan (eds.), *Secession and Self-Determination,* pp. 19–49. New York: New York University Press.

Owen, David (1995). *The Balkan Odyssey.* New York: Harcourt Brace.

Pascal, Louis (1986). "Judgment Day." In Peter Singer (ed.), *Applied Ethics,* pp. 105–123. Oxford: Oxford University Press.

Pateman, Carole (1979). *The Problem of Political Obligation.* Chichester, NY: John Wiley.

Patten, Alan (2002). "Democratic Secession from a Multinational State." *Ethics* 112: 558–556.

(2003). "Can the Immigrant/National Minority Dichotomy Be Defended? Comment on Ruth Rubio-Marin." In Stephen Macedo and Allen Buchanan (eds.), *Secession and Self-Determination*, pp. 174–189. New York: New York University Press.

Philpott, Daniel (1995). "In Defense of Self-Determination." *Ethics* 105(2): 352–385.

(1998). "Self-Determination in Practice." In Margaret Moore (ed.), *National Self-Determination and Secession*, pp. 79–102. Oxford: Oxford University Press.

Pogge, Thomas (1992). "Cosmopolitanism and Sovereignty." *Ethics* 103: 48–75.

Rainbolt, George (1990). *The Concept of Rights*. Ph.D. dissertation, University of Arizona.

Rawls, John (1964). "Legal Obligation and the Duty of Fair Play." In Sidney Hook (ed.), *Law and Philosophy*, pp. 3–18. New York: New York University Press.

(1971). *A Theory of Justice*. Cambridge, MA: Harvard University Press.

Raz, Joseph (1998). "On the Authority and Interpretation of Constitutions." In *Constitutionalism: Philosophical Foundations*, ed. Larry Alexander. Cambridge: Cambridge University Press.

Renan, Ernest (1939). "What Is a Nation?" In A. Zimmern (ed.), *Modern Political Doctrines*, pp. 187–205. Oxford: Oxford University Press.

Ross, W. D. (1930). *The Right and the Good*. Oxford: Oxford University Press.

Rousseau, Jean-Jacques (1987 [1762]). *The Social Contract*. In *The Basic Political Writings*, ed. Donald A. Cress. Indianapolis: Hackett.

Rubio-Marin, Ruth. (2003). "Exploring the Boundaries of Language Rights: Insiders, Newcomers, and Natives." In Stephen Macedo and Allen Buchanan (eds.), *Secession and Self-Determination*, pp. 136–173. New York: New York University Press.

Salmond, Sir John (1920). *Jurisprudence*, 6th ed. London: Sweet and Maxwell.

Sandel, Michael (1982). *Liberalism and the Limits of Justice*. Cambridge: Cambridge University Press.

(1984). "The Procedural Republic and the Unencumbered Self." *Political Theory* 12: 81–96.

Sartorius, Rolf (1981). "Political Authority and Political Obligation." *Virginia Law Review* 67: 3–17.

Scheffler, Samuel (1994). "Families, Nations, and Strangers." (The Lindley Lecture). Lawrence: University of Kansas.

(1997). "Relationships and Responsibilities." *Philosophy & Public Affairs* 26: 189–209.

Schmidtz, David (1990). "Justifying the State." *Ethics* 101: 89–102.

Shafer-Landau, Russ (1997). "Moral Rules." *Ethics* 107: 584–611.

Shue, Henry (1980). *Basic Rights: Subsistence, Affluence, and American Foreign Policy*. Princeton, NJ: Princeton University Press.

(1988). "Mediating Duties." *Ethics* 98: 687–704.

Simmons, A. John (1979). *Moral Principles and Political Obligations*. Princeton, NJ: Princeton University Press.

(1996). "Associative Political Obligations." *Ethics* 106: 247–273.

Singer, Peter (1972). "Famine, Affluence, and Morality." *Philosophy & Public Affairs* 1: 229–243.

(1986). *Applied Ethics*. Oxford: Oxford University Press.

(1987). *Democracy and Disobedience*. Oxford: Oxford University Press.

Smart, J. J. C. (1963). "An Outline of a System of Ethics." In J. J. C. Smart and Bernard Williams (eds.), *Utilitarianism: For and Against*, pp. 3–74. Cambridge: Cambridge University Press.

Smith, Patricia (1998). *Liberalism and Affirmative Obeligations.* New York: Oxford University Press.

(2003). "Bad Samaritans, Acts, and Omissions." In R. G. Ferey and Christopher H. Wellman (eds.), *A Companion to Applied Ethics*, pp. 475–486. Malden, MA: Blackwell.

Snyder, Louis L. (1977). *Encyclopedia of Nationalism.* New York: Paragon House.

Steiner, Hillel (1998). "Territorial Justice." In Percy Lehning (ed.), *Theories of Secession*, pp. 60–70. London: Routledge.

Sumner, Wayne (1987). *The Moral Foundations of Rights.* Oxford: Clarendon Press.

Sunstein, Cass (1991). "Constitutionalism and Secession." *University of Chicago Law Review* 58(2): 633–670.

Tamir, Yael (1993). *Liberal Nationalism.* Princeton, NJ: Princeton University Press.

(1997). "Pro Patria Mori – Death and the State." In Robert McKim and Jeff McMahan (eds.), *The Morality of Nationalism*. Oxford: Oxford University Press.

Taylor, Charles (1990). *Sources of the Self.* Cambridge: Cambridge University Press.

Tocqueville, Alexis de (1988[1835]). *Democracy in America.* New York: Harper Perennial.

Waldron, Jeremy (1993). "Special Ties and Natural Duties." *Philosophy & Public Affairs* 22(1): 3–30.

Walker, A. D. M. (1988). "Political Obligation and the Argument from Gratitude." *Philosophy & Public Affairs* 17: 191–211.

Walzer, Michael (1977). *Just and Unjust Wars.* New York: Basic Books.

(1983). *Spheres of Justices.* New York: Basic Books.

(1992). "The New Tribalism." *Dissent* 3: 164–171.

(1996). "Spheres of Affection." in Joshua Cohen (ed.), *For Love of Country: Debating the Limits of Patriotism*, pp. 125–127. Boston: Beacon Press.

Weinstock, Daniel (2001). "Constitutionalizing the Right to Secede." *Journal of Political Philosophy* 9: 182–203.

Wellman, Carl (1985). *A Theory of Rights.* Totowa, NJ: Rowman and Allanheld.

(1995). *Real Rights.* Oxford: Oxford University Press.

Wellman, Christopher H. (1995a). "A Defense of Secession and Political Self-Determination." *Philosophy & Public Affairs* 24(2): 142–171.

(1995b). "On Conflicts between Rights." *Law and Philosophy* 14: 271–295.

(1996a). "Divided We Stand; United We Fall? An Essay on Size, Citizenship, and Secession." *Good Society* 6: 21–23.

(1996b). "Liberalism, Samaritanism, and Political Legitimacy." *Philosophy & Public Affairs* 25(3): 211–237.

(1997). "Associative Allegiances and Political Obligations." *Social Theory and Practice* 23(2): 181–204.

(1999). "Liberalism, Communitarianism, and Group Rights." *Law and Philosophy* 18: 13–40.

(2000a). "On Liberalism's Regarding Nationalism." in Nenad Miscevic (ed.), *Nationalism and Ethnic Conflict*, pp. 115–131. Chicago: Open Court.

(2000b). "Relational Facts in Liberal Political Theory: Is There Magic in the Pronoun 'My'?" *Ethics* 110(3): 537–562.

(2001). "Toward a Liberal Theory of Obligation." *Ethics* 111: 735–759.

(2003a). "Nationalism and Secession." In R. G. Frey and Christopher H. Wellman (eds.), *A Companion to Applied Ethics*, pp. 267–278. Malden, MA: Blackwell.

(2003b). "The Paradox of Group Autonomy." *Social Philosophy & Policy* 20: 265–285.

(2003c). "The Truth in the Nationalist Principle." *American Philosophical Quarterly* 40: 251–268.

(2003d) and Lindsay, Peter. "Lincoln on Secession." *Social Theory and Practice* 29: 113–135.

(2004) and Altman, Andrew. "A Defense of International Criminal Law." *Ethics* 115: 35–67.

(2005) and Simmons, A. John. *Is There a Duty to Obey the Law?* New York: Cambridge University Press.

Unpublished manuscript (coauthored with Andrew Altman). "Democracy and Group Self-Determination."

Wertheimer, Alan (1987). *Coercion*. Princeton, NJ: Princeton University Press.

Williams, Bernard (1981). "Persons, Character and Morality." In his *Moral Luck*, pp. 1–19. Cambridge: Cambridge University Press.

Williams, Patricia (1991). *The Alchemy of Race and Rights*. Cambridge, MA: Harvard University Press.

Index

Made in the USA
Middletown, DE
28 October 2017